Everything I Need To Know, I Learned in Go-Go

How a Preacher's Daughter Pole-Danced Her Way to Finding Her True Self

Sydnee A.

With a Spin Publishing

First edition: February 2023

The positive affirmations that appear in chapter four are copyright © Farnoosh Brock (ProlificLiving.com), used with permission.

Cover design, illustration, book design and formatting by Gareth Southwell (art.garethsouthwell.com)

ISBN (paperback): 979-8-9869580-8-8
ISBN (ebook): 979-8-9869580-9-5

Published by With A Spin Publishing
www.withaspinpublishing.com

CONTENTS

*This book is dedicated
to all the dreamers.*

*Dare to make every one of
your dreams come true!*

PROLOGUE

HAVE YOU EVER found yourself in a place where you were staring into the future you knew you were destined to follow, yet you were stuck in the space between scared shitless and super excited to start?

Comfort zones are funny things. For most people, standing in front of a room full of strangers topless would be far from "comfortable". For me, when I was hiding behind the persona that I had created, I was most comfortable in that arena. One night in particular comes to mind.

Rivers of sweat were running down from my face, traveling between my exposed breasts as I drew in then forced out breath after breath. Squinting from the blast of the stage lights, I peered through the smoke and into the eyes of the faces staring back at me. I grasped the cold, brass pole that had become a source of security for me with my right hand and used it to keep me steady. I needed a moment to collect myself.

The date was December 22, 2008, and it marked the end of a personal era.

Moments earlier, I had finished my last performance as a professional exotic dancer, and I had given it my all. I was physically and emotionally spent. As I heard the applause and saw the twenty-dollar bills flying through the air and landing on the stage—thrown from a crowd that was up on their feet—I knew that my thirteen years of working in gentlemen's clubs had not been in vain. I looked to my right and saw the man who would become my husband smiling from ear to ear and clapping enthusiastically. He was proud of my swan song, for sure, but he was also thankful that this would be the last time I would take off my clothes in front of strangers for money. He had always supported me fully, no matter the endeavor. I smiled at him from the stage, knowing he had my back in that moment.

As I moved my gaze throughout the bar, seeing each person and thinking of how they had all impacted my life in some way, I knew that the time was finally right for me to hang up my heels and walk away. I had performed on many stages over the years, and those spaces had become the places where I learned so much—not only about myself, but also about the other people I share the planet with. Who would have thought I'd have grown so much as a woman and a person as a result of my years working in go-go bars? The middle school me who was convinced I was going to be the first United Methodist nun because no boys liked me certainly did not see this coming!

I am grateful for this opportunity to share those lessons with you, as well as some of the wild stories that inspired them. I have spent hours with men who were drunk out of their minds, but still managed to be kind. I have made friends with the other girls I've worked with and drawn inspiration from their journeys. I have had many shifts where I have fallen on my face (sometimes literally!) and managed to keep pushing forward. But for you to fully appreciate my journey, we need to rewind and see how someone like *me* wound up half naked in front of strangers on stages in the first place.

I never in a million years dreamed that I would become an exotic dancer. I wasn't sexy enough, I had no rhythm, and I'm an introvert, for goodness' sakes! It turns out; you really don't need to be sexy or have rhythm—or have teeth—to be a successful exotic dancer. I had much to learn.

I grew up in southern New Jersey in the eighties. I was grateful to be born in 1975 because we were the last generation to have a childhood before the internet was in every home and pocket. We played outside, walked or biked everywhere, and spent our teen years sneaking phone calls way into the late-night hours.

My friends and I would sit in one of our bedrooms and listen to the radio for hours, waiting for our favorite songs to come on so we could record them onto a cassette tape. We wound up irritated every time the DJ talked over the very beginning or very end of the song. We passed carefully folded paper notes in class, had the biggest hair, and wore the brightest neon colors in history! Everyone thinks of their own childhood as being the best time to grow up, but we had the Cabbage Patch Kids, the A-Team, and MTV, which played music videos all day long!

Not that I was allowed to watch MTV . . .

Being a preacher's daughter, I was brought up in a strict religious household. In my younger years, I believed that everyone must have also had parents as strict as mine and lived like us. My friends at school and friends at church came from a variety of backgrounds. Other than feeling confused when a friend's family didn't say grace before dinner, nothing stood out to me to let me know that my upbringing was a little different. Eating a meal without first giving thanks to God would have never happened in my house. We said grace before every meal, no exceptions. In the rare times when we would go out to eat, my dad would have us all hold hands and say grace in the restaurant as well.

That was just "life" to me, and I never questioned anything. That was, until I was in my tween years and the "preacher's daughter" comments started. Before then, I had been called a "PK," short for "preacher's kid." It had a little bit of a negative edge attached to it, but overall, it sounded cute. However, "preacher's daughter" gave off a completely different vibe. The stereotype had much more of a stigma. It came with images of rebellion and promiscuity—the preacher's daughter was expected to be "naughty." I'm not saying that that was the reason I wound up topless in front of strangers, but people do learn to behave according to the expectations you place on them.

I saw that play out with a family for whom I babysat as a teenager. The parents warned me that the three boys—aged five, three, and one—were hell spawn, that they wouldn't listen and were generally "bad kids." The first day I watched them, the three-year-old put his one-year-old brother in the dryer, and the five-year-old ran around on the furniture like his ass was on fire before smacking the three-year-old in the nose with a He-Man sword, causing blood to spray out everywhere. For the finale, the three-year-old stuck a peanut-butter-and-jelly sandwich in the VCR because he had seen someone do that in a TV commercial. They refused to listen to me, so I threatened to tell their parents what they had done. The oldest answered, "Go ahead, they won't do anything." I asked if they had ever received any consequences for their actions, and he explained that their parents threatened them a lot but never followed through. From then on, I tried to encourage them to play on their strengths instead of following the belief that they were "bad kids." It wasn't perfect by any means, but I like to think that I'd helped them see that they were not hopeless and were capable of doing better. Just as I knew I was so much more than the stereotype of a "preacher's daughter," I wanted these boys to know they could be more than the label they had been given.

I love my dad dearly, but during my childhood years, his priorities were always the church and parishioners, and he directed most of his energy into being a good preacher. In the past few years, we've had good conversations about how that affected me and my brothers. Knowing that I was always less of a priority to my dad than the church left a lot of deep scars on my psyche.

My mom, on the other hand, worked as a nurse in a hospital before I was born. After she had me and my brothers, she became a stay-at-home mom until I was around seven or eight years old, often doing crafts with us— cutting out fish from construction paper and securing a paper clip to them so we could go "fishing" on the front porch with a magnet that was tied to a string from a dowel rod "fishing pole"—and letting us help her cook. When we got a little older, she began working in the school district as a teacher's aide. My fondest memories of my mom were of how she would always make a big deal out of the holidays.

During my childhood, we moved a lot. Instead of having memories of a single house, we made memories of the traditions and decorations that were consistent during each holiday in every house where we lived. To this day, my mom decorates every inch of my parents' house for every occasion, from Halloween and Christmas to Valentine's Day and St. Patrick's Day, and I love seeing so many of the same decorations from when I was a child still on display every year in their house.

The many happy memories from my childhood include birthday parties, Girl Scouts, youth group, being in school plays, and just hanging out with my friends. Our family took road trips and went camping, first in our van and later in a pop-up camper and then in a thirty-five-foot vacation trailer. My dad used to read the funnies to us, and we spent a lot of time visiting our grandparents, too.

Even though we moved a lot, we lived in one town from when I was eight to when I was sixteen. I had a group of friends in school, as well as friends in the neighborhood who went to a private school. We all got along, so it wasn't divided into "my school friends" or "my neighborhood friends." We would spend hours playing outside, mostly games that we had made up.

Some of the houses in our neighborhood had lawns that looked like they could be featured on the cover of *Better Homes and Gardens* magazine. Ours wasn't one of them, but my dad took excellent care of the yard; it wasn't trashy. My parents didn't mind that we wound up playing games at my house, wearing a path around the house with our running, because they understood that childhood was fleeting. I think they also liked being able to keep an eye on all of us. If all the neighborhood kids congregated at our house, then they knew what we were up to.

Our favorite made-up game was called "Ninja," a combination of hide-and-seek and ball tag. The person who was "it" had to first find another player and then hit them with a tennis ball to get them "out" before they made it to "base," our front steps. While nailing someone with a tennis ball after you find their hiding spot may sound mean, it helped to build a lot of different skills. We learned how to duck and weave, how to run fast, and how to not be a big crybaby if we got hit with a ball. Sooner or later, everyone was going to get hit. It was part of the game, nothing personal.

When I was a Girl Scout, during our after-school meetings, we would have a great time earning our badges, going out and selling cookies, and going to sleepaway camp. The other girls and I became close and spent time together outside of Scouts as well. The one rule was that I was not allowed to go to sleepovers at my friends' houses on Saturday nights unless their parents agreed to have me up and dressed to be ready for church pickup on Sunday morning. It annoyed me. I guess there were more things that stuck out to me as "different" than just saying grace before meals, after all.

I was a good kid, at least until middle school. I don't think I necessarily became a "bad kid." I was just a "normal" one. The difference is when you do normal, stupid things that a lot of teenagers do and your dad is the minister, those normal, stupid things tend to be given more weight. I would hear the following from the parishioners quite frequently:

"You shouldn't smoke; you're the preacher's daughter!"

How about I shouldn't smoke because it will kill me no matter what my father's occupation happens to be?

The opposite was true as well. During our church youth group meetings, I would be chosen to say the prayers because my dad was the pastor. I got in trouble with the leader once for asking, "If my dad was a carpenter, would you want me to put an addition on your house?" I didn't see how my father's job made me more qualified to lead a prayer than any of the other Christian kids who supposedly were praying daily.

At the age of fourteen, one of the church members cornered me in the back hall of the church. He was an older man I knew from church but not someone I saw outside of church activities. He backed me up against the wall, looked me dead in the eye, and said, "You're going to wind up pregnant before you're sixteen, and I want to be there to see your father's face when you have to tell him." Then he laughed in my face and walked away.

First, when that conversation took place, I was still a virgin. Second, what in the fuck would possess a grown man to say that to a young woman as he backs her up against the wall? (Or think he has the right to?) Years later, this man's son came into a club where I was bartending. That night, I had been wearing a mesh top with nothing under it and leather pants. I used to wear leather or pleather when I bartended because if I spilled anything on myself, it was easy to wipe off. I wore mesh tops with nothing under them because . . . more tips! On that particular night, the presence of his son made me feel a little icky in my outfit because I had known this young man since he was a little kid. But, to tell the truth, a little part of me would have loved to have seen Mister High-and-Mighty's face if his son had told him that he had been out looking for some T&A—and got to see my T!

I certainly wasn't perfect, and I'm not saying that I never dreamed of becoming a missionary, either—well, not after age ten anyway. Missionaries used to come and speak to us at church, and they would share their tales of living out in the wild and converting the locals to follow Jesus. I was pen pals with a few of those missionaries over the years, and it all seemed very exotic. But truth be told, I was too spoiled by running water to be able to stay in a country without it for too long. Instead, I always chose to send monetary donations to help those with the fortitude to be in those places for any length of time.

Not wanting to be a missionary is one thing, but there are a lot of steps between missionary and exotic dancer, which was the career path I would soon find myself on. Aside from laughing with my friends in middle school gym class in the late 1980s about who was going to take center pole at The Cat House—something we had only heard of by following our favorite hair bands (I'm looking at you, Mötley Crüe)—exotic dancing was not something I'd ever considered as a serious profession. Until I found myself staring down a brass pole six years later when I was twenty years old.

When I look back on my younger years, I had no idea what I wanted to be when I grew up aside from being a mom. From the time I was a little girl, I knew I was meant to have kids someday. I could feel that calling in my very being, and my soul told me that I was meant to have three children. The Universe works in mysterious ways. Today, I have two biological children and a stepson whom I love as much as if he were my biological child. I was right about how many kids I would be meant to have; I just needed to be open to receiving the kids who needed me in their lives.

When I was considering occupations that I wanted to pursue after graduating high school, I never experienced the same kind of pull in my gut. I met with the school's career counselor, and we evaluated my answers on the standardized "What career would suit you?" test, but "stripper" was not one of the answers I was given. I had considered a future in all kinds of careers, from driving a big rig to practicing law as a prosecuting attorney, but I never pursued them because I didn't feel passionate about them.

My mom suggested several times (indirectly and very directly) that she thought I should become a social worker. I gave it a lot of thought, but I knew that environment would kill me because of my personality. As an empath, I feel too much and would have wanted to kidnap—I mean adopt—every child in the system.

Back when I was nine years old, my parents had become foster parents with an agency in New Jersey and would continue to do so for over twenty years, continuing the family tradition. My father's parents were foster parents through that agency, as were my great-grandparents. I saw firsthand the results of abuse and neglect on children before they were given love and proper care by a family. When I heard what those children had endured, all I wanted to do was hold them and never let them go! I can't speak for all foster parents, and I have heard plenty of horror stories about kids in foster care, but what I know is that the foster parents from the agency associated with my family gave the kids in their care nothing but love and a chance at a better future.

The alternative to being such a bleeding heart would be teaching myself to not feel as much, and I didn't want to do that, either. Not when it came to children in need. I knew I could help these children in other ways without it being my full-time job as a social worker.

So, it was back to square one. I wasn't idle. I went to college to study psychology and sociology and worked several jobs, from a cashier at a card store to a gas attendant. But I never felt fulfilled or like I was exactly where I was meant to be. Little did I know that every one of those experiences was a step forward on the path that would lead me to working in go-go bars off and on for thirteen years. Those dark rooms filled with loud music would turn out to be the classrooms for the many life lessons that I still hold dear today.

Gentlemen's clubs are interesting places filled with a plethora of people. If you've never been inside a gentlemen's club, you'll need to use your imagination (or maybe a scene from a movie) to form your opinions. I'm sure you'll have your own assumptions of what the average patron of a go-go bar looks like—what physical features they may have, what kind of job they do (if any), the type of place where they live, how they talk, and how they smell. It's a common stereotype that the people who go to these clubs are scumbags, deviants, and troubled. Sure, some of them are, but some of the people in your local supermarket, coffee shop, and church are, too. Like a lot of areas in life, assuming makes an ass out of you. Judge not, lest ye be judged!

Like most humans, patrons of go-go bars are regular people who just want attention. They want to feel included.

Or they just want to cop a feel.

Bachelor parties aside (that's a chapter unto itself), most of the guys I met along the way were just looking for a place to unwind. They wanted to enjoy the view and a drink or two for a couple of hours before returning to their realities. Most of the patrons were male, but there was always a sprinkling of female and gender-fluid customers as well. Having female customers at the bar was more common on the weekends, and most of them came in as half of a couple. They ranged from the shy and curious to the ones who believed they could stick their hand down my pants because they had the same parts as me. That's a definite no with most dancers, especially if there is no foreplay. Side note: if you are a woman and are going to a club, please don't assume you can do whatever you want just because you have lady bits, too. Of course, there might be some dancers who will welcome that sort of interaction; I'm not saying I've never hooked up with a female customer during a couch dance. I'm just saying you can't go exploring in other people's G-strings uninvited. That's bad manners.

There were plenty of other crazy things that went on in the private rooms of gentlemen's clubs. Most places followed Chris Rock's take on what kind of sex happens in the champagne room: none. In some clubs, the customers were not allowed to touch the dancers during private dances at all, while others allowed contact but only if it stayed above the waist. But no matter what the rules were, there would always be customers who attempted to push the boundaries and get more than the rules allowed; and there would be girls who would let them. There was always a girl or two who paid off the bouncer to look the other way while she was back there so she could cross the line. The odds greatly increased when you added alcohol to the equation. I believe that most of the women who wind up working in the adult industry are there because they are seeking attention, primarily from men. I have come a long way, but I would be lying if I said that I don't still seek approval and attention from the men in my life. Daddy issues is a common theme, and more than a few of the dancers I knew had histories that included some sort of abuse. The bars gave the girls a sense of empowerment while still getting the male approval they were seeking. Myself included.

A guy I dated from the time when I worked in my first bar and whom I am still friends with sometimes tells me the stories that he remembered from back then. "I always found it a bit funny when I would tell people I was seeing a dancer, and they thought how awesome that was. But once I explained to them how it was a job, the magic was gone. I had moved the curtain."

That's why while it is wrong to make assumptions about the type of people who frequent gentlemen's clubs, it is also wrong to make assumptions about the types of women who dance. At the end of the day, it's just a job. A means to an end. A way to pay the bills. A girl I worked with in 2008 liked to dance to a song called "Dancing for the Groceries" (feel free to Google it if you are not familiar). Kenny Chesney is great, but I would have never danced to a song that blatantly honest. I don't know about you but going out to the bar and watching a woman dancing to a song that explains the hardships of dancing would not make me moist! If it worked for her, good on her. And if it didn't work for her, then hey, good on me! That meant more money in my pocket.

I had never been one to try and work the "pity tip" angle. I preferred dancing to songs like "User Friendly" by Marilyn Manson. I wasn't pretending to be looking for a long-term relationship or anything romantic. I was just pretending to be interested in a short-term sexual one.

It takes all kinds to make the go-go world go 'round. And musical tastes weren't the only things that varied when it came to the girls dancing in gentlemen's clubs.

I have worked with underage girls with fake IDs who had no business being in a club and women in their sixties who, some would say, also had no business working in a club. I have worked with students, moms, grandmoms, accountants, nurses, and even teachers who weren't able to make ends meet on their day job salaries. I clearly remember two of the women from my first club because they both worked in disguise. One was an elementary school teacher. She wore fake glasses and a wig, making her look like she was trying for the "sexy teacher" look. Hiding in plain sight, I suppose. The other woman wore a wig and colored contact lenses, used special makeup to fully cover her tattoos, and told me that she drove over two hours from home to work at the club so that no one would know who she was. She could have been CIA; she could have been totally full of shit; I have no idea! I just remember her being kind to me when I first started dancing and was completely clueless; the rest of her life was none of my business.

I've worked with single girls, married women, and recently divorced ladies. I have worked with super-skinny girls and super-voluptuous ladies. My coworkers have been gay, straight, bi, pan, and asexual. They've ranged from virgins to super sexually active. I used to have fascinating conversations in the dressing room with a girl who had only had oral and anal sex so that she could say she was technically a virgin. The old Catholic loophole. I worked with one girl whose day job was being a dominatrix, and several others who taught Sunday School. Women of every skin tone and every hair color shared the stage with me, and more than one was not born with female genitalia.

I appreciate the friendships that I have made over the years and am grateful for the men, women, and non-binary persons with whom I have kept in touch. I would not have been able to write this book without the countless characters who have made my journey more colorful and more fun, and who, when they pop into my mind, bring a smile to my face. We still laugh when we talk about the good old days. When I started out, the bars were much different than they are now. Some of the stories that my friends who still work in the bar scene tell me make me shake my head in disbelief. Are things really that different? Or am I just older now and more easily shocked?

Surely not the latter!

Just as the truth comes out at the end of the night when the DJ turns on the "cellulights," this book may also reveal some truths that you may not be ready to hear. Especially if you believe that exotic dancers:

1. Are all whores that either want your cock (or if you are a heterosexual lady or gay man: want your man's cock)
2. Walk around "in real life" wearing stilettos and lingerie
3. Are all drug addicts
4. Are all stupid

There are many more misconceptions about women who dance, but this list is a good start. If you believe any of them and are steadfast in your beliefs, stop reading now. You are bound to wind up sorely disappointed.

"Cellulights" was my nickname for the house lights. When you are on the stage dancing during regular business hours, the only lights on in the club are black lights, colored stage lights, or strobe lights that conceal your flaws. I guess the non-go-go equivalent to the stage lights would be social media filters. You know what you really look like, then you pick a filter, and your teeth are whiter, the wrinkles disappear, your stretch marks are faded, and the zits are gone. Black lights, strobe lights, and stage lights offer the same effect, just while people are looking at you in real life. But when the night is over and the bright white overhead lights come on, there is no hiding what you truly look like as you stand there in your undies—the cottage-cheese thighs, pimples, stretch marks, and dimples are all out on display. Most girls would scatter like roaches. I didn't care! I figured if I scared a customer that bad, maybe he would jump in fear and drop his wallet.

My life is multifaceted, and the dancing portion of my past is only one of many pieces that make me, me! While there are a lot of life lessons in the other pieces of my life as well, most people would not be as interested in reading about the wisdoms that struck me out of the blue while scrubbing the toilet or sitting in the school pickup line. I have learned so many things in the time that I worked in gentlemen's clubs, which have helped me to grow as a person. My sincere hope is that by sharing those lessons in this book, they can help you to learn and grow as well. My goal is to share some smiles, inspire you to make positive changes in your life, and help you to find your own path to confidence and become the best you possible. I also have stories from my go-go years that are just plain funny and shocking, and that are worth it for the entertainment value alone.

I have not always had a positive headspace. I spent the last seven years of my life actively diving into my own personal development, committing to exercising, and focusing on better nutrition. I have come a long way from my years of living on Marlboro Reds, Mountain Dew, and having the only squats I did be the ones over a man's lap. (Or woman's lap. I love my ladies, too!) The only thing that is constant in our lives is that things are always changing. Just because you may have gotten into a bad habit or find yourself on a bad path doesn't mean you can't change your life's direction to one that better serves you. I put in work daily to move myself forward and grow as a person. And I am immensely proud when I see the new chapters I have added to my life that have made me a happier and more confident person.

I would not be who I am today if I did not have the go-go chapter of my life. And it all started in 1995 with three little words . . .

ONE

"I Dare You!"

NEVER UNDERESTIMATE THE power of peer pressure. It's not just a condition that affects teenagers. How many times have you found your adult self buying something, eating something (or not eating something!), or going to an event that you never would have, just because the other people in your circle or the people you admire on social media are doing it?

I like to think that it's something we outgrow. And maybe some of you have. If you do not feel pressured to do things because your friends and family expect it of you, then kudos to you! You are stronger than a lot of us.

I admit that at twenty years old, I wasn't there yet.

My best friend at the time and I were interested in getting an apartment. We'll call her "Marissa" because that was the name she eventually used in the clubs. (This is a book about go-go dancers, so no one is using their real names.)

Marissa and I were both living at home at the time. Me with my parents, younger brother, and whichever foster baby or babies my parents were taking care of at the time.

Marissa was living with her single mom who was a couple of cabbages short of a garden and had major anger issues. I completely understand why Marissa wanted to break free.

To put it mildly, Marissa's mom was "nucking futs." She had OCD and had habits that included washing the soup cans in the sink, and then washing them again in the dishwasher, before throwing them in the trash. She had multiple daily cleaning rituals in the house that ensured there were always vacuum lines in the carpets and never a speck of dust on any surface at any time. She spent the majority of her waking hours cleaning and recleaning.

I'm all for having a clean house, and who doesn't love vacuum lines on the carpet? But it is possible to become consumed and take it too far. I was afraid to wear a skirt in their house because the tile was so shiny. If the floors in my high school were shined to the same level of reflection, the boys wouldn't have had to put mirrors on their shoes to see up the girls' skirts!

Affecting how someone decides to dress was not so much the issue when her mom's OCD reached out into other areas of Marissa's life. Marissa would make coffee and sometimes not get every coffee ground out of the pot when she washed it. Marissa's mother told her that if the coffee pot wasn't spotless, she was going to take it to work with her so Marissa couldn't use it. The next time she found a coffee ground left behind, the pot was in the trunk of her car.

Her mom also bought and owned lawn chairs that no one else had permission to sit in. Chairs, as in more than one. Her mom had one ass and didn't allow people to come over. One afternoon when she came home from work, Marissa was sitting in one of the chairs. So, she put them in the trunk of her car along with the coffee pot, and off to work they went! Her trunk was filled to the brim with household items that she didn't want her daughter to touch.

Additionally, Marissa's mom would not allow any of her friends in her house when she wasn't home. (Though now that I am a parent, I can understand that rule.) One day, I stopped by to see Marissa, but her mom wasn't home, so I followed the rules and didn't go into the house. Instead, we stood in the driveway talking. But apparently (even though she had never mentioned this when she would go through her list of rules), her mother did not want anyone in the driveway, either. This grown-ass woman attempted to run me over with her Corolla because I was in her driveway!

I had not assaulted her, I had not killed any of her family members, I had not even spoken a word to her. Marissa had her issues for sure (don't we all?) but considering her environment and having lived alone with this woman for her entire life up to this point, she could have turned out a hell of a lot worse.

But before we get into that story, let's rewind two years. After I graduated from high school in 1993, I spent my summer as a counselor at a Christian camp and then immediately started my adventure as a college student in southeastern Kentucky. It was a bit of an adjustment going from southern New Jersey to a small, very rural town in Kentucky. I had been brought up in a very strict household, so when I found myself hundreds of miles from home with no parental supervision . . . to put it mildly, I went a little crazy.

Within two weeks, I had made an appointment at Bessie's Beauty Parlor to get my naturally brunette hair bleached blond. Well, at least that was what I had gone into Bessie's to have done. After hours of processing my hair, the result was various shades from dark yellow-orange at the ends to white roots. One of my friends (also from Jersey) affectionately called me "piss head" until I dyed it brown again. In addition to Bessie's, the small town where I had gone to college had a tanning salon that charged $1.50 for fifteen minutes in the tanning booth and $3 for a half hour in the tanning bed. I went fake baking several days a week. I was a crispy critter within a month!

When I was still in high school, my eighteenth-birthday present to myself was a rose tattoo on my ankle. My parents flipped! They were not even a little bit pro-tattoo (see Leviticus 19:28), so a small rose on my ankle was not acceptable. By the time I had returned home from college for Thanksgiving break, I had gotten a few more tattoos.

One of my friends in college found a local tattoo artist, and several of us would go together and hang out at the house. Yes, we had these tattoos done in someone's house —talk about dumb coupled with peer pressure! I am very grateful that the person knew what she was doing and used sanitary tattooing practices. One of us would get tattooed while the rest of us would watch, just talking and cracking each other up. I wound up getting a butterfly on my left breast, a heart with a sword and cross on my left hip bone, and a heart-cross-rose tattoo combo that had a ribbon with my name on it on my right shoulder blade. To put it mildly, my parents were even less pleased with tattoos number two, three, and four than they were with number one.

We were all attending college in the early nineties in rural Kentucky. As freshmen, none of us were permitted to have a car on campus. We would walk to the video store next to the Walmart (this took an hour and a half), rent a video camera, and walk back (another hour and a half). Video cameras in 1993 were large. I'm talking designed to be carried around on your shoulder, a "TV news cameraman"-sized camera. We would haul the camera back to campus to make our own music videos and silly home movies. The variety of entertainment we recorded on VHS tapes includes a video of my friends and I lip-synching to "What's Up?" by 4 Non Blondes in one of the common rooms in our dorm, me lip-synching to "Me and Bobby McGee" by Janis Joplin on the flood wall in town, and a spirited rendition of "Bohemian Rhapsody" by Queen performed by me and one of my besties in my dorm room. We would have had a gazillion videos if we had iPhones in college.

I also brought my Cobra CB radio to school and used it to talk to the local truckers driving through town. If you have never used a CB radio before, it is similar to talking on a walkie talkie, but it reaches a longer distance. Before social media, it was not only a way to meet new people, but also a great way to get instant traffic updates. My intention had been just to bullshit with the truckers (aka get attention from men), but as a bonus I also got in touch with the local bootlegger. Hand to god, I thought bootleggers were a made-up thing on *The Dukes of Hazzard*! I didn't think they really existed. This man would deliver bottles of Boone's Farm to my dorm room window for the bargain price of only six times the price of a bottle in the liquor store. Considering I was eighteen and had no business buying it anyway, we were good.

My plan of continuing to purchase alcohol for myself from the bootlegger for my newly formed weekend drinking habit was working out flawlessly until I got in trouble because my CB conversations were coming through on every phone line on campus. We had to move to plan B. My friends and I would walk down to the local park with the CB radio and plug it into the gazebo that had electrical outlets. We talked to all kinds of characters, and once, we all took a ride with a truck driver to the local McDonald's.

Again, I was an idiot and am very grateful that I did not become the subject of a show on the Discovery ID channel. Kids! Do not talk to strangers on CB radios or social media or apps, and definitely do not ever get into a vehicle with a stranger and . . . why are you reading this book? Put the book down and walk away, now!

The bottom line is I was doing all kinds of things except studying or taking my classes seriously.

I made it to class most days, but that didn't mean that I was staying awake throughout my entire class. I had a Basic Statistics class at 7:55 a.m. First, are you serious? Math before eight in the morning? Even on the days when I was taking my studies seriously, it would have been difficult for me to concentrate on learning basic statistics at that hour;

and on the days when I had stayed up all night because I could, drinking way too much Mountain Dew and eating too much sugar, there was no way I was going to be awake and coherent enough to take that class seriously. Second, I have never been a math-minded person, and I just could not grasp the concepts that our professor was teaching. It wasn't his fault; I just wasn't interested. I found myself putting my head down on the table and taking a nap more times than not.

The issue, aside from my not paying any attention in class because I was out cold, was that I snored like a bear. More like the sound of an entire family of bears hibernating in a reverberating cave for the winter while simultaneously revving a bunch of chainsaws. (I think the ceiling on my side of the bed is a little lower than my husband's side from my super snoring.) Not only was I not learning anything, but my log-sawing symphony was distracting the rest of the class. My professor finally reached his limit and sarcastically suggested that I bring a pillow to class if I insisted on sleeping through his lessons. He wasn't nearly as amused as I was when I showed up to the next class with a pillow under my arm.

Looking back, I believe I would have benefitted from taking a year off in between high school and college. I was an immature eighteen-year-old; I wasn't ready to be responsible for my own time in any way that would result in positive outcomes. If I had taken a year off, in theory, it would have given me a chance to let out some of that stored energy. Furthermore, if I had gotten a full-time job, it would have given me a chance to become more responsible and mature. I had only ever worked as a babysitter, a part-time job at a grocery store, and a camp counselor before going away to college. (I could write a full second book on the summer I was a counselor.)

If I had been able to have had more independence before moving so far away from home, I would not have immediately gone nuts the second I tasted a drop of freedom. But realistically, I don't think I would have had that freedom in my parents' home. When I came home from college for the first time for Thanksgiving break, I was expected to be in the house every night at 10 p.m. at the latest. Independence wasn't my parents' style. For shits and giggles, I've often fantasized what would have happened if I had had a year to grow up a little more and do typical young adult things. If that had been the case, I more than likely would have taken the academic side of college more seriously because I wouldn't have been so focused on the things I was missing out on socially. My mother, whom I love dearly, still brings up the "she went crazy when she went to college" stories several times a year to anyone who will listen. "We dropped her off at school, and within two weeks, she was blond and got tattoos . . ." Yet she never brings up the crazily strict, and sometimes confusing, rules in their house that led directly to my craziness.

When I was young, I was not allowed to watch *Mighty Mouse* and *Knight Rider* because they were too violent, yet Bugs Bunny cartoons and *The A-Team* were acceptable. I was forbidden to read Stephen King, but *Flowers in the Attic* and the Dollanganger series was fine. I never dared to ask how my parents decided on the things we could and couldn't watch or read. That may have resulted in me losing the things that were permitted.

I do confess that now that I am a parent, I understand that sometimes we decide not to let our kids watch or listen to certain things just because they annoy the piss out of us. I'm sure that the reason my dad confiscated multiple copies of my Guns N' Roses *Appetite for Destruction* album was because he wasn't a fan of the music, not because he had "spent his entire life building up the things that were important to him and didn't need anyone with their 'appetite for destruction' tearing it down," which was his answer when I asked him why he had taken them.

My parents also eventually adopted a completely new set of rules for my sister, who is twenty-six years younger than me. Some said they'd just given up as they were older now and not as willing to spend their time in battles with their kid. But the most notable change was with my parents' approach to sex education.

Sex education for my brothers and me when we were growing up consisted of one sentence: "Not until you're married."

It took me a while to figure out what I wasn't supposed to do until I was married because I had never been given any details of what sex was. I had just been told that it was expected to be a flat "nope" in my life until I was a married woman. We would go to Christian youth rallies where they would preach about the evils of premarital sex. I even got a T-shirt—the back of the shirt was covered in phrases proclaiming why the wearer was not having sex, things like: "I respect myself" and "I'm not ready for junior yet." In bold capital letters diagonally across the back panel, it said, "I'M NOT DOING IT!"

Now, don't get me wrong: if you are not ready to have any kind of sex for any reason, married or not, that is your choice. You should never let anyone else pressure you into doing something you don't want to do. It's your body, and the only person who has the right to make that decision is you. However, conditioning someone to believe that their decision to take that step with someone else means that they have no respect for themselves, or even worse that they are a "slut," is wrong. Especially when you use guilt and fear to make young people feel ashamed for taking control of what they do with their own bodies. The fact of the matter is just saying "It doesn't exist before you take your vows" doesn't keep it from existing. It doesn't stop any normal urges you have and can leave you in some very confusing predicaments when you don't have any idea what is going on in your body.

Kudos to the public school system and their health class for finally educating me on what sex was and how to do it safely. And luckily, my parents have now taken up new measures with my younger sister to at least lessen the chances of unwanted pregnancy in case she also does not wait until marriage. (For me, I went to a teen clinic in high school to get condoms and the pill, which I paid for myself and had to hide in my room.) Abstinence is a great choice if that is what you decide to do for yourself. Decisions need to be made based on facts. The mechanics of the "birds and bees" should be taught as well so no one finds themselves in a place of confusion where they do not have the information necessary to make the right decision for themselves.

In defiance of that T-shirt—and honestly, I had already "done it" before getting the shirt—I went full speed ahead and excitedly lived life by my own terms.

I wish that I had taken the "Live my life on my own terms" approach to more than just my sex life. Rather than taking the opportunity and time to explore who I was, work, and become more mature the year after graduating from high school, I went straight to college. Then, in 1994 after my first year of college, I decided to take a year off.

And I kind of forgot to go back.

Instead of returning to school, I spent a few ill-fated months cohabitating with an abusive boyfriend, moved back in with my parents, got a job at a convenience store, quit working there, and got a job pumping gas. Eventually, I wound up being a secretary at a stock brokerage.

While I was working there, Marissa and I started talking about getting our own place. I loved my parents dearly but living with them after a year plus of experiencing more freedom than they had ever allowed in the parsonage was tough. I'm sure that it was no picnic for them to have me back home, either.

Marissa was a waitress at the local Pizza Shack. We didn't exactly make enough money to be approved for an apartment, even when we combined our salaries. We had tried to convince a friend of ours to get an apartment with us, but he turned us down. Even though I was twenty, Marissa was only seventeen at the time. Looking back, I don't know what we were thinking! No matter what odds were stacked against us, "Operation Apartment" was in full swing, and we were pushing to make it happen.

We had looked at several sample apartments to see where we would like to move, but we still weren't in a financial position to get an apartment of our own. Our parents wouldn't cosign for us, so we had to figure out a way to make it work ourselves. I asked my boss for a raise but was shot down. We figured that getting second jobs was the only way we could make enough money to get approved on our own.

I put in applications at every gas station and restaurant within a half hour of my house. Since I could only work the later shifts after my office job was done, they had nothing available for me. I needed to find a different type of job that offered late-day and night hours.

I knew that the guys in my stock brokerage office would meet up at a local gentlemen's club every week (we'll call it "Sunsingers"), and they had invited me to come along several times. I always turned them down using the excuse that I was underage and that it was a bar. To be honest, I had absolutely no idea what a gentlemen's club meant. But now that I was on a mission to get an apartment, I considered the following:

- I knew that Sunsingers was open after my workday at the office ended since that was when my coworkers would go.
- I also knew that they served alcohol in the establishment. I wasn't old enough to go into bars legally as a customer, but

you don't have to be twenty-one to be
an employee.

I was an avid television watcher. I particularly enjoyed soap operas, and the characters in those shows always hung out in fancy clubs drinking alcohol. Since all my knowledge of clubs came from TV, I thought, *Maybe they're hiring cocktail waitresses*, since all the TV shows I had seen with club scenes featured cocktail waitresses walking around with trays of drinks. They always wore cute, little, sexy outfits, and that was appealing to me. To me, a club was a club was a club. In my naivete, I shared my need to find a second job with my coworkers and asked them for the address. I'm pretty sure I heard snickers as I walked away; I just didn't know why.

I walked in the door of Sunsingers, and it was black as night, the air was thick with smoke, and I was immediately smacked in the face by the smell that seems to be embedded in every part of every jiggle joint I have ever entered in my life. The smell permeates the air, no matter what state you're in or if the building is a smoking or nonsmoking establishment. It is entrenched in every fiber of the casino-style carpet, in every cell of the drywall, and it hangs from the ceiling tiles. It is unlike any other mix of sweat, funk, and sometimes smoke you will ever smell anywhere else. I call it "Eau de Go-Go."

The music was blaring, and a young woman was on the stage. When my eyes adjusted to the darkness, I could see that the stage was a large rectangle with a mirrored wall on the back. There were two large potted plants, one on each side of the stage. Two poles with a crossbar pole across the top took up the center of the rectangle. The dancer was wearing a red thong bikini with fringe that swayed as she moved. She was swinging around one pole and gyrating to a dance song that kept repeating the word *Egypt*. She would then glide over to the other pole and spin some more. I had no idea how she was able to move so effortlessly in stiletto heels.

My jaw hit the floor!

I turned to Marissa, my eyes huge, and said, "Oh my god! Her ass is sticking out!"

New Jersey go-go bars allow you to have either naked boobs or booze. Not both. Sunsingers served alcohol, so this wasn't a topless bar. I probably would have had a heart attack and died on the spot if that had been the case. Don't get me wrong, I really was not a prude at all! At this point in my life, I had already been to a nude beach, worn lingerie for boyfriends, and seen pornographic movies. (This was pre-internet, so you had to work a little harder to watch porn in those days. I vividly remember going to an adult bookstore with a friend and walking through the beads to the grown-up-movie section. Every other person in the room was looking out of the corner of their eyes to see what titles we were checking out. "Butt Woman Does Budapest" always got a laugh from my friend and me.)

I had just never seen an exotic dancer in real life before, and I suppose that when I had first walked into the "club," it just wasn't what I had expected to see.

We asked the bartender if we could speak to the manager. His name was Luke. He came out to the bar from an office in the back. We introduced ourselves and asked if they were hiring cocktail waitresses. He looked at us and laughed as if to say, "Stupid, stupid, girls." Then he replied, "No, not waitresses, but you could audition to be a dancer. We are always looking for new girls to dance." Luke had one of those big smiles and eye twinkles that you would expect from the manager of a go-go bar. He made us feel comfortable and seemed really nice.

"Come into my web," said the spider to the fly . . .

In that moment, I did think about auditioning to be a dancer. But there are some facts in the whole "me dancing onstage in front of strangers" scenario that could not be disputed.

I was naturally a very clumsy person. I fell up flights of stairs, tripped over thin air, and had a constant bruise on my thigh from the corner of my bureau, which had been in the same spot in my bedroom for over a decade, yet I slammed into it with the same meaty part of my thigh several times a week. In summary, I was not the type of person who had any business putting on heels and walking anywhere, let alone dancing, gyrating, and all that jazz.

I was also not a trained dancer. If I had been asked to provide any past dance or athletic experience on a résumé to be an exotic dancer, I could have fudged the following:

- I had taken a few years of gymnastics classes as a child.
- In the eighties, my BFF and I used to pretend we were *Solid Gold* dancers while putting on extravagant performances in my parents' living room to our favorite 45s.

- I was a cheerleader in high school until
  I was dropped and broke a vertebra in
  my back.
- I was in school musicals, which involved
  dancing to show tunes and following
  choreography.

I couldn't imagine the Charleston, grapevine or ball change being useful dance steps in this situation. And the stage wasn't big enough for cartwheels.

Then there was the whole bare ass thing . . .

I had just about talked myself out of the audition when Marissa turned to me, looked me dead in the eye, and said the three little words that would alter the course of my life forever:

"I dare you!"

She assured me that she would audition if I did. Her statement didn't take a whole lot of guts to make because, again, she was only seventeen and couldn't audition until the next month when she would turn eighteen. I'm sure she thought I would chicken out and that this would be something she could bust my stones about for the rest of our lives.

Angelique, the dancer who had been onstage when we walked in, came over and said, "Hi!" We wound up chatting for several minutes. She was super sweet and told me I should audition. I said, "There is no way I can move like you do! You are amazing!" She flashed a big smile and told me it took practice. She offered to teach me a couple of moves.

That's the thing with peer pressure. You find yourself doing things you normally wouldn't do just to save face, seem cool, or not be called a wuss.

Luke explained that they only held auditions on certain days, so I could either try out the next day or in two weeks.

"Two weeks, please!"

I had to come up with a plan. I always felt better whenever I had a checklist of the steps I needed to take in order to achieve a goal. I used those same steps when it came time to make sure I would be prepared for my audition. I knew I needed an outfit (complete with heels), makeup, a sexy hairstyle, music, and a dance routine. I went to the Frederick's of Hollywood store in the mall and bought the exact same bikini that Angelique had, only in black. I put it on and practiced in front of my bedroom mirror for hours. I channeled my inner Charo and practiced my "cuchi-cuchi" moves. (I'm totally dating myself. If you are not familiar with Charo and her signature "cuchi-cuchi" moves that captured everyone's attention, please consult Google. She is an icon!) I created a routine and after several days of practicing it, I was starting to feel confident. I was happily surprised with how my butt looked in a thong bikini. Hanging out in all its glory and not looking like a couple of mud flaps.

In the mirror over my bureau, things were looking good!

Luke told me that the audition would consist of me dancing to two songs. I had picked the songs: "The Only Time" by Nine Inch Nails and "Slice of Your Pie" by Mötley Crüe. When the day arrived for my audition, I showed up at the club and was brought back to the dressing room. They allowed Marissa to come back into the dressing room with me and help me with my makeup—and my nerves!

As I walked into the dressing room, everyone looked up and checked me out. The room was filled with many different types of women of different ethnicities, from the Barbie-doll types to the crackheads. A couple said hi, but most ignored me. Angelique wasn't working that shift, so I didn't talk to anyone except Marissa.

The "dressing room" was made up of two decent-sized rooms connected by a small hallway and an attached bathroom. Each room had nasty old carpeting, and there was a counter that went along two of the walls of each room. The counters were covered with overfilled ashtrays and empty glasses, in addition to the bags of makeup and G-strings. The walls were mirrored above the counters, and between the tops of the mirrors and the ceiling was a row of fat, round light bulbs. One out of every four lightbulbs worked!

The back room had lockers and more privacy. That was where the more popular girls, as well as the drug addicts, got ready for their shifts and hung out in between their sets. The front room was where the bathroom entrance and pay phone were located. I always picked a seat in that room when I worked because I didn't want to get involved with the drama of popularity or drug use.

I made my way to a back corner of the front room and put on my fringe bikini and my super-high, way sexy, three-inch heels. To be honest, walking in my heels on slippery tile wasn't as easy as when I had worn them on my bedroom carpet. By the time I realized this, I was so crippled with anxiety that the floor surface was the least of my worries.

The DJ came into the dressing room and asked me what songs I would like to hear. I was surprised to see a female DJ. I don't know why I assumed that all go-go bar DJs were men, but that made an ass of me! She was very nice and told me to relax and that the manager would let me know when it was my turn.

I began chain-smoking and talking to myself. In my head, I mean. I was noticing that I was getting a lot of side glances from the other girls. I ignored them and stared at my reflection in the mirror. I gave myself a talking to: "I can do it! It's just dancing," as well as, "It's not brain surgery. No one is going to die if I screw it up. Except me from the embarrassment," and finally, "Oh god, why am I doing this?!"

The manager popped his head into the dressing room and told me I was "on deck," which is fancy speak for "up next."

I forced myself to leave the safety of the dressing room and walked to the edge of the stage where I could watch the dancer onstage performing before me. She had the grace and elegance of a gazelle, effortlessly floating from pole to pole and captivating the audience. She would make eye contact with a customer and smile a sexy, little half smile. She had his undivided attention the whole time she commanded the stage.

Her song ended, and it was my turn.

The cold, hard truth of this situation was that no matter how many times I had danced in front of my bedroom mirror and thought I knew what I was doing, getting up onstage in a go-go bar was something I had never done before in my life. I was basically jumping off a cliff and hoping I would learn to fly on the way down. Much like riding a bike or driving a car, you can listen to other people share their experiences, you can read books about it, and you can watch videos, but until you do it yourself, you will never truly understand what it is about or learn how to do it.

I climbed up the steps and took to the stage with the grace and elegance of a baby rhinoceros. I grabbed the pole for dear life and moved my hips in a serpentine movement, down into a squat and then back up to standing. This shimmy down-and-up movement seemed to be the natural go-to move for anyone who was inexperienced and trying to dance while holding a pole.

I started strutting back and forth and doing the moves I had practiced, carefully keeping my gaze on the pole to which I was heading. My goal was to make it back and forth between the poles without falling on my ass. By the end of the Nine Inch Nails song, I was starting to calm down and feel better.

Then the DJ played my second song . . .

And the only problem was that it wasn't *my* second song! She had gotten the band right, but "Shout at the Devil" started playing instead of "Slice of Your Pie," and I panicked. I hadn't practiced that song in my room; what was I going to do?

I just kept strutting and sweating and doing my best to not topple over onto my face. When the song was just about over, I went back to the shimmy move, holding on to the pole so tightly that I almost left indentations in the brass.

Then, out of nowhere, I was overcome with a sudden feeling of bravery. The song was almost over, so why not try a big finale? It was not like I was ever going to do this again, right? I was just fulfilling a dare.

I walked to the space between the poles and did a wiggle with my arms over my head. The guys went wild! I thought, *They like me! They really like me!* Then I turned around. When I saw my refection in the mirror, I realized exactly why they had been cheering.

My right boob had popped out of my bikini top.

I was mortified. I ran off the stage to the sound of my breast being applauded and decided that I just had to die. There was no other option. Seriously, how embarrassing had that been?

Instead, something even worse happened. I had never imagined this for all of the times I had fantasized about my audition: I got hired!

To quote *National Lampoon's Christmas Vacation*, "Are you serious, Clark?" They wanted me to come back and do this again? Several nights a week?

I'm not sure why it never occurred to me that I could just walk out the door and never return. I guess a part of me was flattered that I had gotten hired. It was a whole new world that was certainly more exciting than the few months I spent in an office full of stockbrokers and their ass-stinging rubber bands.

Before I went home that night, I went into the bar's office with my new boss, and we worked out what shifts I would be working. There would be a lot of late-night shifts at the beginning of the week and lunch shifts on Saturdays. I learned that the more experienced girls and the ones with seniority got Friday and Saturday nights, and very few girls wanted to work on Sundays.

Soon after my embarrassing first step into the world of working in gentlemen's clubs, "Sydnee" was born. I had used another name for the first few weeks, but it didn't feel right. I sat in the dressing room with one of the dancers and the shift manger, trying to come up with a name for me to use. Our conversation sounded like:

Me: "Nikki?"

Manager: "Got one."

Me: "Brittany?"

Manager: "Got one."

Me: "Desdemona?"

Manager: "No!"

Girl: "You look like a Cherokee!"

Me: "No!"

After coming up with several other suggestions for a stage name and being turned down over and over, I came up with Sydnee, spelled just like that in a "stripper" way. It was a much better fit for me than any of the names the manager had suggested. At that moment, my alter ego was born. (The next year my chosen name came back to haunt me when the movie *Scream* became a huge hit. If one more customer asked me, "What's your favorite scary movie, Sydnee?" I was going to, well, scream!)

I would have never created a character named Sydnee or danced on various stages in front of strangers for years if

I hadn't been courageous enough to go through with the initial audition. I credit my breast for landing me the job because it certainly was not my dancing ability that had gotten the manager's attention.

So where is the lesson? If you want something, flash a little tit?

No! Don't be ridiculous. That's just for getting out of speeding tickets.

The lesson is to surround yourself with people who will dare you to make changes in your life for the better. I'm not saying that you should start dancing in gentlemen's clubs—unless that is something you would like to either do for a living or experience once during a club's "Amateur Night."

Instead, I want you to take a moment and answer this question: What is something that you'd like to try but don't think you ever could? Or something you know you could do if you weren't too scared to pull the trigger and make it happen? Have you ever wanted to take a dance class? Start painting? Form a nonprofit to help others? Become a volunteer firefighter? Join the local community theater and perform?

What is the one thing that you don't want to wind up saying, "If only I had _____"?

Don't wait until it's too late! Go out there and chase your dreams, no matter if your dreams are:

- Starting a new business
- Starting a family
- Learning a new skill

- Running naked across the field at the
  Superbowl, knowing you have a friend
  with enough bail money to get you out of
  jail after the game

If the people you surround yourself with aren't pushing you to achieve your dreams and move your life forward, then I DARE YOU! Take a deep breath and take that first step. The first step is typically the scariest one. Once you get past that and are moving forward, you will be unstoppable.

Fear is an illusion. If you spell it out, fear stands for "False Evidence Appearing Real." Yes, the sensations you feel in your body and the physical responses you have to the thing you fear are real; I am not discounting them or saying they don't cause you to feel badly. However, those responses are brought on by scenarios you create in your mind to deal with the fear of the unknown.

There have been plenty of times in my life when I have felt terrified. I have dealt with people who used whatever they had in their arsenal to attempt to frighten me into doing what they wanted me to do. And I admit that it used to work. Afterward, I would feel badly about myself and beat myself up for once again giving in and letting my fear dictate my life instead of believing in myself.

Then one day, I decided to change my mindset, and I used an image from a movie to build up my belief in my own worth and give me strength.

In the 1986 movie *Labyrinth*, David Bowie played the role of Jareth, the Goblin King, and Jennifer Connelly was cast as Sarah, the sixteen-year-old girl trying to solve

Jareth's labyrinth and get her baby brother back. Jareth does all kinds of things to keep her from succeeding and was quite the bully, though the camera angles of him waist-down in his leggings made most of us forgive him . . .

There is a point in the movie where Sarah realizes that her fear is not serving her at all. It is not only making her feel bad, but it is also giving Jareth the upper hand. When she finally realizes that she is the one who controls her life, she looks him dead in the eye and says, "You have no power over me." In that moment, all the lies and fear she had believed were true (as well as the labyrinth) crumble around them both.

When I feel like someone is trying to force their will on me, I hear Sarah in my head and imagine that I am her, saying, "You have no power over me." Then I watch the false evidence crumbling around me in my mind's eye.

It's understandably easier to stand up to your fears and follow your path in a one-on-one situation or when you know you have someone on your side cheering you on. It is harder when you are surrounded by people who do not have your best interests at heart.

It's important to claim your own power because some-times the people in your life who were cheering you on in the beginning will also go back and forth with their support. Marissa immediately began talking shit about me after I started working at Sunsingers and she was still working as a waitress. I don't know what prompted the one-eighty when she had been the one who had initially dared me, but she flipped her position after seeing the difference in dancer income and waitress income. Luckily, she auditioned soon after her eighteenth birthday and was hired on the spot. She quit her waitressing job and began working the same shifts as me so we could carpool and have fun while we worked, and I didn't let our earlier tension get in the way of my goals.

If you don't succeed in reaching your goal when you first try something new, odds are you will learn and gain skills to help you do better on your next try. Make sure you take the time to look for the lesson, and don't be discouraged or afraid to keep trying. I mean, it's not like you're onstage in front of a packed bar with your boob hanging out, right?

What matters is that you follow your heart and be brave enough to make your dreams come true.

I DARE YOU!

TWO

Fake It 'Til You Make It

MY GO-GO CAREER began in New Jersey, and in the beginning, I worked in several bars in the Garden State where dancers were not permitted to work topless. For the longest time I fought against crossing the Delaware River and working topless for two reasons.

First, the truth was I was embarrassed to take my top off. I had decided that I would rather spend ridiculous amounts of time and money on gas to work in a club in the Garden State than set "the girls" free in front of a bar full of strangers. I worked in just about every club in South Jersey and checked out several in Central Jersey to keep from making that leap across the Delaware River.

Second, I had a phobia of being on bridges. When I was a child, my family went on a road trip to New England. We had been hiking and came to a spot with a huge bridge. We walked out onto it, and I peeked over the edge. I picked up a rock and threw it over, watching it fall, down, down, down . . . it seemed to fall forever! My older brother snuck up behind me and grabbed me, yelling, "Ha!" while quickly pushing me forward and back to make me think I was going over the edge and falling to my death.

That scarred me. For years, any time I drove across a bridge, whether I was the passenger or the driver, I would scream my head off. That had to be annoying to everyone else in the car, but I couldn't help it. I immediately felt that panic, and in that moment, I believed that I was going to fall to my death.

In time, however, I eventually did cross state lines and work in topless clubs. It is normal for dancers to work in several clubs over the course of their careers. Bars can be shut down, the money can dry up over time, or you just may need a change of scenery. When we were ready to make a move, Marissa and I scanned the locally published magazine that was free for the taking in the lobbies of most of the bars in eastern Pennsylvania, southern New Jersey and northern Delaware (more on that later). We looked under "the club directory" to see which bars were within a comfortable driving distance. We did not want to work in the city of Philadelphia, having preconceived ideas that parking would suck, that traffic would be terrible, and that it would be crowded and awful, so we looked for places that were not in the city but that we could drive to in under an hour. We made our list of prospects and decided to check them out.

One of the bars we decided to check out was located so far off the beaten path that we dubbed the super-long driveway that led up to the club "Rape Road" and promptly turned around and left. Another had a sign with a giant painted face of a woman that resembled Rosie O'Donnell. Curiosity got the better of us, so we walked in but promptly turned around and walked right back out. It was a weekend night shift, and the first thing we noticed was that there were only a handful of customers and that the girls were dancing to music from a jukebox. It was my first time auditioning in a topless joint, so I was being picky.

We finally decided to audition in a club in a town a little further north than where we had previously looked. It had a parking lot, which was a plus. We scheduled our auditions, and when the day came, I was really nervous about having to take my top off. It helped that this time I knew that I could dance, a skill I had not had during my first audition. Also, this time Marissa would be auditioning at the same time, so I would not be entering the world of topless dancing alone.

This club had two rectangular stages that were inside a large rectangular bar. The stage closer to the rear of the bar was where we were told to dance to our first song. They explained that during the first song, you were able to leave your top on. Then you would move to the second stage where you would dance to a song with your top off.

As I listened to the manager, I felt my heart rate start to skyrocket. I knew I needed to emotionally prepare myself for this audition because my nerves were starting to get the better of me. I gave myself the internal pep talk that had worked so many times: "I can do it! It's just dancing." "It's not brain surgery. No one is going to die if I screw it up. Except me from embarrassment." "Oh God, why am I doing this . . . again?!"

Then I promptly sent Marissa out to audition first.

She headed out to do her first song, and as it wound down, I knew it was show time for me.

I stepped onto the first stage and saw Marissa dancing on the second one. She flashed a big shit-eating grin at me and whipped her top off. Of all the words that I could use to describe Marissa, *shy* was not one of them. She had a killer body and had no issues showing it off. After a couple of years of dancing, she eventually ditched the giant granny thongs for bottoms that were barely an eyepatch. I don't recall what songs she and I danced to, but I can tell you I was wearing a black crochet thong bikini and thigh-high black leather boots.

I got to the second stage, and I knew what was coming. I was ready! When you put yourself into a position where you must do something, not because you want to but out of necessity, it can actually make you braver than you otherwise might be if you didn't feel the pressure to make it happen.

I got through the first verse of my second song and knew it was go time. I reached behind my back and grabbed the bikini tie.

Here goes nothing, I thought.

I pulled, and nothing happened. The knot keeping my bikini top tied was stuck!

I had a boob pop out during my first audition in a non-boobie bar, and then my top got stuck during my first audition in a topless bar. What the actual fuck?

I grabbed the two crocheted triangles that were covering my breasts, pulled them open Hulk-style to set the girls free, and kept dancing. I finished my audition and made my way off the stage to where Marissa was waiting. The manager came over to let us know that we were both hired and that we could go around for tips.

I hadn't realized that the tiny bit of cloth covering my breasts had acted like a security blanket in the past. One advantage to working in the Jersey bikini clubs was that you were able to wear padded bras, and no one was the wiser, whereas in bars where your top is destined to come off, it would be silly to wear a padded top. I used to say, "What am I going to wear? A WonderBra? When I take it off, the customers will wonder where my tits went!" The first few weeks of dancing topless and being more exposed were definitely uncomfortable for me. But in time I got used to it, and it was just another day at the office—just an office filled with a variety of boobs.

There really aren't as many fake breasts in go-go as you may think. At least there weren't many in the bars where I worked. Marissa and I were both au naturel in the breast department. At the time, I was a full B and Marissa was an A. She was such an exotic beauty that it wouldn't have mattered if her breasts were concave. Most of the girls I worked with had natural breasts ranging from ten-year-old-boy size to totally racktacular. Their boobies came in various natural shapes and sizes, from perky little chest planets to onions in socks. Of course, there were several dancers who had implants, too. You could usually tell not only which girls had fake breasts, but also which ones had made a hefty investment and who had gotten a Bargain Basement Boob Job. One girl I worked with had boobs that looked like they were going in two different directions—one nipple pointed east and the other looked west. Another girl had one boob that had dropped post-surgery and one that didn't. She would spin around the pole, and lefty would stay put while righty swung back and forth like a pendulum.

If you have ever considered implants, please investigate all the pros and cons. I have friends who have happily gotten implants and have never had a problem. I also have friends who have gotten very sick from their implants and ultimately had explant surgery. It is your body and your choice; I am just suggesting that you go into a decision this major with as much information as possible to keep yourself safe and healthy. You must also be careful because, like everything else in this world, someone out there is "the worst" at it. You want to make sure you are not going to have surgery performed by the world's worst plastic surgeon. As I type this, someone is doing exactly that.

No matter what risks may be associated with getting breast implants for cosmetic reasons, some girls will always crave the attention that comes with a big ol' set of tits. If you do decide to go ahead with it, make sure that you go with a breast size that compliments your body type. If you go too big, you'll wind up looking like you have a couple of those big eyes from the Visine commercials.

To quote Ben Stein, "Wow!"

It's also possible that you may wind up going so large that you develop back problems.

I worked at a bar we'll call Warlocks with a girl who was one of the nicest people I had ever met when she was flat-chested. When she got implants, it was like they implanted a bitchy attitude along with them. She went from sweet to salty overnight. Confidence is amazing—and I highly encourage it!—but it does not mean treating other people like shit because you're getting off on all the attention and you've decided you are now better than everyone else.

Some of the customers also tried to use the topless environment to their advantage. You had to be smart enough to not fall for the old "Are those real?" trick.

The customer who inquired about the authenticity of your chest wanted you to answer, "Yes," so they could fake disbelief and say, "No way! I don't believe you!" To which you would say, "Yes, they are!" To which they'd say, "I don't believe it! Let me feel them to see . . ."

Nice try, Skippy! It's not happening.

I would always shut that down immediately with "If I'm paying thousands of dollars for implants, my boobs would be walking into the room before me. I wouldn't have gotten Bs!" There are advantages to having tweeters instead of hooters.

While you should always stay true to yourself and reaching your own goals, there will always be times when you can use a little boost. In the world of gentlemen's clubs especially, but not limited to only those places, that may mean implants. Or hair extensions, or fake nails. If any of that is your thing, god bless you! I'm a mani-pedi fan myself, and I also routinely make sure my "granny hairs" are covered to match the rest of my dark-brown hair to give the illusion that I am years younger than I truly am.

When I say fake it until you make it, I'm not just referring to outward appearance and physical things. I also mean internally, the things that are going on in your mind. Imagine someone who has the qualities that you would like to achieve. Then pretend that you are them in the situation you are navigating.

I am in no way suggesting identity theft; what I mean is that you should channel their energy and make it your own.

How would they handle the positions that you are finding yourself in? What skills do they have that you would like to have as well? If you are a Christian, it is the same idea as asking yourself, "What would Jesus do?" This is not about religion; you just need to insert the name of the person who has the skills and qualities you would like to have also: it could be Jesus, Betty White, Brian Boitano . . . whatever person fits you and your goals.

Channeling the confidence and swagger of someone you admire is a good way to practice and gain the skills for yourself while not having to risk as much. When you are just trying out the vibe, you don't have as much on the line. You're just acting after all, right? It's a great way to give yourself the confidence to branch out when you may not really feel that way yet. The cool thing about being the master of your thoughts is that no one else has any clue what is going on between your ears. If you are just repeating, "I am brave. I am successful. I got this!" in your own head, the only one who can hear that conversation is you.

Here's an example of how I did this while dancing. Earlier, I mentioned that the local magazine was available for free in the lobby of most of the local clubs. We'll call it *Undressed*. The magazine editors would do articles in each issue featuring photos and information about a specific club or girl. They also had a special section that included girls from many clubs: the "Best of" section. The girls featured in this section won an award each month for things like "best smile," "best breasts," "most fun," etc. The winner would have her picture featured, and several other girls would be named as honorable mentions. I started to collect several of the magazines in which I had won an award or had been given an honorable mention. My "best smile" award included a picture of me smiling in a Santa hat. In another issue, I was given a co-"best couch dance" award with one of my coworkers. I was also picked for mentions in various categories over the years. I used to love skimming the names each month to see if the magazine mentioned me or my friends in that issue.

When I was still a newbie, one of the local DJs was given a page in the magazine to write his own articles. Some of the subjects he covered were "Pickup Line of the Month" or the "Top 30 Songs" he had been playing. He would also feature a few of the dancers and ask them questions like "What songs are you dancing to right now?" or "What is your big dream?" One month he asked me, Marissa, and our friend Morgana if we would be willing to answer questions for his article. (Of course, we would!) He asked us about our current music selections, what our big dream was, and "What goes through your mind while you're onstage."

I'm sure a lot of the guys in the crowd with whom I made eye contact while I performed thought that all kinds of dirty things must have been going through my mind while I danced. I would lock eyes with them, run my hands down my body and over my breasts, make my best "oooh" face, and have them believing I wanted nothing more than to ride them like a Harley on a bumpy road.

However, my answer in the article got me more attention than if I had lied and said I was thinking about sex. What I thought about when I danced was: "One, two . . . kick my leg. Three, four . . . touch myself."

Most of the time while I was onstage, I was also making a mental list of what I needed to pick up from the grocery store on my way home. Other times, I would replay a conversation in my head from earlier in the night and get angry about all of the awesome comebacks that were easily coming into my brain now that it was too late.

The point is, I could have answered that question any way I wanted because the only one who knew what was going on in my own head while I was onstage was me. Just like you are the only one who can hear your own thoughts.

If you do not feel these things already: act brave, act confident, and pretend that you aren't afraid.

As you are developing these new skills, make sure that while your inner strength and bravery are coming from a "fake it 'til you make it" place, you are still being genuine with your intentions. Faking an air of confidence when you are terrified internally is not the same as lying. It's learning. The more you pretend to be confident in times that you are scared, the more confident you will become.

Dancers telling lies to people comes with the territory. Dancer lies typically start with answering the question, "What's your name?" (Yes, there are girls who use their real names, but those girls are few and far between.) I am fairly certain that the number of women in the outside world named after recipe ingredients is quite small compared to the number of them in gentlemen's clubs.

You have the girls who choose their dance names based on bakery ingredients and products: Sugar, Cream, Cinnamon, Cocoa (or Coco), and Cupcake.

Your fruit names: Cherry, Peaches, Berry, Apple.

Then there are random foods like Candy, Caramel, Sage, and Ginger, as well as brand names like Hershey.

I even worked with a "Puddin" once.

Car makes and models were popular choices—Mercedes, Lexus, Porsche—as well as precious jewels and gemstones like Diamond, Sapphire, Emerald, and Onyx and geographical names like Savannah, Dakota, and Dallas. Some girls went with names that described what they might be providing to the customer, such as Fantasy (or Fantasia), Destiny, and Delight. The most popular was any name you could "stripperize" by changing the *y* at the end to an *i*: Brandi, Mandi, Nikki, Brittani, etc.—or in my case, an *ee* for Sydnee.

I once worked with a girl named Charmon. It was spelled differently than the toilet paper, but you could pronounce the word "asswipe" as "Ass-wee-pay" and still have to put up with the same crap (pun intended) from the customers. When I became a manager, Charmon was one of my regular girls (we had previously danced together at another club and had gotten along great; I loved working with her). One night, she was in the couch room giving a lap dance before she was supposed to go onstage. The customer had apparently gotten a little too excited and . . . "shared the love" on her leg. She asked me to stall for her so she could clean up before her set. (I didn't ask about the logistics of how that happened. I didn't want to know.) I told her that it was fine; just be quick.

Since we had a history of working together, I knew that she had a sense of humor. I could not resist the opportunity to mess with her. She danced to hip hop and dance music.

When she got onstage, the DJ was already playing a song that she typically danced to. Little did she know that I had spoken to the DJ while she was in the dressing room baby-wiping her thigh. Once she was onstage, comfortable that it was just a regular set, I had the DJ switch her music to the song "Come Baby Come" by K7. I couldn't help myself. If you are unfamiliar, the chorus of the song is the title repeated over and over. She stopped mid-dance to shoot me daggers. She was fake mad at me for a little while, but I could tell she thought it was funny, too.

The pièce de résistance of "Why would you pick that out of all the names in all of the communities in all of the countries and cities and villages in the entire world when you are given the chance to make a new name for yourself?" was, and I swear I couldn't make this up if I tried . . . "Tweety Bird."

When they weren't requesting to see her "Putty tat," guys would still ask her, "Is that your real name?"

Seriously?

Whenever I was asked if my real name was Sydnee, which happened frequently, I would flat out answer, "Nope." This would inevitably lead to the next question, "Then what *is* your real name?" I would look them in the eyes, completely straight-faced, and answer, "Bertha, that's why I go by Sydnee." (No offense to anyone named Bertha!) I never understood why it mattered. Most of the customers couldn't remember the name Sydnee in the five minutes from when the DJ said it to when I walked up to them for tips, so why did they care?

For a brief period, I had a regular customer who got couch dances from me every week and moaned, "Oh,

Tatiana!" There was a Tatiana who worked there, but it wasn't me. I corrected him a couple of times, then decided I didn't really care. Tatiana used to sneak up behind me, grab me, and moan, "Oh, Tatiana!" like the customer. More than once, she would be giving a couch dance at the same time I was in there with the guy, and Tatiana and I wouldn't look at each other or we would just start giggling.

When it comes to wanting to know a dancer's real name, I imagine there is a certain excitement about knowing things that only a select few have been privy to. It makes you feel like you are part of a secret society. But most of the customers called us "Baby" or "Hon" anyway, so it didn't really matter what our names (or stage names) were.

I didn't know it at the time, but my choosing "Sydnee" as a stage name would later make me the subject of a very personalized pickup line.

Pickup lines are as common in go-go bars as they are in regular bars, so it never surprised me when I heard them while walking around for tips. They ranged from "If I could rearrange the alphabet, I would put *U* and *I* together" to "Was your daddy a terrorist? Because you are DA BOMB!" I heard some of them so often that it was easy to come up with a quick reply. If a customer asked, "Hey baby, what's your sign?" My usual replies were "Stop!" or "Do Not Enter." My favorite generic pickup line is to ask the person you're interested in, "Do you like apples?" Most people do and would answer, "Yes," to which you can ask the follow-up question: "I'm gonna fuck you tonight. How you like them apples?" (I'm completely joking; I've never used that line on anyone! If you do and you get slapped, don't come crying to me. It has the same success rate as "My face leaves in two minutes—you better be on it!")

One night in 2000, while I was bartending at Warlocks, all the TVs in the bar were on the sports channels spotlighting the upcoming Summer Olympics in Australia. I was chatting with one of the regulars when he told me that he really wished he could go to the Olympics. I thought nothing of it but asked, "Oh yeah? Why's that?" He looked me dead in the eye and said, "So I can say that I've been in Sydnee [sic] at least once!"

I lost it! I gave him kudos (and bought him a beer) for coming up with such a timely line. Even though he will never be able to say he's ever been in Sydnee. Not even once!

In my experience, the rotation of dancers went smoothly most of the time, no matter how silly the names of the girls working that shift happened to be. However, in one of the clubs where I used to work, the name game became a huge source of confusion. On any given night, four of us worked together and we had chosen terribly similar names: Cindy, Cynthia, Sadie, and me, Sydnee. The DJ was a big guy who was always either eating or sounded like he had a mouth full of food. He would call "Sadie" to the stage, but it sounded like "Sydnee," so I would make my way there only to have him yell at me because it wasn't my turn. This happened with all four of us because, through a mouthful of shit, our names all sounded the same.

One day, I decided enough was enough after being hollered at once again because of the DJ's inability to enunciate. I marched into the DJ booth and told him, "That is it! From now on, I am Bob." I figured this would end the confusion, and I would know exactly when he was calling me to the stage.

It worked! In addition to clarifying when I was supposed to be onstage and lessening the number of times I got yelled at, it was a riot to see the customer's faces when the DJ announced over the microphone, "Up next . . . please welcome the very sexy . . . Bob!"

Some of those guys probably still think that was my name. If nothing else, I made a lasting impression.

You can also make a lasting impression in your own life. If you don't have the confidence right now to take the steps toward your goal, too bad! Fake it like you've already made it. If you train your brain to believe you are the things you want to be, it will naturally start thinking and acting that way. I'm not saying pretend you're a brain surgeon and waltz into an operating room with a scalpel. I mean if brain surgery is your passion, mentally think of yourself in that space. When your brain believes that you have already accomplished your goal, it will find you paths to get you to that place and help you to become successful.

You also need to make sure that while you are on this path, you are remaining true to yourself. When I started dancing, I observed the other girls purring into the guys' ears while they walked around to collect tips. They whispered all kinds of dirty things to convince their customers that they wanted to get naked with them. The customers ate it up because they were being so sexy. I thought that if that was what everyone else was doing, that must be what I was supposed to do, too. So, I walked up to a guy and said in my sexiest deep voice, "Hey baby . . . how are—"

That was as far as I got before I burst out laughing. I literally busted my gut laughing in this poor dude's face because I knew I was full of shit. I couldn't even keep a straight face!

From that point on, I was myself, just a more confident version. I would walk up to a guy and give him a hug (I am such a hugger—no perfume or glitter for me!) or just punch him in the shoulder and say, "Was sup?" After a few years, I learned how easy it was to make a few extra dollars by walking up behind a guy and rubbing his shoulders and giving him a massage. Massage money was great, but most of the time, I made my money though humor. I was, and still am, a huge fan of dad jokes. The cornier, the better. If a guy said to me, "I like your tits," I'd reply, "Thanks! I'm kind of attached to them myself." If a customer looked at me and said, "You've got great legs!" I'd answer, "Thank you! They go all the way up and make an ass out of themselves." One that always got a big laugh was whenever there was a bald man sitting at the bar. I'd sneak up behind him and rub the top of his head, saying, "Don't tell the manager that I'm giving head at the bar!"

There is a balance to be achieved between simply faking it to succeed, and making sure you still retain your core values. Another way a lot of girls fake it in go-go land is by pretending they are bi or lesbians. Not to let the pussy—I mean, the cat—out of the bag, but guys aren't the only ones who can be "gay for pay." I mentioned earlier that I am bisexual. Honestly, when I look at the female form, I don't know how every person on earth wouldn't find the female body hot as hell. I love my men too, but women of all shapes and sizes are just beautiful! I played "pretend girlfriend" to a lot of girls over the years. Want me to kiss you in the couch room so we both make more money? Sure! Want me to feel you up so we both make extra money from a customer? Twist my arm and make me feel your boobies . . . okay.

At Warlocks, we had a giant rectangular main stage with three poles—a center pole that was rarely used, a pole to the right where you would dance to your first song, and another to the left where you would take your top off and dance to the song picked by the girl onstage after you. In the multiple years I worked there as a dancer, bartender, and house mom, I had gotten to know many different girls and their personal cause-and-effect triggers. Generally, the girls would respond with an eye roll or complain under their breath whenever they were called to the stage. One dancer sticks out to me more than the others because of her specific trigger. I'm not normally attracted to blonds, but April was a cutie-pie with an awesome body. Not too thick, not too thin, small chest, round butt, and most important—hilarious! She had a Pavlovian response to the song "Dancing Queen" by Abba. That song just rang April's bell. If April was behind me in the rotation and I heard Frida and Agnetha hit that famous first note, I would see April running at me from the other end of the rectangle main stage at full speed, arms stretched wide, screaming, "Let's dyke out!"

I'm not going to pretend that I wasn't a willing participant. She was a hottie! But there is only so much you can do onstage in front of a club full of customers and stay within the parameters of "keeping it legal." After the initial kissing and heads motorboating between each other's boobs, she would lie down, and I would get on top of her. I would start by kissing her and then work my way down, running my lips and tongue over her neck . . . down her chest . . . to her belly, and finally resting at her thong with my hair covering her crotch and lower belly. If you have long hair, it increases your ability to give the illusion of sexual contact that may or may not be happening between you and the other person involved. I moved my head back and forth in the right way, I was able to create a convincing illusion that I was going down on her, especially to the men who really wanted to believe they were watching lesbian sex happening in real life in front them. A couple of times I gave her a zurbert on the inner thigh, but that usually ended with her smacking me in the head with her leg or bucking her hips and cracking me in the face with her pelvic bone. Neither of those moves felt pleasant, so I concentrated more on the illusion we were providing than being a smartass and making her laugh.

Pardon the pun, but the customers ate that shit up! They would throw money at us, and we would split the take evenly when the song was over.

I never had any kind of relationship outside the bar with April other than a few trips to the diner for some after-work grub and giving her rides home. I'm not sure if she was truly bisexual or if ABBA just did it for her. I was never invited in when I gave her rides home, so maybe she was bi but just didn't find me attractive. Either way, we had a hella lotta fun rolling around onstage together and made a lot more money than we would have done if we hadn't put on those shows. Neither of us ever forced the other one to participate.

You don't ever want to sell out when it comes to your own values and morals. Don't fake it into a way that will land you on the therapist's couch. If "dykeing out" on a stage in front of a bunch of people isn't your thing, then by all means, don't do it! It's hardly a situation that most of the population would ever find themselves pressured into participating in. What I am suggesting is to find that balance and "pretend yourself" into a more confident version of the best parts of you. Especially if they are parts you don't have all together right now. Don't do anything you're not comfortable with, but the secret is to not let yourself become *too comfortable*, either.

I know I have already used a shellfish illustration, but the online video of the Rabbi and the lobster is a wonderful illustration of the benefits of being uncomfortable in order to grow. It would be "shellfish" of me to not share this story! You can search for it on YouTube, but here's a little summary:

> Lobsters have soft, squishy bodies under their hard shells. Their bodies grow, but their shells do not. At some point the lobster's body will get too large for its shell, making it constricted and uncomfortable.
>
> For it to continue to grow, the lobster must find a safe place to hide. There it can abandon the shell it has out-grown and grow a new one that is a better fit.
>
> It will continue this process repeatedly in its lifetime as it continues to grow and change. Being guided first by

feeling uncomfortable and then achieving something greater. Not just once, but multiple times in its life.

It's the same for us.

You are only as good as your next achieved goal. When we get complacent and rest on our laurels, it can all go to shit very quickly. Staying in our comfort zones keeps us from moving forward and causes us to never reach our goals until we are so uncomfortable that we have no other choice.

You need to keep improving yourself: mentally, physically, and financially. We all have room to learn and grow. When you are feeling the most uncomfortable, that is a signal that you are ready to grow. Don't be afraid to shed your old shell. (You can hide naked behind a rock for a bit while your new shell is growing or just let it all hang out—whichever is more your style.) Don't interpret the feelings of discomfort to mean something negative. Instead, get excited because it means you are ready to push forward and get closer to achieving your goals. It is all for your greater good.

You can find all kinds of resources that can help you on your journey, from self-help books to classes to YouTube videos. No matter what skills or knowledge you are seeking, odds are that either the skill itself or the guidance to lead you to where you can acquire the skill are available to you right now. (There are so many podcasts, videos, and blogs that are designed to teach you, and all you need to do is search. A lot of them won't even cost you a penny!)

I completely understand that trying to find balance can

be hard. Sometimes it can seem like no matter what you try, you continually hit a wall, hear "No" and it may feel like your dreams are unreachable. There were certainly nights when I was a dancer that I wanted to hang up the heels. Customers told me I was fat, or ugly, or that they were only there to see someone else. As tempting as it was to want to quit and find a new path, I knew deep down that I had to take the good with the bad. I had to be strong and push through the negative to reap the rewards that I knew I would achieve with perseverance.

I recently heard another example that helps me to visualize not only where I want to be but what I will realistically need to go through to reach those goals. If you think of life as a pendulum, it can help you to assess what you are realistically willing to do when it comes to the life you want to lead. The pendulum swings freely left and right. When the pendulum swings to the left, that is where all the joy and amazing feelings live. When it swings to the right, that is where all the pain and hardship lies. The amount it pulls in one direction is the amount it will automatically swing to the other.

So many people choose to live in the narrow middle territory where the pendulum only swings a tiny bit left and right. This ensures that you never really feel pain or hardship. The flip side is that you never really feel true joy or success, either. You're just existing, doing enough to get by in your day-to-day. The downside to this life is that while you ensure that you never experience deep pain, you never get to experience true elation, either. If you work hard and push the pendulum hard to the left, you are going to be rewarded with intense joy and success. But eventually it will swing to the right, and you will feel pain and struggle.

Like most jobs, dancing in gentlemen's clubs had pendulum like times. January, for example, would be slow. Credit card bills were coming in from buying holiday presents, and New Year's Resolutions had been made that often included giving up alcohol.

The flip side was the Spring when tax return checks were flowing and there was money to spare followed by an influx of bachelor parties. I had to recognize that there were times when my income would be lean, but if I pushed through, I would make it to the times of plenty.

While you can't get blood from a stone, the most important factor to my success or failure was me, my work ethic and my attitude. I had to do my best and know that sometimes that would yield more than other times.

Are you willing to deal with the pain and struggle for a time so that you may also experience immense joy and success? Or do you want to stay in the narrow comfort zone, so you don't get hurt, but also don't get to experience anything extraordinary?

If you understand that extraordinary success comes with dark times, it makes it easier to swallow whenever those dark times surface. You will realize that the negatives are only temporary and part of the process when it comes to leading an overall balanced life. This will give you confidence that, in time, the pendulum will swing back, and you will find yourself in the land of awesomeness once again.

Everything in life is temporary. The good stuff as well

as the bad. In the times when things are good, remember that you need to strive to keep them going. Never get complacent. Know that when you are in a difficult season, it isn't going to last forever. So, never lose hope. Be brave and be willing to take on the occasional pain and dark times in exchange for an overall extraordinary and amazing life. It is so worth the trade-off.

It's also important to point out that even if you are living in the middle of the pendulum, true balance is a myth. Especially for those of us who are trying to juggle momming, having a job, keeping a house, and simultaneously having any sort of life aside from those three things. When I started an online business in 2013, it required tons of my time. I started to feel guilty because no matter how hard I tried, I couldn't find a way to put my effort into everything at once. In the times I was a successful online fitness coach and giving my attention to my clients, I felt guilty because I couldn't give my kids 100 percent of my attention. If I was pouring all my energy into my kids, I was not giving enough time to my husband. All of this resulted with me spiraling into a state of depression where I was not able to give any of myself to anyone in a meaningful way.

It can be difficult to block out the negativity from strangers but being treated poorly by people you love is a thousand times worse! Thankfully, even though my parents did not approve of my dancing, they told me that I was old enough to make my own decisions. The same did not hold true for some of the people in my parents' circles, particularly the "Christians" who ignored the verses in Matthew 7:3-5 about planks and specks in eyeballs. I had to remind myself that when it came to those situations, I needed to consider the source.

In time, I learned that I will never be able to achieve a state of total balance every day of my life. I realized that not only is it not possible to do everything myself, but it is okay for me to admit that. It is necessary for me to ask for help in times when I need it and to not feel bad about reaching out to others. So many of us feel like we need to be Wonder Woman—and that if we are not, it means we are failing at life. That is just not true.

Get organized and plan out your time so that you can be present in the times when it is most important and can call for backup when your attention needs to be focused elsewhere. Make sure that your partner knows in advance the times when you must put your energy into your business or your kids. Make sure to schedule date nights and one-on-one time so they do not feel ignored and neglected. Communication is key!

Remember that being uncomfortable, like the lobster, is a natural part of the growth process. It can be scary to push the pendulum into the side of the swing that is painful, but just remember that the pain will be temporary. In time, the pendulum will swing away from that place of being uncomfortable, and you will be enjoying the rewards of your sacrifice. If you really want to live the kind of life that will bring you extraordinary joy and make you feel amazing, take that leap of faith—and fake it 'til you make it! Tell yourself you are brave over and over until you believe it in your very soul, and you allow that destiny to manifest.

THREE

Don't Let Anyone Put Your Fire Out!

IT CAN TAKE a long time to find your passion, but when you do, you need to make sure you stoke that fire inside of you and continue to make it grow into an unstoppable inferno.

For some people, their passion can be found in their work. Certain people seem to be born to do awesome things, or they feel a pull in their heart tugging them to their purpose in life. I have tremendous respect for people who have a talent or who have known since childhood which path they want their life to take.

I don't fall into either of those categories.

Sometimes when I am out and about, I stop by the deli my husband owns to see him. My husband is a fan of the local public radio station, and it plays in the store often. Once, my ears perked up when my husband mentioned that the song playing through the speakers was written by a guy who had graduated from the same high school as he did, but when I heard what the DJ said about the artist, Devon Gilfillian, it resonated with me even more. According to the DJ, Devon knew that he *had* to make music. It was not a choice. It was an all-consuming desire inside his very being that could not be ignored, which resulted in his song "Unchained."

I wish I had that kind of inner guidance in my life. A sense of longing to not only know what my destiny is but to also have the inner GPS to guide me on the path to fulfilling it. The fact is I still don't know what I want to be when I grow up. I've always felt that I can do several things decently, but I don't feel as though I have an actual "talent." My kids are musically and artistically gifted, and I love watching them hone their crafts and use the talents they have been given. But in my forty-plus years, I have never really discovered one in myself. Sure, I am a decent cake decorator, and people have encouraged me to sell my cakes and cupcakes out of my home, but since I'm also currently working as an online health and fitness coach, I think selling cupcakes to people and then encouraging them to buy fitness and nutrition programs might be bad karma!

I also love to sing . . . but trust me, that most certainly is not a talent. I was in my school chorus and show choir, but there would be no Broadway debut in my future. Once, I went out to sing karaoke with friends and did my best Alanis Morrisette impression. I single-handedly cleared out an entire Chili's! (Even though I cannot sing like a professional, I sing at some point every day because I enjoy it. One of my favorite things is harmonizing with my daughter while we're driving in my truck.)

To be honest, I wasn't an extraordinarily talented dancer in the traditional sense, either. I was pole dependent! In time, I learned how to spin and shimmy and do a variety of pole tricks. When I wasn't holding on to a pole, I was crawling on the floor or leaning up against the mirror.

Basically, my sets contained no dance moves that didn't involve the safety of the pole or a mirror.

Hmm . . . fake it 'til . . .

Singing, dancing, and decorating all make me happy, but when I started writing this book in my mind, it finally ignited a fire in my gut and excited me!

The thing about personal joy is that when other people find out about it, they tend to want to poop all over your dreams and try to bring you down. It is imperative that you protect the flame of your passion and not let the people in your life—or even strangers on the internet—shit your fire out.

Most of us consider bullies to be an issue that school-aged children deal with. The table of "mean girls" who say we can't sit with them or the mental image of the big kid beating up the small kid to get their lunch money is typically what comes to mind when I hear the word *bully*. Unfortunately, there is so much more to bullying than one awful stereotype. Bullying is multilayered. The sad truth is bullying does not always end when our school years do. Any person who uses fear tactics, insults, or any other form of intimidation to take advantage of others or coerce them into doing things is a bully. It doesn't matter how young or old the meanie is.

So many people are like crabs. I don't mean cranky; I mean like the actual animals. I heard this story a while ago,[1] and it's stuck with me:

There was a man walking along the beach who came upon another man standing in the surf. As he got closer, he saw the man was crabbing. He put each crab he caught in a bucket, but the bucket had no lid.

The first man asked him why he didn't have a lid on the bucket. Wasn't he worried that the crabs would escape?

The second man explained that if there was only one crab in the bucket, it could crawl out. However, when there are multiple crabs in there and one tried to escape from the bucket, all the other crabs inside would pull it back in and not let it leave.

People are like that too. When they see that someone is trying to crawl out to a better life by working hard, doing well in school, starting a business, getting healthier, etc., others will try to pull them back down. They would rather have that person share the same fate as the many rather than help to elevate the one to something better.

Those people are usually doing that out of fear. If you better yourself and move your life forward to a better place, it forces them to face the hard truth that they are capable of doing the same thing. They are just too lazy, scared, weak, or comfortable in their current situation to try. It is a lot easier for those types of people to tear down others who are being successful in the hopes that they will fall back to the crab life, rather than taking the effort to work toward improving their own lives and escaping the bucket, too. Misery loves company!

Don't surround yourself with crabs. Or with people who will give you crabs.

Make sure that the people around you will lift you up,

push you forward, and dare you to reach your dreams.

Why is it easier for so many people to tear others down than to elevate themselves? I think it's because most bullies are in the position that they are in because they have no self-worth. Perhaps they grew up in an environment where they were torn down every day by the people who were supposed to love them. In time, they began to believe the bullshit they were being fed and as a result were convinced that they were unlovable and powerless. Those scars run deep. And even though they are not happy with who they have become or where they find themselves in life, they don't have the cojones to do the work needed to lift themselves up to be in a better place. So, in order to make themselves feel empowered, they feel the need to tear down other people. The even sadder fact is how many of these kids, and later adults, have learned this behavior from the adults in their lives who had been treated that same way as children themselves. It's a cycle and a learned behavior.

The age of social media has made this behavior even easier to participate in because you don't have to have the balls to bully someone to their face. I'm not saying social media creates bullies; it just exposes them. These platforms open the opportunity to showcase that behavior more easily if it's part of your makeup. Also, bullying is no longer confined to school hours. Internet bullying is possible twenty-four seven. You can hide behind your screen and anonymously be a dick. You need to develop a thick skin and not let them get to you. Or better yet, turn off your device and walk away. You cannot be bullied online if you block, avoid, or ignore the person who is trying to get to you. In my experience, when a troll realizes you are not going to give them a reaction, they'll go somewhere else.

When you are setting and working toward your goals, just remember that it's your dream, and if someone else doesn't share your passion, just bless, and release.

When you first fall into the initial excitement of following your dreams, it's so easy to feel unstoppable, and the first few days or weeks can be immensely exciting! However, inevitably, people will come out of the woodwork to start picking your passion apart.

"What if you fail?" they may ask.

"But what if I succeed?" you answer.

"But what *if* you *fail*?"

Let me let you in on a little secret: anyone who is great at something has failed multiple times before they got great. It's just the way it works. You need to make sure that when you do fail, you learn and then try again. Don't give up when the going gets tough. That is the naysayers' wet dream and will result in you being buried under a pile of "I told you so!"

I heard an acronym for *fail* that has helped me to rethink how that word makes me feel—it's a "First Attempt in Learning." When you look at failure as a learning experience instead of a negative experience, it can make it easier to handle when things don't work out the way you planned. You can take the lessons from the experience and move on rather than beat yourself up for failing. It's just all part of the process. While you are attempting new things, you don't succeed or fail—you succeed or learn!

Dr. Seuss's first book was rejected by twenty-seven

publishers before being published. Stephen King's book *Carrie* was rejected by thirty, after being rejected by himself! Can you imagine what would have happened if either of these men decided, "Well, I guess writing just isn't my thing," and never tried to get a book published again? I can't imagine my teenage years without reading *It*, *Christine*, *Pet Sematary* . . . or never seeing the movie *Stand by Me*. I also can't imagine my kids not celebrating Dr. Seuss's birthday for an entire week in elementary school. Or growing up in a world where I'd never read *There's a Wocket in my Pocket* and *Oh Say Can You Say* at bedtime.

Instead of Stephen King and Dr. Seuss packing it up the first time they were told no, they pressed on. They didn't let other people's opinions keep them from pursuing their dreams, and they each achieved massive success in writing, selling millions of books.

Most of us have already taken this approach to life without even realizing it. For any person who is blessed with the ability to walk, there was a time when we had to learn that skill. We didn't come out walking out of the womb. If, when we were babies, we gave up the first time we fell on our butts while taking our first steps, none of us would be walking now.

We didn't let literally falling on our asses hold us back when we were little, so why should we let a figurative fall on our asses hold us back now?

When people in your life say things to try and hold you back, even if they are coming from a place of love, you need to hold fast to your dreams and keep following your passion. Close your eyes, stick your fingers in your ears, and say, "La la la la la la la la la," if you must. Put your foot down, put your walls up, and don't let the negative energy in. When you let the fog of negativity permeate your mind, it can choke out all the progress you are making.

There are two types of pooh-poohers. The first are the people who legitimately care about you. They really do believe that the things that they are saying and doing to you are for your own good. Their pooh-poohing is based on a place of love and comes from worrying about your well-being and having your best interests at heart. These people are so afraid that you will get hurt that they will throw all kinds of things at you to get you to stay where you are instead of blossoming into who you are meant to be. They are not taking into consideration that transformation isn't always easy. Sometimes it can hurt! You need to continue to learn and keep on your path, despite the pain.

The second type of pooh-poohing comes from those who just want to see you fail. Narcissistic people who believe they are better than you can be are the most hurtful because they are motivated by wanting to knock the wind out of you. Seeing you fall brings them joy. They are just waiting in the wings to say, "I told you so!" and laugh every time you are forced to take a step back.

I hate those fuckers!

Then there are those with low self-esteem who will try and take you down in order to make themselves feel better. Send in the crabs!

If you posted about your passion on social media and got 499 encouraging, positive comments and one negative one, which of those comments are you going to think about?

It's human nature to take the negative stuff to heart because it makes your heart hurt. But no matter how much you want to lash out at the negative and hurtful commenters, don't feed the trolls! That is exactly what they want. Learn to ignore the bullying. I recently shared my opinion about a news story that was trending on social media. I got over one hundred reactions and fifty comments, and most of them were positive. A couple of people disagreed with my opinion but said it in a way that was respectful. No worries! I don't post opinions expecting that everyone will agree with mine; that's what makes it my opinion. (When I say *opinion*, I mean how I feel about questions like: Does pineapple belong on pizza? Who's the all-time best eighties band? Opinions can be open for discussion. Things like racism and discrimination against others based on race, gender, or sexual orientation do not fall into the opinion category. Human rights are just that: rights.) But while some people have the skills to express a conflicting opinion in a respectful way like an adult, others do not. One of the people who commented was so worked up that they contradicted themselves with ridiculous "worst-case scenarios" and half-formed sentences and ultimately negated their point. That's when I knew the reaction was all about them and not me. If you call them out on it, they will typically get angry and leave the conversation, throwing a few insults at you on the way out for good measure.

It's okay to not agree, but some people take having a difference in opinion as a personal attack. There was a time when I would have taken that sort of criticism to heart and allowed it to shut me down. I used to give too much weight to the thoughts of others, and it would cause me to abandon my path and cave rather than cause a disagreement. My friend Dom says, "Don't be a cavewoman!" meaning specifically, "Don't cave and give up when you feel the pressure from other people." Stick to your principles.

I've learned that if I know in my heart that I am following my passion, the people who are trying to stop me are merely speed bumps on my way to success. I need to stay on my path.

Sometimes when I feel like the negative opinions of others are starting to break through in my mind, I like to sit back and imagine the day that my dream is finally achieved. I picture the faces of the people who have told me I'm stupid. More specifically, the ones who've said I'm not as smart as they are because I never got my college degree, as if what I've learned during my other life experiences cannot be counted as valuable. I think about the people who have called me names, cut me down, made me feel "less than." I especially see the faces of the people who I know have smiled to my face while talking shit about me behind my back, blissfully unaware that I know all about it—what was said and to whom, and when, and where . . .

In my daydream, I see all these people gathered in a large room. I am standing at the front of the room at a podium on a stage. When they have all seated, I thank them for coming to hear what I would like to share. Then I give them all a big raspberry and a finger eleven, throwing up both middle fingers because one just isn't enough for these people, before I walk off the stage and into my happy life.

Shallow? Sure. Immature? Definitely! But every once in a while, when I am really stuck and don't have the motivation to sit down and type, the thought of proving every single one of those assholes wrong gets my motor running, and I get to work.

Overall, I am very into positivity, the Golden Rule, and leaving things better than I found them. Sometimes though, I just need to take all the resentment, hurt, embarrassment, and anger that I have felt over the years and transform it into fuel to drive my dreams. It's a way for me to take the negative energy that is being thrust into my life and turn it into something positive.

There is no better feeling than being so much more than what the bullies told you you couldn't be. Don't buy into the bullshit. The *only* person who decides what path your life takes, how successful you will be, and what is best for you is *you*! Not your parents, not your spouse, not your friends, and especially not strangers.

The inspiration for the name of this chapter came from a story that makes me laugh to this day. I used to work with a gorgeous girl named Fire. I can picture her now in a red gown she wore frequently. It clung to her curves perfectly and showed off all her assets. On top of that, she was a super-nice person, and we always had a lot of fun when we worked together.

Unfortunately, even though Fire loved to drink, she could not hold her liquor. I'll always remember one shift in particular when she had a few too many. She was doing her best to try and act sober, but it was not a good act. She held on to the pole with one hand and kind of swayed back and forth with a faraway look in her half-crossed eyes. She turned my way and gave me a little half smile, bent forward, and then bent back up to standing. She wobbled back and forth before regaining her balance by placing her back against the pole . . . and then the waterfall started. She peed herself onstage!

This happened not once but on two separate occasions while we were working together.

The second time it happened, the bartender turned to me and said, "I guess she put her fire out!"

I laughed and laughed because I wasn't the one who had to clean it up.

While I would never suggest drinking to excess and wetting your pants (legs, shoes, etc.) onstage in front of a crowd of people, I do love that when Fire did just that, it didn't deter her from coming back to work the next night with her head held high. She had to be so strong to not run away and hide forever and to instead come back to the club and work her next shift like nothing had happened the night before. I would like to hope that after strike two she didn't do that again, but I have no idea. Wherever you are now, Fire, I hope you are happy, healthy, and dry!

She wasn't the only dancer I've worked with to come back to work after an embarrassing night. I have had a few myself. Thank god I never peed myself, but there was one time when I did my signature back somersault and flipped myself right off the stage and into the rack of well liquor. I've tripped and landed wrong and had wardrobe malfunctions . . . but I've always laughed it off and kept going.

Once when I was bartending, a girl managed to fly sideways off the stage, which was four feet from the ground, taking out several bottles of liquor before she came to a stop. The only thing that stopped her was the interior back wall of the bar. It was as if she had gone sliding into home base, only midair. The first thing she did, once she made sure that all her body parts were intact, was hop up and ask me if I was okay. I was shocked but managed to ask, "Me? I'm fine, are *you* okay?"

I genuinely believe that all bartenders who work in gentlemen's clubs should be required to wear helmets. The amount of legs swinging around poles with stiletto-heeled feet, frequently right at skull level, is dangerous. I have been kicked in the head several times while bartending, and it hurts like a mofo! I am sorry to say that I have kicked my fair share of bartenders as well. Never on purpose, of course. It got to the point where I would yell, "Fore!" before spinning if one of the bartenders was nearby so she wouldn't accidentally walk into the space where my heel was soaring by.

After a few years in the business, I worked in a club where the dressing room was on the second floor. We would head upstairs to get changed into our costumes and enter the stage by way of a spiral staircase leading from the second floor to the stage. I have seen more than one dancer come down those stairs at the speed of light, compliments of alcohol and gravity. Some of them would recover immediately and try to play it off by jumping to their feet and starting to dance. Others required some time to get their wits about them. None of the girls whom I saw fall down the stairs when I was working required medical attention, thankfully. Drugs and alcohol have a way of enabling you to bounce.

Marissa and I had auditioned and very briefly worked at a club where the stage was so high you had to climb a pool ladder up the side wall to get to the actual stage. By "pool ladder," I mean that it was literally the kind of ladder that is sold to go on the side of the deep end of a swimming pool. Not only that, but the stage was also a platform that was six to eight feet off the ground. There was no railing or raised edge to keep you within the bounds, and the stage floor was so slippery it was as if it had been waxed. That was the only place I ever worked where I had to sign a waiver that made me swear to them that I wouldn't sue if I fell off the stage and got hurt. Marissa and I only worked two shifts there. I believe that my total income from the two shifts was twenty-four dollars. When you spend more in gas and tolls to get to your job than you make at work, it's time to find a new place. (The club has since become an Indian restaurant.)

When Marissa and I had exhausted most of the bars in South Jersey, we headed north and decided to check out a club in central New Jersey. We called and set up a time to audition. When we walked into the bar, we were shocked by the two-story pole. Girls would enter the stage by a trap door in the ceiling and slide down the pole to the stage. Not every girl was comfortable doing that, and they had the option of getting to the stage by way of walking behind the bar and up a couple steps. In addition to having the biggest pole I've ever seen, this club was unique for having a shower drain in the center of the stage floor. It was a metal circle with several holes in it. The first time I saw a drain like this was in the floor of the shower house at summer camp. Why would there be a drain on the stage? I don't know if the building was prone to flooding or if they hosed the girls down during their sets . . .

When we showed up to audition, we cozied up to the bar to get a feel for the place. We looked up just in time to see one of the girls flying out of the ceiling and down the twenty-foot pole, stopping nineteen-and-a-half feet down. We were extremely impressed by her skills! Until she finished dancing, walked away from the pole, got her heel stuck in the drain hole, and face planted.

When we did our auditions, Marissa and I both politely declined using the ceiling hatch to make our way onto the stage and instead walked up the steps behind the bar to perform. We danced to our songs, and that was that. Marissa and I were both hired, but we never went back. We just got a weird vibe from the place and went with our guts. The manager had pushed way too hard trying to get us to not only schedule shifts but start working right then and there. I didn't like the desperation. Plus, I knew in my heart that sooner or later I would have attempted a hatch entrance and broken my neck.

In all my years in go-go bars, I have only seen one bad injury during work hours. It wasn't from falling off the stage, though. A girl named Clarissa got into a fight with a customer and kicked him. I still don't understand how this happened, but she kicked him and broke her leg. The mixture of anger, alcohol, and whatever drugs she had had in her system at the time made her blissfully unaware of the unnatural angle in which her leg was pointing until several people ran over to see what had happened. She gave her leg a cross-eyed glance and insisted it wasn't that bad. The managers forced her to get a ride to the hospital.

I have seen plenty of girls continue to dance with injuries. When you are in a position where you need to make money every night to survive, calling out of work just isn't an option. It's not like dancers get benefits or paid time off. I have worn knee and wrist braces at times when I have needed them. It was a little crazier when I worked with girls who had casts. Unfortunately, the "slip and fall" stories that most of them told as the reasons for their injuries were made-up stories to hide the physical abuse they were enduring at home.

There will always be people in this world who think that it is completely acceptable to view the people who are being abused as "less than," but I don't. People go through all kinds of things, and you never know what someone is dealing with until you walk in their shoes. Try walking in six-inch or higher heels for hours at a time while keeping a smile on your face as you put up with all sorts of unsavory situations. It's not easy! (Of course, I'm being a smartass here.) When you visualize what someone else is going through in their life, it can help you to be more accepting of them. If you imagine how you would feel if you were in the same situation, it can help you to be more compassionate in general. Also, please don't take the "I would never be in that situation" approach because there are so many unseen twists and turns in life that none of us may see coming. Just ask anyone who started a new business in March of 2020. You can't always tell what kinds of struggles others may be dealing with by looking at them from the outside, so it's always better to err on the side of compassion.

I found myself in an abusive relationship in my late teens and stayed in it way too long. Like so many people, I just wanted to be loved. I believed the lies he told me and considered that to be "Love." Many of the girls I worked with over the years were born into situations where all they ever experienced while they grew up was abuse. They witnessed their own mothers being abused by man after man, so they learned that being abused—physically, emotionally, and sexually—was either acceptable or expected. They did not have examples of healthy relationships to model their own lives after. A lot of them were thrown out of their homes at a young age and had to fend for themselves or for themselves and their own children.

In addition to the many girls who grow up abused, many boys are raised seeing men abuse women and believing that this is how they are expected to behave to be considered "a man." They wind up repeating the pattern of abuse in their own relationships when they get older. If no one is willing to step in and try and break the cycle that so many people are finding themselves in on both sides, how can it be expected to change?

We need to be able to help the people who have been abused find the fire that will light them up to see that they are worth so much more than they have been led to believe. That change is not only possible, but attainable. That just because they were in a horrible situation, they don't have to stay there. Physically or mentally.

Luckily, there are so many organizations leading the way in making change; RAINN, NOVA, The Trevor Project and the Office for Victims of Crime[2] are just a few organizations that are available to help. Nothing is going to shift until we stand up for those being abused and say, "Enough!" We also must realize that people who have been abused need to relearn the reactions and behaviors that have made up their lives for so long, which takes time and compassion.

If you are a victim of abuse, you need to stand up for yourself and reach out to the resources that are available to you. That can be terrifying, and it may seem impossible. Do not allow your abuser to put your fire out and make you feel like you are unworthy. You deserve to be loved, accepted and if the person that you are with does not feel that way it is time to be with someone else, even if it is just yourself for a while. It can take a long time to come out on the other side, but it will be well worth it.

On a personal level I have been called names and been disrespected by customers every night that I worked. In the years that I danced, my body changed drastically over time. When I started, I was only a baby adult, not far past my teenage years, and when I decided to quit, I was in my thirties and had had two children. But no matter what insults a customer threw at me, I would not allow them to put my fire out. Even if I had to repeat the words in my head until I believed them—I was beautiful, I was worthy, and I was loved!

Many of the people I worked with were able to rise

above the crappy hand they were dealt to fight for a better life for themselves and their kids. While being called a "stripper" can be seen as derogatory, these women ignored the naysayers to provide for their families. They fought through injuries and abuse and never let anyone put the fire out in their bellies to care for themselves and their kids. They know that done is better than perfect.

The next time you feel like you've failed, stop! It doesn't matter if your self-doubt is the result of abuse or has been brought on by something in yourself with no outside influence. Remember the fire that is burning inside of you and the person you want to be. Remind yourself that in order to make those dreams a reality, there will be a lot of twists and turns. Not everyone is going to be on your side or be kind, but that is not a reason to quit. Don't ever let anyone or anything put your fire out.

And if they ever try to hose down your fire, watch out for the drain!

FOUR

"No" Is Not the End of the World

I WANT TO dive a little deeper into how important it is to recognize that objections are not the same as dream killers.

When chasing dreams, we cannot take the first or twentieth or hundredth roadblock as an excuse to quit. Especially when you know in your heart and soul that the path you are on is the one you are meant to take because it will guide you to your dreams.

It is perfectly natural to have ups and downs when it comes to being motivated to do the actions it will take to accomplish your dreams. We can't have our "very best day" every day. All we can do is be our best every day. Whatever your best is varies from day to day. Some days, my best is reorganizing the basement while I have a tray of cookies baking in the oven and laundry moving through the washer and dryer, with a notebook beside me where I keep track of new ideas for a book. Other days, my best is getting the bare necessities done to move closer to my goals and then lying on the couch scrolling through social media because I need some downtime. When the roadblocks seem to keep hopping in front of you, or you're tired, or you are struggling financially and emotionally, or you are just not in the mood, you may be tempted to say, "Fuck this!" and give up.

Don't!

The best way to get a step ahead of those feelings is to write down the reasons why you want to achieve your dreams. Don't just think about why or type your "why" into your phone—sit down with a pen and paper and write out all the reasons by hand. Studies suggest that handwriting things on paper creates a deeper impression in your brain than when you type it. When you write down the reasons why you want to achieve your dreams, I want you to dig deep. Peel through the layers like an onion and really describe not only the goals you want to achieve but how you will feel when you achieve them.

For example, a common reason someone may want to reach a goal may be: "To make more money."

Well, whoopty-freakin'-do! You and pretty much everyone else on the planet would like to make more money. How is that motivating you? How is that making you dig deep and do the hard work when the motivation has left?

It won't.

Motivation is not enough to get you to your goals. It's a great way to get started, but just like eating when you're hungry, bathing when you're dirty, or shaving your . . . whatever when things get a bit too hairy, motivation is not something that lasts long-term. You need to work on it often.

First, it is important to create an emotional attachment to your goal that will light that fire under your ass when you want to give up. What is the driving force behind your goal? Would it make you feel like a super parent if you are able to pay for your children to go to college? Will you feel like a super kid if you can raise enough money to pay for your mom's chemotherapy? Think about how it would make you feel to reach that goal, and you should be able to tell the person driving you that you did it for them, even if that person is yourself. Picture the look on their face, think about how much they mean to you. Imagine the way that you could change their life for the better and the impact that it would have.

Now, imagine the look on their face and how it would feel when you tell them, "I'm sorry, you just aren't worth the work I would have to put in to reaching this goal for you."

Second, to make this motivation last, you need to get more specific when you are creating goals. Having a clear, detailed, specific goal can help you to stay on the right track. Instead of saying, "I want to make more money," you need to speak in specific terms. How much money do you want to make, and what will your end result be?

For example, let's say you are passionate about animals. You want to start a rescue for senior dogs, and you know that in order to pay for all the dogs' medical expenses, you will need to make at least $100,000 a year. That is a tangible goal. So, now instead of having a goal to "make more money and start a senior dog rescue," you know you need to "make $100,000 a year because it will cost $40,000 for food, $45,000 for medications, and $5,000 for miscellaneous expenses, toys, and blankets." (I am making up numbers for this illustration, so please don't contact me to correct my made-up expense amounts.) This amount can be broken down into how much you need to make monthly, weekly, and daily to make your dream a reality.

From there, you can plan out exactly which steps will get you to your goal. If you make an hourly wage, how many hours (after taxes and other expenses) will you need to put in to make the money? If that winds up being more hours than most people could work in a lifetime, think larger. What resources are available to you that can help you to attain your dream? Are there grants? Celebrities who could back your cause? Are there philanthropists who would be interested in donating money? What kinds of fundraisers can you organize, and who do you know who can donate time? Is a GoFundMe page appropriate for your goals? Baskets to auction? Raffle prizes? There are so many options out there in addition to clocking in and out of a nine-to-five job.

If you hit some speed bumps and start to feel like it's not working or that you just don't want to put the effort in, you can picture the fourteen-year-old pug looking at you with those big eyes. All he needs is someone to love on him in his twilight years . . . how could you say no?

Another thing you need to remind yourself when the going gets tough is this: while you are desperately trying to get people to contribute to your senior dog rescue, there will always be people out there who just don't like dogs.

You can't take a "no" to heart. It's going to happen. And it's going to happen a lot! The more you put yourself out there and hear "no," the more you will learn to not take it personally. People are rejecting ideas and situations; they are not rejecting you.

When I was a dancer, I had a routine to follow. I would dance onstage and then walk around the bar from customer to customer in order to collect tips and ask for lap dances. I heard "no" a lot of times. I also heard, "Nah," "Get outta here," "Fuck off," etc.

To be honest, I'd have rather heard any of those rejections than have a customer turn his head away and pretend I wasn't even there. If you are running an online business, that is the "real life" equivalent to being ghosted in messages. It's always better to be turned down than ignored.

In all those situations, I did my best not to take it to heart. I knew there were many reasons why I did not get a tip. Maybe they were budgeting (then don't come into the club perhaps?). Maybe they were there to see another girl. Maybe I just wasn't their cup of tea. That's okay, I prefer coffee.

Other times, people just suck, and they get their rocks off telling people no. It gives them a false sense of importance. The person they have turned down might have to put themselves in a position of revisiting the topic later. Or, if the person wants it badly enough, they may feel like they need to beg for the naysayer's acceptance or approval. Some naysayers have self-esteem so far in the toilet that the only way they are able to feel power is by dangling a prize in front of someone that they treat as "less than" to make themselves feel "more than." And some girls had fallen so far down into the financial and lack-of-self-esteem hole that they felt they had to do whatever the customer said in order to get every dollar possible.

That didn't work with me. I would just say, "Thanks anyway!" and go on to the next customer.

In the years that I worked in gentlemen's clubs; I must have been told no thousands of times. Not taking it to heart and being upset about it was one of those skills I developed through repetition. It's the only way to get better at moving forward. You must continue to put yourself out there at the risk of being turned down.

The same is also true when choosing the situations where it better serves you to be the one saying "no." Saying no to the dollar danglers is a great example, but there are so many more.

Women, especially, have been groomed from the time we were young girls to smile and be polite. We were taught to not rock the boat and not hurt anyone else's feelings, even if that meant we would feel like we were dying inside. I'm here to call bullshit on that way of thinking. The more we realize that we are valuable and worthy of respect, the more we can feel more comfortable saying no ourselves. Particularly in the situations where we feel like we must go along with what is happening even when we don't want to.

When we keep exposing a part of our skin to friction, it develops a callus over time and gets thicker and stronger. The same is true with building emotional skills. The more we expose ourselves to the friction of being told no, the thicker it makes our emotional skin. In time, with more and more exposures, it gets less painful when we hear "no."

A friend of mine posted a picture on social media of three acronyms. I've referenced the first one earlier, *FAIL*. You should never be upset when you fail at something because that stands for "First Attempt in Learning." Then we have *END*, which is not the end because it means "Effort Never Dies." But the third one struck me the most because it was simply the word *NO*. When you are told no, remember that it simply means "Next Opportunity," and move along.

When we realize that the things we may perceive as dream killers, goal smashers, or reasons to quit are in fact ways for us to learn, we can move forward with more confidence because we have gained additional knowledge. Even if the lesson is to not take every objection to heart. They are objections, not rejections. Just hold your head up high and keep moving forward.

That being said, it never felt good to have a customer tell me he wasn't interested, especially the customers who were more creative at turning me down than others. But before I could ever be turned down, however, I had to learn how to be tipped to begin with.

The first time I went up to a customer for tips was after I had danced for my audition at Sunsingers. *Clueless* does not even begin to describe how inexperienced I was. Thankfully, the first customer I approached was an older man in his mid- to late sixties. He walked me through the tipping process and was very kind. He could have easily taken advantage of me; I had no idea what was expected of the girls. I was in an emotionally unstable place in that moment. My breast had just gone rogue after all! I don't think I would have had the wherewithal to question it if he tried to go past the boundaries of what was acceptable.

Luckily for me, he was genuinely nice and gave me the time I needed to compose myself, breathe, and try to relax. Most important, he kept his hands to himself. We talked for a few minutes. When it came time to get my tip, he explained the process. He said, "Okay, see the girl over there?" He pointed to another dancer across the bar who was leaning in and pushing her boobs together around a dollar to collect it from a customer. I nodded my head. "That's how you go for the first dollar."

He took a dollar bill and placed it in the spot on my ribs between my boobs. I squashed them together around the dollar and he cracked up. He let go of the money, and I had officially made my first dollar.

Yay me!

He then explained how to go for the second and third dollar, but I'll talk more about that a little later. After showing me how to get the initial three dollars, he placed a five-dollar bill in my hand and wished me luck. If only every other customer I had ever met was like him . . .

But alas, the night is dark and full of assholes.

Many of these assholes thought that it was fun or funny to be insulting to the girls when we walked around for tips. They would make up games among themselves, giving each other points for the most creative insult or cheering each other on for bad behavior.

I learned the hard way to always keep my guard up. After a while, I had built an emotional callus so thick that it was rare for anyone to break through. That took years! But like most fortresses, my emotional callus was built brick by brick and was not completely impenetrable. There were times when, depending on the circumstances, I would be more sensitive. If I was overstressed or overtired, or if the hormones were parading in with a vengeance, I still got hurt. Overall, though, I took most of the negative energy in my stride and adopted an "I'm rubber, you're glue; whatever you say bounces off me and sticks to you" mentality.

In my years of walking around collecting tips, I had gotten good at not taking "no" to heart and moving on to the next customer. But sometimes I would be feeling saucy and would decide to stir the pot for my own entertainment, especially if someone was being a drunk asshole. These people were easy prey because they made stupid arguments to justify their behavior. (Much like a lot of people on social media.) What can I say, I'm only human; sometimes starting shit for the sake of starting shit can be fun, especially when you're young and dumb and are in a room with a lot of people you know have your back. If I had just started working somewhere, I held my tongue until I felt that I did have people around me who supported me. It is not wise to come into a club running your mouth when half of the other dancers working that shift are already angry because you just got hired and are "taking their tips," and the rest don't know you well enough to get involved in your shenanigans.

Not everyone is a nice person or understands that the women who are taking off their clothes and dancing for them are doing it for money and not because we're lowly women whose duty it is to perform for the almighty possessor of the penis. I've reached into the back of my G-string expecting to pull out a dollar only to discover a Burger King coupon. I've been told various things, including: "I don't tip brunettes." "I can't tip you because the money in my wallet is for my rent." "I don't have any money for you, but could you tell [fill in the name] to come over so I can get a couch dance?" "Nah, your tits aren't big enough." "I don't like girls with tattoos." "If I give you a dollar, I'd have to give everyone one." "My wife would kill me!" One guy looked me dead in the face and told me he was unable to tip me because he had "just gotten hit by a truck." Really? I think I would have gone to the ER before going to the titty bar, but that's just me.

I think my favorite excuse of all time was "I can't tip you because I'm a priest." I responded, "If I were a little boy, I bet you'd give me your tip," and walked away.

The sad fact about humans is that so many of them get off on tearing other people down. It's easy for a man to make fun of the size of my exposed boobs when his penis is securely hidden in his jeans. Or if he is a real dirtbag, wearing sweatpants with the worn-out crotch sans undies so he can get the most out of a lap dance. If you have ever been mean to me in a club, I will believe that the reason why you are so nasty, whether it's the truth or not, is because you have a microphallus and it makes you feel insecure. Why else would you need to lash out and be mean? Just say, "No, thank you," and I would have been on my way.

Most of the time after being treated that way, I would say nothing and walk away. It just wasn't worth getting into it with a customer who believed they didn't have to pay me to do my job. It's the club equivalent to getting into a fight on social media about politics or religion. No one changes their opinion, voices get raised (a.k.a. someone starts using the CAPS LOCK), and everyone winds up in a tizzy.

When you are not in a situation of collecting tips for a performance but instead are trying to build a business or side hustle, there is another layer to the scenario to keep in mind. When you are approaching someone about a business opportunity or are trying to sell a product, most people will not be open to what you're saying the first time. This is true both offline and online.

On average, a person needs to be exposed to a message or experience seven times before they are open to saying yes to learning more about it. That doesn't mean they will say yes to what you're offering at that point. It just means that they are in a place where they are willing to hear more. It is called the "Rule of Seven" and is well known not only in multilevel marketing circles, but also by parents introducing their children to new foods.

It is a natural reaction for most humans to say no when they are first approached with an idea or opportunity. Sometimes it is because they are busy, and they feel like they can't possibly take on one more thing, even if it's devoting a small amount of their time to hearing more about it. Other times, it is because they haven't received enough information to know if they are interested or not. Or it could be that subconsciously they believe that answering "no" is always the appropriate first response in those situations—"No one is going to take advantage of me!

I'll shut them down before they get the chance!" Some-times, someone might have had a bad experience in the past, which leads them to look at all things with a negative perspective without digging any deeper to see what makes you and your opportunity different. Or maybe it's because you're six months old, and green beans just aren't as yummy as applesauce.

Whatever the reason, the Rule of Seven does not mean assaulting someone with your cause seven times in the same day. It just means don't get discouraged if someone isn't open to listening to what you have to say the first time you approach them about it. Keep sharing your message publicly. Then every month or so, when a natural opportunity opens, reach out privately to see how they are doing. Be genuine in your conversation. People can smell if you are being disingenuous like a fart in a car. If their circumstances have changed in a way to make them more open to what you are trying to share, that is the appropriate time for you offer to give them more information.

This advice is more specified to those who have multi-level marketing businesses or people trying to share a cause or belief. In the go-go bar, the customers are either tipping in that moment or they're not. A split-second decision can be made when they have boobs in their face. However, how you react in that moment can also lay the groundwork with a customer who may come back another time. I have had multiple customers who were unable to tip me the first time we met, only for them to come back another time and tip me generously for being kind to them during our first encounter.

Press forward. If you hear "no" from one person, just move on to the next. Try and take the perspective that every "no" you hear is one step closer to hearing a "yes." When you turn it into a game, you'll be happy every time you hear a "no" because that just means you're getting closer to your goals while you move on to the "Next Opportunity."

There is a whole big world out there full of people, most of whom are kind, like my first ever customer. It's your job to sort through the assholes and find the good people. It takes time, and there are moments when it will be extremely frustrating. Never forget your end goal! Picture those big pug eyes or whatever it is that will spark your emotions and keep moving forward toward your dream.

During my years in the go-go business, I held just about every job title available minus "owner." That's not to say that I never considered owning my own club. I just knew enough about the industry to understand that owning a gentlemen's club would be a headache I never wanted to have. The process of climbing the go-go corporate ladder started out for me with the position of dancer. Eventually, I climbed up the rungs to bartender and then manager. When I was pregnant with my kids, I worked as the club's house mom. I also physically removed patrons (bouncer) and hopped into the DJ booth when the scheduled DJ was running late or a no-show and played the music for the girls to dance to during their sets.

I have always been a hard worker, and I love to learn as much as I can about every facet of the jobs I've held. Having the skills to cover other people when they fall short is also a great asset to have, and it made me more valuable as an employee. From my go-go days, I learned to make myself invaluable. I did more than I was asked, or at least learned how to do more than I was asked so that I could always step up if someone else faltered. I also learned that there are always plenty of people who are making more money than you by doing a lot less, so don't be afraid to add to your own skill set to become a bigger asset to your company. I then used those skills to put myself in a position to ask for more.

In addition to working hard, I do positive affirmations daily. The one I chose for today I will continue to use when the going gets tough. I found it (as well as a bonus affirmation) on Prolific Living.[3]

The first one is, "It is always too early to give up on my goals."

I followed that with, "Giving up is easy and always an option, so let's delay it for another day."

I love the idea of telling your doubts and fears, "Sure, sure . . . there may be a time when I am ready to throw in the towel. But now is not the time." Until you have exhausted every single option—and there are an infinite number of ways to achieve goals, by the way—it will always be too early to give up. So, go ahead and delay giving up for another day.

FIVE

Go for the Booty Dollar

IN THE PREVIOUS chapter, I mentioned that the minimum goal for most dancers while collecting tips was to get three dollars per customer. Occasionally, the go-go gods would shine upon you and bring you a customer who wanted to "make it rain." That meant they would throw fistfuls of dollars at you while you were on the stage, making the bills fly up into the air and "rain" down on you.

In Sunsingers, there was a regular who was known for his practice of showering the girls with dollars while they were onstage. I have no idea what he did for a living. He looked like your average everyday guy. Most people would probably not even give him a second glance. Until he started tossing dollar bills, one hundred at a time, onto the stage multiple times a night. The first time he picked me, I was so thankful! My gratitude doubled because he never expected anything in return. He was just a cool dude who liked to share his wealth. He also loved to give the dancers shoulder massages. He never tried to grab anything else, and he was really good at massaging shoulders! I was always incredibly grateful to receive a free massage at work.

The instances of money getting thrown at you onstage were few and far between on most nights. You could encourage more onstage tips by getting a customer's attention and pulling your bottoms out to make a "basket" for them to try and throw the money into. It was always a good thing if the first try missed because you could encourage them to keep trying until they made it. Not only did this increase tips, but it also allowed you to eat up stage time and use a lot less energy than you would have if you had to dance during your entire set.

Also rare, but much more annoying, was when a customer would throw something other than money at you while you were dancing. One night, some drunk douche beamed me in the forehead with a lime wedge while I was in the middle of a song. He must have had the "micro-iest" of microphalluses.

Since being thrown money while you were onstage was not the norm in the bars where I worked, you were required to walk around the bar and go up to the customers to collect your tips. Most customers would only tip one or two dollars, as inflation had affected everywhere but go-go bars. Three dollars is the desired result of the "tip dance" that the girls learn about very quickly when they begin working in gentlemen's clubs.

Let me also clarify that I can only speak from my personal experience. I know that there are places where you can only legally put money in a garter on a dancer's leg or in their hand. That was the law in New Jersey, but it was rarely followed. (More on that in the next chapter.) For now, we'll talk about practice rather than the letter of the law.

The way that tipping worked in the clubs where I worked was simple. You approach a customer and get their attention. I'll use masculine pronouns for the customers just because majority rules. You can say, "Hey sweetie!" or place a hand on his shoulder or poke him in the ribs with your fingernail; everyone has their own style. Some girls straight-up start dick grabbing. Every club has a couple of those; it's just the way it is.

When the customer turns to face you, grab a boob in each hand and shake them up and down, like, "Here boy! Look here! Who likes boobies? Do you like boobies? I know you do!" to ensure that you have their full attention. Most customers have been around the block a few times, and if they are tipping, they will automatically place a dollar between your boobs for you to squeeze and take like a breast claw machine. Don't be surprised if he leaves his hand there for a little "slappy slappy" between the girls before pulling his hand back.

Some topless clubs allow you to walk around topless or flash nipple while getting tips. Others only allow you to be fully topless or show nipples onstage. It's all up to the club and the laws of the state in which the club is located. Legally, you couldn't show any nipple at all in the bikini bars because they were not topless; however, a lot of girls would flash regardless. There are also different rules as far as if you are permitted to walk around for tips inside the bar or outside. I worked in one establishment where you were only allowed to be topless behind the bar. So, when we were done dancing, we would go around for tips inside the bar, just collecting boobie tips. Then we would go double-dip around the outside of the bar.

There were always customers who would try to ignore me when I walked around for tips. I was not that easily dismissed, so I would start pushing my boobs together and then opening them back up like they were breast puppets talking. I would say in my highest falsetto voice, "Hiiiiiii! Would you like to give me a dollar?" It was completely ridiculous that their decision to ignore me motivated me to turn into a titty ventriloquist. Most of the time, my ridiculous tactics resulted in my getting a laugh and then a tip. At the end of the day, I may have been silly, but I wound up with more money than if I had been offended and walked away.

If a guy is particularly nasty, he may put the money in his mouth to put it between your boobs. Whether putting money in your mouth to give a tip is permitted or not varies by club and dancer. He may be thinking, *Yay, potential motorboat situation!* while I was always thinking, *God, I really hope that dollar was in the sweaty ass crack of a male stripper before it got to you.* Money is filthy, and you should never put it in your mouth. Didn't we all learn this as toddlers?

Once you get the first dollar by hand or mouth or whatever creative vessel the customer has come up with, it's time to go for the second dollar. The thong is the logical next place to offer up as a dollar-collecting site after getting the booby dollar. This is done by continuing to face the customer and pulling out the side of your G-string. The strap that goes over the top of your hip. Helpful tip: always make sure to do this yourself. If you allow a customer to be the one judging how far your thong will be pulled from your body, you will more than likely end up with all of your "down below" on display and a super stretched-out thong elastic. Exceptions of course being anyone you have known for a while, and you trust to not be a totally disrespectful asshat.

Some girls go left, some go right. Some girls pull it out to the side and front so far you can get a full view of her snapper, others put one hand over the front of their thong while pulling out the side to keep all of her lady bits locked up tight. Some girls do a snatch flash, and some have their hairy hatchet wound on lockdown. Others fall somewhere in between. Some ladies like to show a bit of their hairstyle if there is one. Others would do a lil' peek then slam it shut. It was ultimately up to the girl how much she was willing to share.

I never did the whole peekaboo. I never danced nude, and I was certainly not showing off my hoohah for a dollar (or less!). I had standards after all.

As a side note, while the idea of being entirely on display in front of a room of strangers was never something that I aspired to make a reality, the main reason I never wanted to dance nude was for hygiene reasons. When the girl before me had just gotten done smearing her 'gina juice up and down the pole, I had no desire to be like, "Me next!" I don't care if there was a bucket of Lysol sitting on the stage to wipe the pole down. That was a hard "no."

The very few times I have stepped foot into fully nude clubs to visit friends, I have been horrified to see girls onstage "catching" dollars in their vajayjays. Don't get me wrong—your anatomy, your rules; and if you can suck a bill up into your lady cave, then you do get the Kegel Award! However, I can only imagine the number of germs the dancers in those clubs were introducing into an organ that has a very delicate pH balance. I, personally, would not have taken the risk.

Also, I find it completely embarrassing if I am out and about and discover that I have picked up some toilet paper on the bottom of my shoe after using the public restroom. What if I were dancing nude and had a day when I didn't shave as close as I could have and wound up with a little nub of toilet paper stuck to my coochie? It would totally glow in the black light, a brightly shining vagingleberry. Would anyone tell me? Or would I find out later that I had accidentally wound up with some "clitty litter" while using the bathroom? Ultimately, it would be yet another situation where I would just have to die.

While we're on the subject of hygiene and pole cleanliness, I feel compelled to debunk yet another myth: no one in real life licks a stripper pole. At least no one I have ever seen in all my years in the clubs. I don't know what movie started the trend of showing women pole dancing and running their tongues up and down the pole, but that is just foul. If germs collect on brass doorknobs, it's safe to assume that brass poles would collect even more germs as they are being touched by more than just hands. Just as there is not enough Lysol on the planet to make me touch a pole after a girl has danced nude on it before my turn, there isn't enough Lysol on the planet to make a brass stripper pole lickable. Nasty.

If you managed to clear level two, it was time to attempt the booty dollar. (I have a friend who not only calls it the "poop dollar" but actually sings the words "poop dollar," so

I am laughing as I type.) Going for this dollar puts you on your guard because it requires you to turn away from the customer, and it requires a bit of trust. I have had guys in the past betray that trust and try to get into places where they have not been invited and are certainly not welcome to visit. Overall, most customers are respectful, and it usually wasn't an issue.

The way you go for the third bill depends once again on the girl and on club rules. I guess it could also depend on your outfit. At any rate, you stand with your back to the customer and lean forward so your butt is facing them. Don't be surprised if you then get pulled into said customer's crotch for a little grind. They like to make you work for those ten dimes after all. When you feel you should go for the kill, you open up the top of your thong—or if you're feeling more adventurous, a little further down the rear so they can see your entire ass crack—and make space for a dollar to slide in. Or a Burger King coupon. That bastard!

Again, I had creative ways to sway a guy who may not have wanted to go for the third dollar. I would lean forward and wiggle my butt back and forth at him, trying my best to get his attention. If he didn't bite, I'd holler back, "C'mon now! I'm making an ass of myself!" Or I would do the butt version of the boob ventriloquist and channel my inner Ace Ventura: "Let me *ass* you a question . . . you're really not going to give me another dollar? You don't want me to make a stink about this!"

Was it sexy? Not even a little bit. But as I've stated before, I was more about humor and getting a laugh or reaction than trying to be sexy.

Once you get your three dollars, you can push for a fourth by spinning back around and going for the other side of the thong or the boobs again. It's worth a try, but those dollars are few and far between. Just like the guys who tip five-dollar bills or more.

To this day, dancing is the only job I've ever had where I have gone to use the restroom and literally had money fall out of my ass. Sometimes you'd get a few dollar bills in the top of the back of your thong and miss one when you took them out. With outfits that covered more space, like teddies for example, it was possible to have several dollars hiding up in there that you didn't find until you were taking the outfit off. Nothing like found money to put a smile on your face.

The significance of the third dollar is this: there were several times when I was walking around for tips when I was tired or just not in the mood to be at work. Once I got to the second dollar, I would move on to the next customer because I couldn't be bothered to try for the third. I don't even want to imagine the total sum of money I had left behind (pun intended) over the years just because I was too lazy to go for that third dollar.

Every tiny step you make in the direction of your goals will add up to so much ground covered, money raised, and skills learned. You may not see a huge change all at once, but the little steps add up to covering lots of ground on the way to reaching your goals.

A great example is when someone is on a journey to lose weight. If they eat healthy one day, they aren't going to wake up ten pounds lighter. If they make the small step of giving up soda, then in a few weeks add another step of walking thirty minutes each day, and then a while later they add another step of drinking more water, in time they will notice the scale moving little by little until they reach their goal. If you don't start taking steps, you'll wind up staying in the same place where you are and never going anywhere.

Laziness is second only to fear as the biggest killer of our dreams. We get comfortable in our situations, and it's easy to put off the crucial goal-achieving steps until "tomorrow" or "Monday" or "as soon as I . . ." That mindset just holds us back from achieving our goals. No one ever moved forward by giving in to the lazy side and pushing the activities they knew they needed to do off until another time.

When you are tired and cranky and not in the mood, that is when you need to push even harder for that extra step, the extra person talked to, the extra hour of work put in. The difference between those who are successful and those who fail is this: successful people do the work no matter what, not just when it is convenient.

If you have a goal in mind, whether it is starting a new workout routine, changing the way you eat, deciding to read positive affirmations, etc., imagine that the motivation for these changes is because you want to feel better, look better, and be better!

So . . . why do you want to wait?

On one of his podcasts fitness trainer Shaun T said something that has stuck with me and that is a great inspiration to change your mind set about waiting to start on the path to achieving your goal until Monday, or January 1, or summer, or [fill in your own procrastination-inspired response here]. He puts it this way: "If someone offered to give you ten thousand dollars a day for the rest of your life, would you say, 'Great! I'll start collecting it Monday!' (Or January 1, etc.) or would you start today, right now, this minute?"

What goal makes you as excited as the thought of ten thousand dollars a day? What are the little steps that you are being too lazy to take right now in order to collect on your dreams? Figure out your own version of booty dollars, and then push to get them. Write down your "why" or read it again if you had written it down after reading Chapter Four. Push through the fear, or the laziness, or the self-doubt, and get it done.

A helpful trick is telling yourself that you only need to do the activity for five minutes. Whether it is a workout, reading a textbook, or making phone calls to potential clients, whatever activity your booty dollar is. Often, when you make the effort to do the activity, you will continue past the first five minutes and move closer to achieving your dreams. Collect your booty dollars! They add up to help you be even more successful.

SIX.

Get Creative

HAVE YOU EVER noticed how, on social media, someone will post something utterly amazing? Or funny? Or thought-provoking? Then the next day, a few more people will be posting similar things. In a week or two, you are so sick of seeing the thing that now everyone is posting that you don't care about it anymore.

"Yanny or Laurel?"

The trick is finding ways to set yourself apart.

I gave some advice for running multilevel marketing businesses in Chapter Four. I'm going to venture down the path of using social media to start a business again. It was an area in which I had to be creative in the past and I know many people have at least dipped their toes into the "MLM" world at one time or another or know someone who has.

For example, if your goal is selling makeup online and building a business, don't be one more person sending a copy-and-paste message to someone's inbox. Especially when it's someone you haven't talked to since high school (and quite frankly, you didn't even like them back then) but friended on social media so you could cold message them to try and sell makeup. The days of that being an effective way to get sales or add to your team are long gone.

It's safe to say that most people know that a message in their inbox that starts with "Hey girl!" is going to end with the sender trying to sell them something. I used to answer those messages with helpful tips for how to reach out instead. People would get mad, so now I ignore those messages completely because I can smell the wannabe sale a mile away. Instead of following the cut-and-paste scripts that are given out by many uplines, use your thinking cap and come up with unique ways to showcase your products to spark interest organically.

What has the product done for you? When you put on your makeup, how does it make you feel? What places have you visited, or events have you attended with your face all prettied up with your makeup? Did someone pay you a compliment about your looks that made you feel good? When people get to know you and trust you, it will be a lot easier for them to spend the time to learn about your product (even if they are ultimately not interested). You don't want to waste your precious time with "Hey girl! I started this awesome company and knew you would be a great fit!" "Hey girl" messages are not creative. Copying and pasting is not creative.

Funny story: I was scrolling through the news feed one day when I saw a post from an online friend about how she had just received a "Hey girl" cold message from someone. The woman who had sent her the message said, "I had to reach out because I know that you will just LOVE the new tanning accelerator that I've been using! You can buy it from me directly!" My friend is a gorgeous African American woman who had no interest in a tanning accelerator.

Also, if you are involved in an MLM company that encourages using copy-and-paste cold messaging to reach out, may I *please* give you a word of advice? Before you hit "send," make sure that your message no longer has the instructions from your upline included. I received a message once that literally said, "Hey (add name here), I just started my own business and thought of you! I know that you would be great at this, too!" We must have been so close that she thought my name was "(Add name here)."

When I first started out trying to build an online business, I was guilty of a similar faux pas. I had my script that I had received from my upline and settled into my desk chair to start messaging people. I was terrified! What if I made people mad? What if they yelled at me? My anxiety started to creep in. I changed the part of the script that said "(Add name here)" to the name of one of my friends who I knew was nice and wouldn't judge me. Let's just say her name was "Mary." I did some deep breathing, swallowed the vomit that was trying to creep up my throat, and sent out my first message.

"Hi Mary! I just wanted to let you know that I started a new online business . . ."

First message sent! I thought to myself and went on to send the second. It got easier and easier with each message until I had sent out twenty or so. That's when I realized that when I had copied and pasted the messages after my first one, I had also copied the "Hi Mary" part. All the messages I had sent out after hers looked like this:

"Hi Beth!

Hi Mary!

I just wanted to let you know . . ."

I was mortified, but I had no other choice than to take it as a lesson. I made sure from then on to double check the messages that I sent to people.

At first, sending scripts to safe people or people I didn't really know felt like the right way to begin my new venture of being an online business owner because I didn't know any other way. Honestly, it's a chicken shit way to do things and not creative at all. I wasn't sharing my passion for the company I truly believed in, and I wasn't connecting to the people I was messaging. I was just fulfilling a message-sending quota. But once I got to know people, I began to find creative ways to connect them to how the company I worked with would help them to make positive changes in their own life.

Another way you may have to be creative is when the path to your goal doesn't go exactly as you had planned. Maybe you want to start a company, but there are some legal issues you were not aware of that are preventing your timeline from happening. Instead of opening your business in six months like you imagined, perhaps you need to seek counsel from a lawyer, so you have to have the creativity and openness to decide if your plan needs to be restructured. Maybe you had the perfect building picked out to rent for your store, but the landlord rented it to someone else, and you need to tune in once again to your creativity to deal with this new setback. Would selling your products online be a better option? Is there an existing business that will rent you space in their store to utilize for your purposes? There are a million different hiccups that can pop up and derail your path to success, from legal to logistical to personal. There are also a million ways to try something different to make it work!

With a little creativity, you can find a way around these roadblocks. Is there a loophole that you can use to your advantage? Can you find a completely different path that will bring you to the same destination? Don't be so stuck on one way of looking at things that it prevents you from creatively solving problems when they will inevitably arise. Always try and discover alternative ways to do things. You need to stay focused on your goal but stay flexible when it comes to the steps that you will need to take to achieve it.

It is important to learn from others who have come before you. But be cautious.

I had been working at Sunsingers for several months and had gotten quite comfortable with the routine and the environment. That is, until I experienced my first raid. I didn't realize that raids were something that happened in real life and not only in movies and TV shows. Let me tell you that they most certainly do happen in the real world. Well, as real as the world of go-go is, anyway. If you have never been part of one before, it can be scary as hell!

When everything went down in the bar, it was complete chaos. No one had suspected anything. It was a regular day, business happened as usual, and then—BAM! The cellu-lights came on out of nowhere and a bunch of men screamed, "This is a raid!"

Customers were running out the front door, dancers were running out the back door in nothing but their thongs and heels—it was craziness! I stood there not knowing what I was supposed to do but feeling confident that I had nothing to worry about. I hadn't done anything wrong. I was of legal age to be a dancer, I didn't use drugs, I wasn't a hooker, and I wasn't a thief. I was good!

Or so I thought. It seems that when I was taught how to take tips, I had been given some misinformation.

As you wander down the path of learning a new occupation: double-check everything that you are being told as far as company and legal policy and guidelines to make sure it is the truth. Especially if it is being told to you by someone who has been working there for a lot longer than you. Frequently, people get comfortable and may lose track of the strict guidelines of company policy or the law. Other times, laws and policies change, and they remain blissfully unaware of those changes until they are caught not following the rules.

Before the agents announced that everyone needed to put their hands up and not move because it was a raid, I had been onstage and walked around for tips as usual. I had no idea that one of the gentlemen I had gone up to for a tip was an agent for the ABC—Alcohol Beverage Control. I also didn't know that taking a tip between your breasts—even breasts that were securely in a top with the entire breast, nipples included, remaining unseen—was considered "prostitution 2."

Let me say that again: prostitution *two*.

It was explained to me that the definition of the "prostitution 2" charge was "masturbation for money." I call bullshit because I had not gotten off.

The ABC did not care about my lack of orgasm, and I

got the charge. The thing is when you name something "prostitution 2," no one hears the "two" part. That would be the same as referring to getting charged with slapping someone as "murder 6." The actual action that took place is not anything like the word in front of the number. The good thing (for me at least) was that it was a liquor board charge, which meant that the club had to pay a fine. It was not a criminal charge against me personally, and my record remained unsullied.

The club was on its best behavior after the raid, like a kid who was trying to be good after getting into trouble. The higher-ups made sure all the employees were following every single rule of the ABC to the letter. For a couple of weeks anyway.

During that time, dancers were technically not allowed to touch the customers at all. I walked around and gave customers handshakes, completely being a smartass. The managers didn't say anything about that. For once, I did not get yelled at! But not being able to hug anyone was tough for me. I am a hugger by nature and would always give a big hello hug to the customers I knew, as well as a thank-you hug to any customer who was open to one.

We had a couple of regular customers who were Amish. They were super nice and always tipped well. They always made sure to put the money directly into our hands because they refused to be touched by any of the dancers. I was told that their beliefs state that the only woman who can touch a man in their community is his wife. I guess they took "Look with your eyes, not with your hands" to a new level. After we had been raided, we were only permitted to take tips in our hands or in a garter. While the Amish men were in their glory, the other customers were less than pleased. The best word to describe the atmosphere in the club was *pathetic*. The number of customers dropped daily, and as someone who counted on making money from working in this club to pay her bills, I was frustrated. I would walk around for tips and hold my hand out. If I got a dollar, I would put it in my purse and hold my hand out for a second, giving the customer my puppy-dog eyes and saying in my best Oliver Twist impression, "Please, sir, may I have some more?"

That was the first time I got reprimanded by management for thinking outside the box during super-duper rule-enforcement time; they didn't appreciate my Broadway-musical-inspired way of collecting tips. The second was when I took a Styrofoam cup and wrote "Will dance for money" on it. I walked around collecting tips in my cup until the manager came out of the office and yelled across the bar, "Sydnee! Stop being a smartass!" "It's better than being a dumbass!" I yelled back.

Reprimanded again.

One thing that has been true about me since I was a small child is that I am creative. My strict upbringing gave me a talent for coming up with loopholes and looking for creative ways to accomplish what I wanted to do while technically not breaking any of the rules that were in place. I faced the challenge of dealing with the new bar rules in the same way.

Let's look for the loophole. What had we been told? Exactly?

We had been told that we could only collect money in our hands or a garter.

They did not, however, specify where your hands needed to be.

Aha! Loophole discovered. When I went up to a customer for a tip after I danced my set, I would slide my hand through the center of my top with my palm facing up. The customer could put a dollar in my hand (following the rules) and get the illusion of putting it between my breasts. Then I would stick my hand under the side of my thong and out the top. Then the same with the back. I wasn't breaking the rules; however, I was making more tips than the other girls because I had found a creative solution and given the customers the illusion of getting more for their buck than they were getting from the other dancers.

Creativity served me well beyond just tip collecting. I also made myself flexible when it came to performing. The thing about me is that I can and have danced to just about every type of song there is. I used to tell the DJs, "You could play the Alphabet Song for me, and I could make it look sexy." I became the go-to girl for when a customer would request a random song that no one else wanted to dance to. I have danced to the theme song from the cartoon *Fat Albert and the Cosby Kids*, "Chocolate Salty Balls" from South Park, "At a Medium Pace" by Adam Sandler . . . in addition to the plethora of other songs that weren't really "my style" but I danced to anyway.

Once, the DJ came in with a three-foot-wide afro wig, and he and the manager asked me to wear it while I danced. Why not? Most of the customers thought it was great! I felt like Jan in *The Brady Bunch Movie* when she was trying to reinvent herself. One old man, however, got inexplicably angry and told me to "Take that stupid shit off." I told him to piss off. Some people have no sense of humor.

In addition to dancing to the songs no one else wanted to dance to, management and the DJs would recruit me to do other kinds of stunts as well. I loved getting the crowd into the show and making sure they had a good time. If they didn't think the club was fun, they wouldn't come back. If they didn't come back, I would have no one to give me tips.

I was working a day shift at Warlocks one day when the power went out. Thankfully, there were emergency lights, so we weren't stuck in the basement in total darkness. Despite the hour, there were already several customers at the bar. The bartender had given them each a free drink, but they started getting antsy. I hopped up on the stage in my street clothes and started telling jokes. I am in no way a stand-up comic, but I did my best to keep the customers entertained with every joke that I could think of until the power came back on. Every one of them stayed! I even made a few bucks that I wouldn't have made if I had sat at the bar and bitched with the other girls.

One year, the club owner bought season tickets for the local NFL team as a giveaway for the customers. What better way to give away the tickets than with a contest? Specifically, a "paper football" contest. When we used to have paper football contests in school, the objective was to flick the folded-up triangle-shaped paper "football" through the "goalposts," which were your friends' index fingers pointing up to the sky while their thumbs touched. In the club contest version, the goalposts were my legs pointing up to the sky as I lay down spread eagle on the stage. All the customers who managed to get the football through the goalposts would advance to the next round, which would be me moving farther away, and we would eliminate contestants like that until we had one winner. Occasionally, the customer would flick the paper triangle at the exact wrong angle, resulting in my getting the point of the triangle in one of my most sensitive areas. A paper cut to the nanny-hoo-hoo will wake you right up. Thongs are not paper-point proof.

There were other times when we would give away T-shirts with the club logo from the stage, and some of the girls would stand there for a half second before throwing the shirt into the crowd at no one in particular. Instead, I always made the customers work for it. I would put the T-shirt on over my outfit and walk back and forth across the stage while I was wearing it. I would scan the crowd, putting my hand to my ear to get them to yell louder. Then I would take the shirt off and rub it all over my body as they hooted and hollered, trying to get my attention and, ultimately, my T-shirt. I guess dancer sweat is a commodity!

What is your creative solution to a problem you are currently facing? How can you set yourself apart from the other people in your field? For example, if you have come up with a product or idea that is entirely new, how can you get people's attention instead of just becoming another ad or social media post that gets scrolled past? In a social media world that is built on billions of posts daily, it's easy for people to keep scrolling through the news feed without giving it much thought. When there are thousands of people posting similar things, the news feed becomes white noise until you see something that causes you to stop and look more closely. What kinds of posts do that for you and get your attention? Is it a beautiful scene in nature? A cartoon? A baby animal? See how you can take the scroll-stopping subjects that work for you. You want them to not only check out your post but also be drawn into wanting to know more.

Maybe your goal is not to sell something but to be more assertive. Or you want to lose fifty pounds. Maybe you need to find a way to schedule some "me time" without your kids. Well, how can you start creatively looking for solutions?

Stop what you're doing and create a brain dump page right now. If you tell yourself, "I like this idea, but I'll do it later," you will most likely wind up distracted and not get to it. So, take out a piece of paper and write your goal across the top. Set a timer for five minutes and let your mind wander. Then just start writing down ideas on how you can accomplish it. It doesn't need to be pretty or organized. Even if something seems farfetched, silly, impossible, or completely unrelated, write down every little thing. For example, if you need some "me time" as a mom but don't know how to get started, think of friends who can watch your kids for a couple hours. Is there a local teenager who is a trusted babysitter? Is there a class your kids can take? Gymnastics? Karate? Can you start a mom group (recruit your own moms, mothers-in-law or sweet older ladies in your church for help) and have the grandmoms watch the kids for a few hours while the other moms get mani-pedis? What else? Do not cross out or erase anything during the brain dump exercise! This exercise can open your mind to things that you may not have thought of otherwise, and you never know what may spark inspiration when you read it again later. Keep writing down everything that pops into your head until you run out of ideas. Now, look at what you've written down and see what inspires you.

Look for the loopholes in life that you can use to better yourself and bring yourself closer to your goals. Get creative and find ways to stand apart from the white noise. And no matter what situations you find yourself in, never ever be afraid to be a smartass. It is always better than being a dumbass.

SEVEN

The Art of Visualization

DID YOU DO your brain dump? If you didn't, go back and do it now. If you did, then you can proceed.

This chapter is all about visualization. The definition of "visualization" is as follows:[4]

verb (used without object), **vis·u·al·ized vis·u·al·iz·ing.**
   1. to recall or form mental images or pictures.

verb (used with object), **vis·u·al·ized, vis·u·al·iz·ing.**
   2. to make visual or visible.
   3. to form a mental image of.
   4. to make perceptible to the mind or imagination.

Have you ever visualized something into being? This practice is also called "manifesting."

When I first heard of this practice, I immediately dismissed it as some sort of hocus-pocus bullshit. Over the past few years, however, my opinion has changed. I have been reading a lot about the Universe and energy, and I've learned that stating your intentions daily will help them to manifest into reality—if you are willing to do the work, of course; manifesting is not the same as rubbing a lamp and getting to ask a genie for three wishes. I have also seen it in action several times.

I have also heard visualization or manifestation summed up to "What you believe you will achieve" taken a step further. In order to use this practice, you will need to believe that there is a higher power. What you call that higher power is your choice: God, the Universe, "Source Energy," "Bob," or whatever makes you most comfortable. When we imagine ourselves in the place where we most want to be, or as the person we most want to become, we are sending a message to the Universe (or whichever higher power you pick) that says, "This is where—or who—I want to be. Please help me on my path to achieve my goal."

If what you want most is to be the CEO of your own company, then what does that look like? How do you dress? What does your voice sound like when you talk to your employees? What does your workspace look like? How do you picture your office or other space where you spend your working hours? What is hanging on the wall? Do you have carpet or hardwood floors? Do you have one of those plastic mats under your desk chair that smells like the 1980s? It's your dream, you tell me.

The more detailed you are when imagining how your dream looks, smells, sounds, tastes and so on, the more real your vision becomes. When you focus in on all the minute details of your goal, you are communicating your desires to your higher power in a way that will enable said power to home in on what you genuinely want to achieve.

I wish that manifesting were as simple as that, but of course you need to do the work as well. The difference is, you now have a clear picture of where you want to be and have opened the channels of communication between your mind and your true self. Listen to the cues you are receiving from your higher power. You will start to notice things that you would not have given a second thought to before. You may find yourself meeting people who can help you or find yourself in the right place at the right time. There is no such thing as a coincidence.

Perhaps you've always wanted to be a baker, and as soon as you begin visualizing your bakery, smelling the cakes baking, and imagining yourself with an icing bag piping "Happy Birthday!" on your latest masterpiece, you start getting emails to sign up for cake-decorating classes. Or a mutual friend introduces you to someone who happens to have a bakery they inherited from their recently deceased aunt and who is looking for the perfect person to learn the ropes and run it with them.

Now, if you have an Alexa (or any device with a microphone: laptop, smartphone, tablet, etc.) in your house, and you've been talking about your vision while hanging out at home, you may be tempted to shrug it off as "Big Brother" listening in to your conversations. Fair point.

But how many times have you thought about something, keeping your thought completely in your own head, and then it's shown up in your news feed shortly after?

Take these gifts from your higher power as a blessing and be grateful. Use them as a compass to guide you to do the work that will make your dreams manifest into reality. I wish that just daydreaming about your goals would make them a reality, but you do need to put in the work to make them come true. Fortunately, manifesting brings "helpers" and "guideposts" into your life to get you there. You can still arrive at a new destination on your own, but having a map or GPS is a big help.

Sometimes, the way you are meant to achieve your goals and dreams is different than the journey you imagined. It's important not to question the "how" on your way to the "what." We don't have all the answers, so you need to trust in the guideposts that show up on your path and help to light your way.

And take the time to say, "Thank you!" when these gifts are presented. I pray several times every day. Most of the time, these are prayers of gratitude. Grace over meals, gratitude for getting my kids to school on time safely even though they once again farted around, and we left the house way later than we should have. (On those days, I should not have been able to make it there on time unless I was driving a stock car, yet somehow, we always arrive safely and on time.) I still struggle with my beliefs when it comes to religion, but I do find myself sending up a "Thank you, Lord!" or ending a prayer with "In Jesus's name." Maybe it's just conditioning from my youth, but it feels right to me. I don't think that words are as important as the intention. If God or Jesus is listening and you're truly thankful, I don't think they're going to take away points for not addressing Them directly. The opposite I also believe to be true. The Universe is open to your heart and energy and doesn't care what name you use if you are sincere.

Visualize what you want to accomplish and be grateful for each step you make closer to it, no matter how big or small.

When I first started dancing, I would sit at the bar and watch the girls who could do pole work with wide-eyed wonder. Not all dancers spin around the pole or do any sort of pole work. I once worked with an older woman who never did any pole work, but she must have previously worked as a contortionist. She would lie on the stage on her back and put both of her ankles behind her neck. Then she would spin around like a turtle on its shell. When she stood up, she would tuck a match over each nipple and light them on fire. The scars on her boobs revealed that she didn't always do that trick successfully. Other dancers walked back and forth across the stage for the entire length of their song. I wish that wasn't true because it's not terribly entertaining. Maybe they had always dreamed of runway modeling and were trying to practice.

I didn't want to be lumped into the group of dancers who walked back and forth looking bored. I tried to emulate the moves that I saw the dancers whom I admired doing so I would be able to learn how to do pole tricks, too. I know that there have been memes going around that suggest that dancers don't spin around poles because it's the poles that spin. I can't tell you that is total BS because I have worked in clubs where the poles do spin—some extremely loudly. Whether they are spinning silently or sound like the side of a semi scraping a metal girder, it's friggin' dangerous! Centrifugal force is a real thing, and I have seen girls go flying off the pole like they were on the Scrambler ride at the carnival with no seat belt. Fortunately, most clubs had stationary poles, though some were plastic and filled with water and bubbles. Bubble poles are wider than a standard pole and not as sturdy. In addition to making pole tricks practically impossible, they also tend to leak over time and, in my opinion, are not worth the investment. One club used the building's water pipes as the stage poles. You could hear the water rushing through the poles whenever someone flushed the toilet. Classy!

Luckily, most of the clubs I worked at had brass poles with a standard "stripper pole" circumference.

When I first started out at Sunsingers, I got used to the layout. The club had a main stage and a side stage, or a "satellite stage," for all you schmancy folk. The satellite stage sat unused most nights but was open on the weekends. The dancer who was up would dance to her first song, the song she had chosen, on the main stage. Then she would move to the side stage as quickly as possible in stilettos while pushing her way through the crowd of grabby man hands. Why they designed the club to have you exit the main stage on one side of the building to get to a satellite stage on the other side of the building, I have no idea.

When she made it to the satellite stage, she would perform her second song, which, as I've mentioned, would be the song that the dancer in the rotation behind her had chosen. I would pray that Marissa was behind me in the lineup because I liked her music for the most part. One night, I was stuck with a girl who, hand to god, played "My Heart Will Go On." Yes, the theme from *Titanic*. I started doing mock ballet onstage . . . and got yelled at, again.

When it was slow in the club or on the days when the side stage wasn't being used, I would go there after walking around for tips to practice pole spinning. There are several different styles of spinning and multiple ways to do pole tricks. Some are really complicated, and I was not ready to tackle them at first. So, I began by attempting what I thought was the easiest spin.

To perform the basic spin, you grab onto the pole above your head with your hand, hook the knee pit of one leg onto the pole, push yourself with your other foot, and then keep both feet off the ground, allowing the centrifugal force to spin your body around the pole. With practice, you can land on one foot and stand up, achieving the classic move known as the "Ta-Da!" Without practice, you can end up in a heap on your ass on the stage, achieving the classic move known as the "Aw Shit!" That spin seemed easy enough but looks can be deceiving.

The poles at Sunsingers were stationary, so if you gripped the pole too tightly, you would get stuck and hang there like a fruit on a vine. If you were not used to the sensation of being off the ground and trusting your body to keep you from crashing down onto the stage, it could be intimidating. Did I mention that brass poles can give you a skin burn? It feels horrific on the back of your knee.

I spent hours attempting to spin. I just couldn't get past the fear of picking my foot up off the ground and allowing myself to spin into it. I kept giving a push off, followed by a ridiculous one footed "hop hop hop" around the pole instead the graceful spin I was trying to achieve. Soon, I had calluses on my hands and no skin on the back of my right knee. At one point, I even purchased a bowling glove for my right hand to cover the spot in my palm where I had ripped off all my skin. I could have given up on learning pole tricks and instead moved to Hollywood to make it big in the movie business—I was perfect to play the part of the hand coming out of the grave in horror films. As much as I was banged up and bruised, I really wanted to add spinning to my dance bag of tricks, so I knew I couldn't quit trying.

I started to imagine myself onstage. I could picture myself confidently spinning around the pole, smiling at the crowd. It didn't happen immediately, but one of the girls who had been working at Sunsingers for years offered to show me some pointers. (Find a mentor!) With practice, I was able to go halfway around the pole before dropping my foot back to the stage out of fright. Then a little more, and a little more.

The more I visualized my goal of spinning around the pole, the closer to realizing it I became.

The first time I successfully pulled off a pole spin is etched in my mind. It was a Sunday, so the bar was mostly empty. On Sundays, Marissa and I would go onstage together and entertain ourselves. There were times when hours would go by with one or less customers sitting at the bar. The management didn't mind if we entertained the solo customer with our antics because that was one person hanging out and buying drinks. He was spending money instead of being chased out by every girl in the place coming around for tips. And the other girls didn't mind because they could just sit on their asses instead of dancing for peanuts.

There was a crew of guys who came in every Sunday, but not until later. Marissa and I befriended them, and I really enjoyed spending time with them. They were not only willing to participate in our shenanigans, but they would also buy us drinks. Dan was the leader of the group. He was a mechanic and told the funniest stories and was always up for doing shots. Marissa and I would go out with the group to the diner for breakfast after work or meet up with them at a bar to shoot pool if we weren't working. There was never anything romantic or sexual; we just had fun hanging out. Dan introduced me to Vampire shots (vodka, Chambord, and cranberry juice) and a drink called "Nuts and Berries" (Chambord, Frangelico, and cream or milk). I went through a lot of Chambord in those days.

Dan knew I was trying to up my stage skills, so one Sunday, he dared me to spin around the pole. (We've been over how I was all about dares back then.) So, with my Sunday crew watching, I successfully pulled off the slowest pole spin in history! It may have been painfully slow, but I made it all the way around the pole, landed on one foot, and stood up.

Ta-da, mothafuckas!

I was so excited that I went to the other pole and repeated the painfully slow pole spin. This time, I made it around the pole one and a half times!

In time, not only was I was able to spin faster, but I learned a few different pole-spin techniques. If I hadn't visualized my goal and hadn't seen myself in my mind doing it, I may not have ever achieved it. It certainly took practice and work, but with my vision in mind, I was able to see what I wanted to accomplish, and that pushed me to make it happen. When I pictured myself being able to spin around the pole, I could feel how proud of myself I would be. I imagined how good it would feel to have the customers watching me instead of zoning out at the bar. I opened my mind to receiving the help I needed to make that dream a reality.

What kinds of goals can you see for yourself? Are you willing to visualize them and trust in your higher power to send you the help that you need to make your dreams a reality?

If you are someone who benefits from a physical source of visualization rather than just an image in your mind, take the time to make a vision board. Also called a "dream board," a vision board is a collection of photos, images, quotes, and affirmations. While they can be based on the things you want—a large house, marriage, a baby, a yacht, a platypus, etc.—it is also important to include how you want to feel and use pictures or words to represent those feelings. You can buy vision boards from craft stores or the internet if you want a corkboard or something Pinterest worthy. If you don't want to spend the money on one, a sheet of paper or poster board will do the trick just as well.

You will want to place your vision board somewhere where you can see it multiple times a day. The more your goals are in the forefront of your mind, the more you will be visualizing your dreams, whether you are aware that you are seeing them or not. The more you visualize yourself in your dream job, space, vacation spot, or situation, the more you are sending those messages into the Universe. In return, the Universe will continue to guide you on the path to making those dreams a reality, and you will feel more motivated to do the work to make it happen.

If you have multiple goals, you may want to have more than one board. You can make one for your personal goals and keep that at home. Then have a separate one for your business goals that you can keep where you work. If you are not comfortable hanging up your board in those places, take a picture and use it as your lock screen or background on your phone. We all look at our cell phones multiple times a day!

I had a vision board as my phone background before I got married that included pictures of me and my husband smiling in our wedding outfits—I Photoshopped our heads onto a picture of a bride and groom—an image with the words "Debt Free" on an arrow, a bulldog, and my kids in caps and gowns (my husband and I got together after we had both already had kids). (I also took a photo of our kids and Photoshopped graduation caps onto their heads.) My vision board symbolized that we could pay for their college educations. It also included other photos that represented the future I wanted to create: What kind of home? Cars? How would we spend our time? What activities would we enjoy?

You can also put words on your vision board. Some of my favorite quotes are song lyrics ranging from the musical *Hamilton,* to Brandi Carlile, to Slipknot.

You can use any word or phrase that will inspire you. Such as, "Do your shit," which is my go-to quote for my kids when they are farting around and avoiding doing chores, homework, etc. It works for me as well when I am not feeling inspired to write or work out. "You are now the dangerous one" is a phrase I picked up from an event I attended in November 2019 for the MLM company with which I have been affiliated since 2013. I use affirmation words to symbolize how I want to feel as well: "Loved," "Successful," "Brave," "Validated," "Happy," "Fearless," and *"New York Times* Best Seller." Thank you for helping me achieve that goal! (Wink!)

One of my *all-time favorite* movies is *The Rocky Horror Picture Show*. (Tim Curry just does things to me . . .) I love the lyrics from the song "Don't Dream It, Be It." I can just picture the cast floating around in the pool, repeating, "Don't dream it, be it . . ." as they act out their fantasies in lingerie and fishnets. For the purpose of this exercise, I'll tweak it for my vision board. When it comes to visualization techniques, you need to "First dream it, then be it."

EIGHT

Sometimes You Put Your Foot Down, and Sometimes You Get A Foot Up Your Ass

IT WOULD BE wonderful if there were never any consequences to our actions and life consisted of all of us
bopping around doing whatever the hell we wanted with
no accountability. We all know that is not the way things
are.

As we travel down the road of life, we are going to
make a lot of mistakes. Some are intentional—I don't
care what he says; no chick has ever tripped and landed
on a man's dick, and no dude has tripped and landed in
a female! But intentional or not, our mistakes and wrong-
doings will always bring us consequences. Some are
immediate, others can take years. Some are public while
others are just in our own heads in the form of guilt or
self-hatred. Unless you are a sociopath and are incapable
of feeling empathy or any sort of remorse for your
actions, we all feel bad when we do something bad. Even
if it's temporary.

Some mistakes may be rectified simply by apologizing,
while others require more of a penance to right the wrong.
It has always blown my mind when people are unable

to say the words "I'm sorry." Swallow your pride and just apologize! No one is perfect, so when your human is showing and you screw up, own it. It will minimize a whole lot of drama.

I am a creature of habit. When the managers of Sunsingers announced that they had opened a second club, I didn't know what to think. Especially when I found out that the second club was in the middle of bumfuck nowhere. Management told us that all the dancers would be required to pick up shifts at the second club. Of course, the girls who were the "pets" of Sunsingers weren't required to work at the second club. I wasn't willing to do what those girls did to get that pass, so off to East Jabip I went.

The first thing I noticed when I pulled into the parking lot in the middle of the Jersey Pine Barrens were the trucks with the dead deer strapped on the hoods and the gun racks in the back. I walked into the club, and it seemed decent enough. The biggest downside (dead deer aside) was that there was no DJ. There was a DJ booth, but no one in it. Instead of a human spinning tunes, they had a cassette tape that played the same songs over and over for several hours. It got to the point where I knew what I would be dancing to during my next set even when there were several girls in the rotation ahead of me.

I won't share the real name of the club, but Marissa, Morgana, and I called it "Farts." It was close to the actual name of the establishment and a fair description.

I have a memory from Farts that is clear, until it's not. Frankie, the owner, came in to see how things were going with his new club. I rarely drank in the first several years I worked in gentlemen's clubs, and even more rarely during day shifts. I used to say, "If you need to drink to do this, it isn't the job for you." I kept to that for many years, my drink of choice being ginger ale. Or "Syd shots," when a customer kept pushing me to accept a drink and wouldn't take no for an answer. Syd shots were either a shot of ice-cold water or mixed juices with no alcohol.

When Frankie came into Farts and saw me, he told the bartender to make me a drink. I kindly declined, but he wouldn't hear of it. I finally said, "Okay, I'll have a Woo Woo, but make it light; I'm not a big drinker." He replied, "Make it a double Frankie special!"

For those readers who are not "in the know" of fruity, girly, alcoholic beverages from the nineties, a Woo Woo is vodka, peach schnapps, and cranberry juice. When it is a double Frankie special Woo Woo, it is all vodka and peach schnapps with a tiny splash of cranberry juice.

He motioned to the seat next to him, so I went and sat down. I had a lump in my throat and my stomach hurt. I knew I was screwed. At this point in my "career," he was the only owner I had ever worked with.

Let me pause my story to note that I would have said "worked for," but in all but one of the clubs where I worked, exotic dancers were considered independent contractors. We were required to pay a house fee, which was considered rent for using the stage and club to make money. However, you could only rent the space whenever the club said (in some clubs, they give you bookings without you having any say in your availability), and you could not call out sick without being punished, even if you had already covered the fee for the space.

You would tip the DJ for their services, the bouncers, and in some clubs, a house mom as well. Of course, if you bought drinks and weren't an asshole, you would tip your bartender as well. Most of the clubs in which I worked had extremely strict rules about how you could make your money and what you were and were not permitted to do. Several had physical handbooks that you received upon being hired.

According to the IRS website, "You are not an independent contractor if you perform services that can be controlled by an employer (what will be done and how it will be done)." So "independent contractor" my ass. They found a way to get girls to pay them to work. Good on 'em, I guess.

Every time a dancer started a shift, she was in the hole until all her payments for the night were made. I always brought all my tip-out money with me to the club and paid my tip outs when I got there. There were plenty of times when I didn't make enough money to cover tip outs in my shift, and I hated owing anyone money.

One of the managers at Sunsingers used to come into the dressing room at the end of the night hollering for his "scamolians." That meant everyone needed to fork over the house fee. Some of the DJs would bust into the dressing room for tips. Others who respected that the dressing room was a naked place would wait outside to get paid.

If you didn't pay your house fees, you could get suspended or fired. If you repeatedly stiffed your DJ, they had the power to embarrass the shit out of you while you were onstage, and if you were a repeat offender, you could also get suspended or fired. One DJ with whom I worked in several clubs had a song that he kept on reserve for any girl who repeatedly left without tipping him. It sounded like it may have been from *Sesame Street*. He would play one of her regular songs to get her onstage, then click over to a song that featured a cartoonish voice singing about how there was a cow and you could hear it moo because it weighed twice as much as you. Another DJ would play "You're Pretty When I'm Drunk" by Bloodhound Gang. Over time, I learned to take care of my DJ. If a DJ and I didn't get along, but they still played what I asked to hear, I would usually tip a dollar or two over the minimum. I was a major overtipper if I got along with a DJ and he played the songs that I liked to dance to, so I could be a minor overtipper for one I didn't really like but who did the job.

I worked with a DJ in Sunsingers who also had a successful career as a professional wrestler. He was a friend of the owner and worked the Monday night shift for shits and giggles, not because he needed the dough. This apparently gave him the idea that he could do whatever he wanted.

I once asked him to play a song called "Black No. 1" by Type O Negative. He responded that "Christian Woman," another Type O Negative song, was a better song. I liked that song too, but it wasn't what I wanted to hear in my set. I said, "Yeah, that's a cool song, but please play Black No. 1.'" So he agreed.

Until I got onstage and did my first spin. Then he said over the mic, "Oops! Wrong song!" and played "Christian Woman."

I was pissed! That night, I tipped him one dollar so he would know I hadn't forgotten to tip him but had given him one dollar on purpose. The club minimum for DJ tips was twelve dollars, and I typically gave the DJs twenty. He wound up chasing me out to my car. He was completely flabbergasted that I had tipped him a dollar. I said, "Look, I know this is a fun pastime to you, but it's my job. If you want to hear what you want to hear, stay home and play it in your living room, but I tip you to play the music I want to dance to." He apologized, and we were cool from then on.

Fast forward to the time Frankie insisted on buying me a drink at Farts. We still were dancing to cassette tapes in that club, so we had no DJ to tip. They had also waived the house fee when the bar first opened because they were trying to attract girls to work there. It made it easier to handle the little bit of cash we were making each shift when we were able to keep it all. But it didn't help me the day I was sitting next to the owner and squirming. I was still trying to figure out how to not drink and not insult him. I had worked very hard at being a stellar worker by tipping out consistently, showing up early, being a team player, etc. The fact is, I wanted to impress him because he was the owner, but I also found myself in an uncomfortable place.

He honestly believed he was the South Jersey Tony Soprano, complete with Bada Bing! and the "Fahget-aboudits." I was naive about how active the mob was in the nineties and erred on the side of not wanting my body to be buried deep in the Pine Barrens, never to be found.

I started to slowly sip the drink. *Strong* does not begin to describe the level of alcohol that was in that glass. My breath was probably flammable. Did I mention that I hadn't eaten anything before he had come in? Alcohol for breakfast is a bad, bad idea!

Mercifully, it was my turn onstage within the next few minutes. I headed up to do my two songs, walked around to the couple of customers to get tips, and sat back down.

When I looked at what was in front of me on the bar, I saw a topped off drink. The liquid was once again all the way to the rim of the glass. The thing with alcohol is the more you drink, the easier it goes down. We repeated the "drink, dance, and come back to a refill" pattern several times over until, not surprisingly, I was *wasted*!

When it was my time to go onstage again, I staggered behind the bar and up onto the stage where I tried my best to figure out which of the multiple poles that I was seeing was the one that was real. I'm sure that my "dancing" looked completely ridiculous, even though at the time in my head I thought I was pulling off my set with no one realizing how intoxicated I was. I took comfort in knowing that I had my routine memorized (more on that in the next chapter) so I could run through it, as wobbly as I was.

Until the song got to the second verse . . .

This was the day I did my infamous backflip right off the stage and landed in a heap on the floor. The last thing I remember was the bartender shoving a turkey sandwich in my mouth.

They must have taken me back to the couch in the office to sleep it off because that's where I woke up hours later. The head honcho was long gone. I hung out for several more hours and drank water. When I was sober again, I headed home. I swore that I would never allow myself to be put in that position again.

Did you catch what I said earlier? I had allowed myself to get completely intoxicated and had put myself in a position where I could have been hurt, raped, or worse because I didn't want to offend my boss. I had been able to stand up to the DJ and demanded respect because I was paying them to help me do my job correctly. But when it came to managers and owners, I still put them in a "better than" category because they were men with power who told me when I was able to make money. I was initially afraid to disappoint them for fear of punishment or retaliation. The fact was my upbringing and how I had been taught to see myself compared to a man in charge had put me in that position. My dad is the king of his castle, and it has always been his way or the highway. He called the shots when I was a kid. I was raised with the expectation that in all situations I am required to act in a way that allow people to view me as nice, agreeable, and "good," especially if the other person had a penis. Thankfully as I got older, I realized that I am worth more than that, and I am the one who sets boundaries and decides what I am and am not comfortable with—whether that makes other people angry or not.

From that day on, I never let a club owner, or anyone else for that matter, put me in a position where I went along despite my best interests just to appease them. Whether it was drinking alcohol or shelling out my hard-earned money to pay someone who was not doing their job. I've learned that whether I tipped in cash or time, some people deserve more than others.

Side note: I took several showers when I got home the day after Frankie had bought me all those drinks and I had woken up on the couch in the manager's office. I was always afraid of sitting on that couch for fear of getting pregnant. I had to have been completely wasted to have actually lay down and slept on it. I'm just thankful I didn't wake up to find my face stuck to a cushion.

One day, several customers managed to find their way into Farts. By "several," I mean more than the usual two bodies at the bar. I wanted to make sure that they all stayed while we danced to the music on the infamous cassette tape, so I hopped behind the DJ booth and introduced each dancer as she went onstage. I threw in some funny one-liners between the introductions, and the customers seemed to be having a great time. The girls seemed to appreciate not having to count the songs to figure out when they needed to be onstage. When it was my turn, I said, "Up next, the very sexy . . . me!" and scurried across the bar and onto the stage. After my dance, I walked around for tips and then headed to the booth to go back to being DJ Syd. The manager came out of his office and started yelling at me (again) because no one had given me permission to do that. I have no idea where he had been the previous hour when he apparently hadn't heard me on the mic, but I have a guess or two. (Pssst . . . It rhymes with "the pouch in the foffice".)

After the initial grand opening of Farts, it became apparent that no one wanted to work there. It was a haul to get there, you had to dance to whatever the cassette roulette landed on, and the customer pickin's were slim so the shifts were far from money makers. They managed to hire some girls who worked there exclusively. I imagine they didn't mention that there was another club where the dancers typically made more than less than half of the minimum wage during a shift for fear that they would ask for shifts there. And those of us who had been with the company for a while were able to stay at the first club.

Until they threw us a curveball.

If you did something to get in trouble at Sunsingers, your punishment was having to work shifts at Farts. So, if you were late to work, late to the stage, had called out, or something that the managers invented on the spot, you would be sent to North Wherethehellarewe to serve your time.

I was raised to always help others when I was able, to go the extra mile. The owners and managers picked up on that immediately and used that to their advantage. I was the first one they would call when they were short on girls for a shift, especially at Farts. I just didn't know how to say no, especially to men in what I perceived to be "positions of power". I felt like I should have always dropped everything to help out, even if I hated every second of the time I was helping and really would have rather refused.

Even when Farts had been established for a few months and they had a DJ for the night shifts, I still preferred Sunsingers. I made the most of the time I worked at Farts by amusing myself. I would dance to songs like "Run to the Hills" by Iron Maiden and "Girls of Porn" by Mr. Bungle. I was making the same dollar a set either way, so why not entertain myself? Most days, I left with only a few dollars.

It's really frustrating to spend more in gas to get to work then you make at your job. To their credit, even after they started enforcing it, the managers would waive the house fee when they knew we didn't have enough to pay it.

I could have gotten mad and quit. I could have said, "It's not fair!" and stomped my stilettos and pouted. But if I had to work there, it was for a reason. With me, it was almost always because I was unable to say no when they asked me to pick up shifts, so I couldn't really be mad at them for seeing an opportunity and taking advantage of it. In the couple of instances where I was sent there as a punishment, I put my bitching aside and "took my lumps."

We are all human, so there will be times when we screw up and make mistakes. Just as when we were kids we would be given time outs or grounded for not following the rules of the house, we are given the same kinds of consequences from the Universe as adults. These are the times when our actions have consequences, and we may have to go through a period of suck before we can get back on the good path. But these are also when we learn the biggest lessons. So, don't give up or pout or throw a fit like some preschool kid. Instead, try and learn from your experience.

What can you do differently the next time to avoid being in that same situation again? What did you learn from the punishment that you can use on your journey? Most of life's lessons and rewards come from times of hardship, not when things are easy peasy. Keep your eyes and ears open and educate yourself.

That being said, if you find yourself in a job or relationship where you are being punished or reprimanded and it is completely unjustified, you need to decide if it is in your best interest to remain in that situation.

I can help you with the relationship scenario: if you are being abused in any way—mentally, physically, or emotionally—then you need to get out. I don't care what the person abusing you tells you—they are not sorry, they are going to do it again, it is not your fault, and they are never, ever going to change . . .

You deserve better! Period.

It may be not as black and white if the scenario is you are in a job where your superior is an asshat. If they are jealous of you and are snarky, annoying, and have everyone talking shit behind your back, or if they give you all of the crappy shifts after you have been there long enough to not be the person expected to take the crappy shifts, then ask yourself if it is worth your peace of mind to stay in that job. Can you make a lateral move even if there is nothing available that is a step up? Can you cut back on your spending to get a job that may pay less financially but pays you so much more in terms of happiness and sanity?

Or in my case: if your boss keeps pushing alcohol on you when you don't want to drink, when do you decide to speak up for yourself and draw the line?

Money is not everything. It's nice for sure and can help you to do things, but it should not be the only marker you use to judge your life as "successful" or "unsuccessful." Happiness is worth so much more. And you never, ever deserve to be abused! No matter what the person abusing you would like to make you believe.

Don't be afraid to reprogram your brain to serve you better. It's taken a long time, but I have learned to not compromise myself in order to be viewed as polite and agreeable in situations where I want to put my foot down. This has been especially difficult for me when dealing with men, but I've made progress. You can retrain your brain to create and enforce boundaries in your own life. It will take time and you will feel uncomfortable, but in the end, you will be happier. Leaving situations that are unhealthy can make us feel sad. It can be scary to break away and move on to something better, even when you know you need to. Let yourself go through those emotions. You need to deal with the closing of that chapter of your life so you can move on to the next. Grieve it so you can leave it.

As grownups, we need to be self-aware and use discernment in deciding which situations are teaching us lessons and which are holding us back, hurting us, or just not a good fit. It may take some practice, or in some cases some brain "retraining," but once you are able to see the difference between the times you need to take your lumps and the times you need to put your foot down and set healthy boundaries, it will all be worth it to help you grow.

NINE

Creating Positive Habits

WE'RE ALL FAMILIAR with the word *habit*. It is used most often to describe a negative behavior that is repeated over and over. If you bite your nails, smoke, drink soda . . . you can explain these behaviors away by saying that you just can't help yourself because you don't even realize you're doing it. It's a "bad habit."

Think about this: What if you could start cultivating good habits instead of excusing bad ones?

Habits are born out of repetition and become cemented in your psyche once you start to develop cues for those behaviors. The hardest ones to break are the ones you don't even consciously realize you've created. They are things like a certain activity you began doing at a certain time, and before you knew it, it became a part of your daily routine.

I started smoking cigarettes at a young age and continued to do so for decades, minus stopping during the years when I was preparing to be pregnant through to the time my youngest turned two. When I smoked, I used to have a cigarette before dinner as well as after dinner. As soon as I knew it was time to eat dinner, I would go light up. Whenever I drove to the same places regularly on my commute—work, a friend's house, the grocery store, etc.—

there were landmarks that would trigger me to reach for a cigarette as soon as I encountered them. They were like checkpoints, only for cigarettes. It wasn't even that I necessarily wanted a cigarette at that moment, but it was where I always lit up, so it had simply become a habit. And if there was something I had to do and I really, really didn't want to (such as calling to make an appointment, needing to run errands, etc.), I would have to have a cigarette first. Creating that habit made for a double whammy. I combined the bad habit of procrastination with the bad habit of smoking cigarettes.

Instead of those bad habits, what good habits could I have created instead? What new cues could I use?

When I decided to quit smoking, I took a different route to my usual destinations whenever possible to eliminate passing the landmarks that had been cues for me to light up. When I knew we were about to eat dinner, I would drink eight ounces of water. I have almost eliminated any practice of talking on the phone. (That may or may not be a good habit, but I smoked the most whenever I talked on the telephone. Most people would rather text now anyway.)

I still procrastinate. It is amazing the number of things I can find to do instead of just running the vacuum and getting it over with. Scrolling through social media is my favorite procrastination activity. I have started to intentionally put my phone away and not log on to social media on my computer to avoid going down the news feed rabbit hole. I have certainly not eliminated all of my bad habits, but I am working on making better habits every day.

What good habit can you swap for a bad one? What cues can you change or eliminate?

The biggest problem that occurs when someone decides to change their life for the better is just that. They think, *I want to change my life!* How fricking scary is that? Setting off on a journey to change your entire existence? No wonder so many people fail right out of the gate.

When you make the decision to "start running five miles, follow a vegan lifestyle, wear makeup daily, and read personal development books by next Monday," it is *way* too many new habits to begin at once. Instead of taking on everything at once, break everything down into smaller chunks that you can transform into habits over time. For example, if you want to start doing fifty push-ups a day, and for the last decade you have done exactly no push-ups a day, you are setting yourself up for failure if you attempt to do fifty initially. Even if you are physically able to knock out fifty push-ups on the first day, there is an incredibly good chance that your triceps will not allow you to repeat doing fifty more the next day.

When it comes to habits, start with consistency, not quantity. If you need to start with one push-up a day, that's where you start. But do it at the same time every day.

Create a cue that will help you to form a habit. If we use push-ups as an example, you could:

1. Get out of bed.
2. Go pee.
3. Do one push-up.

That may be good for the first few days, until you realize you can do more than one push-up. So, add on another. Or three! Don't take the lazy way out when you know that you are ready to take on more steps. Keep your routine the same but add a little to it at a time. As time goes by, your repetition of "wake up, pee, push-up" will become a routine, and you will start doing the habit of push-ups without even thinking about it. If you keep adding on to your routine to challenge yourself, you will gradually improve until you reach your goal. Then you can concentrate on surpassing it.

When I was an exotic dancer, that was my daily exercise. I was never a gym person, and I was skinny, so I never thought about adding any additional workouts to my life. Now that I'm in my forties and have quit smoking, I must exercise and eat right to keep my body in the shape I would like it to be. I am still not a gym person, so I am so thankful that I have found a community of people who use at-home workouts to stay healthy. I work out six or seven days a week, but it didn't just happen out of the blue.

In my thirties, I wanted to add working out to my daily routine. Until it became time to work out, and then I didn't want to. I am amazing at planning, coming up with ideas for what I am going to do, and telling myself how awesome the results are going to be. But for the longest time, I sucked at executing those plans. I was the "Queen of Two Weeks." I could do any work out or follow any diet, nutrition, plan, or organizational idea for two weeks, and then I would cave. My bad habits would jump back into the driver's seat. To this day, I like to start new workout or nutrition programs on Mondays. I don't know why that makes my OCD happy, but Monday is the day my brain believes new things should begin.

I just started a new ninety-day workout program this past Monday. I had a week between the last full program I had finished and this one, so I tried out a different workout every day in between to keep myself in the habit of working out. It's a lot harder to start over than keep your momentum going. Now, I could have just waited to start the new workout and coasted for the week leading up to it. I could have made excuses that I needed the time to prepare myself mentally, that I needed to make my schedule and shopping lists, that I needed to rest, that it would be my last time to do _____ for a while so I should just enjoy it and go hog wild until my start date. But remember my story about Shaun T and the ten thousand dollars? Rather than allowing myself to make excuses, I wanted to start collecting immediately!

I mentioned giving up cigarettes earlier. My husband and I both smoked and we decided that we wanted to quit smoking, and full disclosure: I was terrified.

I feared the thought of having to deal with stress in my life without cigarettes. I had been a smoker for decades, and my bad habit was well established. I came up with so many excuses of why I *had* to keep smoking. "Well, so-and-so's wedding is coming up, so you know we're going to want to hang out and smoke." Or "We're going to the beach, and you know we always hang out on the deck of the hotel and relax and smoke." I could even spin it in a way that would make me look like I needed to smoke for the well-being of others: "You know how cranky I get when I don't have a cigarette. I never want to put you through how awful I'll be if I try and quit smoking totally. So, I better keep smoking. You know, for you. Because I love you so much!"

Or, "We're all going to die someday. Watch, I'll quit smoking and get hit by a bus!"

The bottom line was that all my excuses were fear based. I was afraid that I would have to change the person I believed I was. I had identified as a smoker for so long. Who would I be as a nonsmoker?

My biggest fear was that I would become one of the people I knew who had quit smoking and had blown up like a big ol' balloon. I have body dysmorphia and an unnatural fear of gaining weight. The thought of packing on the pounds after I quit smoking scared me more than the possibility of dealing with all the inevitable dangers that threatened my health if I kept smoking. I can trace this back to a previous relationship during which I had gained weight. My partner informed me that I was too fat for him to still be attracted to me and refused to have sex with me when I was that big. Honestly, "that big" wasn't even that big; he was just an asshole.

Despite my fears, I knew I had to give up cigarettes. It was not as if the ways that smoking negatively affects your health were unknown to me, too. I had grown up in the eighties, not the thirties. I had seen plenty of posters hanging in the school hallways and sat through countless health class videos showing us what a smoker's lung looks like compared to a healthy lung. I clearly remember a time when I was a teenager, and a local group representing a nonprofit had set up a table at one end of the mall. Their display included not only very graphic pictures of a smoker's lungs and all kinds of pamphlets explaining the benefits of quitting smoking, but an actual smoker's lung. A real, black human lung from a dead smoker. We used to laugh (and cough) as we walked by the table puffing on our smokes. We were little assholes. I am also dating myself by admitting that I was a teenager during a time when smoking in a mall was still permitted.

A couple of decades later, I was becoming aware of the negative effects of smoking cigarettes on a personal level. I was starting to get a raspy cough more and more often. I woke up every morning hacking and spitting into the sink. I named the glob of ick that I spit out every morning "Harry the Morning Phlegm Ball."

Smoking is super attractive!

When the time came to quit, I knew that for me to be successful on this journey, I would need to set up good habits *before* giving up the bad one.

I bought a home workout program on DVD and started doing the workouts every day in the month leading up to our quit date. We picked the day after my thirty-eighth birthday. Before we decided, I was still trying to make excuses of why I couldn't quit cigarettes yet. "But . . . but . . . it will be Christmas, and I can't quit then! I'll be miserable and ruin the holiday!" "It's Valentine's Day!" "We're going to a concert!" Letting myself have that last birthday as a smoker shut up that bullshit line and gave me a solid quit date.

When I started doing the workouts, it blew! I would have trouble catching my breath doing cardio. I would cough a lot. I would hit "pause" until the coughing stopped, and I could breathe again. Do you know what happens when you've given birth twice and you jump around doing cardio while coughing? You pee your pants. A lot!

I was sore, wet, and tired. I had to fight the negative voice inside me every step of the way. As soon as I thought about working out, my brain would pipe up about what a waste of time it was. My inner voice would rattle off all my favorite excuses, reminding me of why it was more comfortable to keep smoking. It would be easier, it was more familiar, I should just stop trying to change.

In time, I fought through.

Every morning, I would wake up and get into my workout clothes. No farting around! I was out of bed, I peed, and I got into my fitness wear. At the time, my "fitness wear" was a pair of sweatpants and a sports bra that I had bought in a multipack at Walmart. (And a pee pad!) You don't need expensive clothes from specialty stores to work out. You don't even need weights. You can use cans of food until you can get dumbbells. Get creative, remember?

I would force myself to work out first thing in the morning before my brain could come up with excuses for why I shouldn't. There were mornings when I was literally tying my shoes while my inner voice said, "You did three workouts this week, you can skip today!" But I would continue getting changed and then go work out. Sometimes you must go through the motions physically regardless of what your brain is saying. Let your inner voice run its mouth, just don't listen, or take it to heart. Within a couple of weeks, I found myself in front of the TV working out with little recollection of the steps I had taken to get there. It became more and more routine as I repeated the same actions daily.

These days, my morning routine is completely automatic. From the second I open my eyes, I text my husband a "Good morning, I love you!" message, and take a pic with my shaker cup of water and post it in my social media stories to remind my followers to drink water as soon as they wake up. I put in my contacts, brush my teeth, and walk down the hall to the kitchen. I start my coffee, feed the guinea pig, and then make my breakfast.

I have attempted to mix up the order in which I do things, and it doesn't work. Mostly because my guinea pig, Stanton Amadeus Fluffernutter, is aware of the routine and gets a major attitude if I add a step between making my coffee and feeding him. Once, I decided to quickly throw in some laundry before giving him his breakfast. I walked up to his cage to find his Pigloo and food bowl upside down and him in the corner of his cage giving me "the look." I asked, "What is your damage?" and he turned so his butt was facing me. Then he started kicking his bedding and poop at me. For a rodent, he has personality plus!

My fear of pissing off my lil' man has kept me in my routine most days. In addition to making that first cup of coffee, I eat the same breakfast almost every day, so making that meal is also a habit at this point. I fill in my planner for the day to organize my time, do my personal development, and write in my journal while drinking my "momcrack."

That is an all-natural pre-workout drink that gives me the energy to really push through my workout. I also drink "momcrack" at times to push through the afternoon slump. Or push through housework. By the time I am done writing in the morning, it starts kicking in and I'm ready to kick my workout's ass!

At first, every single one of these activities required a conscious effort. I missed some days and had a lot of "day ones" over the course of a few months. Don't take a "do over" as a reason to feel like you've failed. The only way you can be a failure is if you quit!

You may need to adjust the time of day you are doing your activities. It may not be the most conducive during the first time period you tried. For me, exercising in the afternoon is so much harder than in the morning. In the times when I need to, I really must remind myself of all the reasons why it's important for me to follow through.

Make sure you push yourself on the days where you don't feel like it. Motivation is awesome, but as I have said before, it doesn't last. Discipline and routine will overcome when you are lacking motivation, so creating good habits will serve you better in the long run.

When it came to dancing, I had unintentionally created a habit for my routine that would work with just about any song.

I had certain moves I would do through the first verse of the song. Typically, the chorus meant spinning around the pole. Verse two would be when I made my way to the back wall, second pole, or far end of the stage, depending on the bar. I would slide or crouch on the floor and then crawl my way to the front of the stage. Depending on the length of the verse, I would either wiggle my way up to standing or flip onto my back and do a spread eagle then bring my legs back together, pointing them straight up to the ceiling. I would then perform a back somersault, get up to my feet, and go back to swinging my hips and doing more simple spins.

Most songs have a big crescendo moment, which would be when I would flip up and hang upside down on the pole. If there was a long period where the song was quieter, I would climb the pole, cross my knees, point my legs straight out, and lean back. One hand would be holding on to the pole and the other would be outstretched, as if I were showing off the item for bid on *The Price Is Right*.

Ta-da, version two!

These moves were so ingrained in me that it did not matter if I were on my game, feeling like crap, drunk, or tired . . . I could automatically do my routine. It's not as if the customers cared because . . . boobs! I mentioned before about the girls who would just walk back and forth across the stage whenever they did a set. They still made money because the reason most of the customers came in to watch the show had nothing to do with actual dance ability. If they got to see tits and ass, they were happy.

There are no shortcuts when it comes to habit building. It takes time and repetition to lay the foundation for your new habits. Therefore, you need to have a legitimate end goal to justify doing your daily activities. Especially on the days you don't want to. For me, my motivation for doing the same moves over and over was knowing I would always be able to do a routine no matter what kind of day I was having. My routine made me comfortable and being comfortable made me confident. Dancing equaled tips, so I had to keep not only showing up to work but also getting up onstage and walking around for tips to make sure I got the money. That was enough motivation to keep me repeating the habit over and over.

A lot of that has to do with wanting and getting an immediate response. Me: "Look, boobs!" (Wiggle wiggle.) Customer: "Thanks, here's a dollar!" (Stuffs money in cleavage.) I got immediate gratification for my actions, which made it easy to see the results. On the flip side, there are very real goals that we want to achieve that do not give us the payoff immediately. What do you do when your goal isn't something you need as immediately as cash for rent and food? Because it takes a lot of time for them to become a reality, it's easy to blow them off when the going gets tough. For example, we all know that we need to eat healthy and exercise to keep the lifestyle-related diseases away, but when the going gets tough, the donuts are winning.

You may decide you want to lose twenty pounds. Eating a donut isn't going to completely derail your goal. Which is precisely why we find it so easy to say, "It's only one . . ." But it's a slippery slope. If you're telling yourself, "It's only one . . ." several times a week, the compounding effect of so many "only ones" will be one fat ass! If you gained ten pounds every time you ate one donut, it would be easier to turn them down. The opposite is also true. You cannot start a wellness journey and expect to reach your fitness goal after doing one workout or eating one salad. I would love to do a hundred squats and walk away with a lifted, C-shaped, wonderful tush. It's just not going to happen.

However, if you are adding these habits to your life and doing them several times a week, the compounding effect will be one hot ass!

If we set up healthy habits that keep us away from being in situations where we will succumb to temptation (don't keep junk food, booze, cigarettes, etc., in the house), we are less likely to mindlessly do the things that are counterproductive to our goals. Odds are if you think you want a donut or ice cream or something else unhealthy, you won't want it enough to get in your car and drive to the store to buy it.

If you do continuously get into your car and drive to the store to get the unhealthy thing, you most likely have an addiction. When you are dealing with an addiction, it takes a few extra steps to break it, but it is not impossible. You may benefit from joining a group, community, or, depending on the addiction, going to a rehabilitation center to help you overcome it. There is no shame in asking for help!

More than once when I smoked cigarettes, I wound up doing some crazy stuff to get them. My parents knew that I (as well as my brothers and some of our friends) smoked and tried to discourage us to quit by not allowing it on their property when we were teenagers living at home. We would have to walk across the street and stand on the sidewalk like a herd of jackasses to smoke our cigarettes. Their (completely justified) lack of support for our nicotine habits made it pretty obvious that the question, "Can I borrow the car to go to the store and buy smokes?" would be answered with a big, fat "No way!"

One night when my brother and I were almost out of cigarettes, we quietly snuck into the garage. We opened the electric door manually because if you hit the button, the mechanism that opened it was loud enough to wake the dead. Once the garage door had been opened with ninja stealth, we put my father's Honda Accord in neutral and rolled it down the driveway into the street. After taking the extra step to roll it even farther down the street, we started it up and took it to the gas station to get smokes. We brought the car back and repeated the same process in reverse. Other than parking it completely crooked in the garage; we had managed to pull off our scheme with no one the wiser.

Years later, when I was in my twenties, I realized after the blizzard of the century had started that I did not have enough cigarettes to get me through until the storm passed. I have lived in the Northeast my entire life, and I have never been a fan of snow. Especially when it's the completely blinding, ice-smacking-you-in-the-face, Arctic-wind-blasting kind of snow.

As much as I despised the weather, I needed more cig-arettes. I bundled up and walked several miles to the closest store. (I drove a 1985 Camaro at the time that was not snow worthy, so driving was impossible.) By the time I got there, I was a "Syd-cycle." Frozen to the core. The cashier only had cartons of my brand in soft packs. My initial reaction was to be annoyed because I always bought hard packs and didn't understand why anyone would prefer soft packs. (Hello entitlement.) Whether it was my style of packaging or not, there was no way I was going to walk to any other store. To be honest, I was surprised this store was still open! I went ahead and bought the carton, wrapped it up in the plastic bag, and trudged back home through the snowdrifts, victorious.

It just goes to prove that when you really, really want something . . . and it is something that you believe in your very core that you need (positive or negative), you will do whatever it takes to get it.

One could argue that of course I would do those things since I had a nicotine addiction. I would argue that addictions can be broken. Or ignored for a time, even if it means that during that time, you're a total bitch because you want your fix. The trick is to get your mindset to the place where your *dreams* become an addiction. It's easier to try and ignore the pull of reaching your highest potential and stay where you're comfortable. Only crazy people would trudge through the blizzard to reach their dreams or sneak a car out of their parents' garage, right? Wrong! Only passionate people who want to achieve their goals are crazy enough to do whatever it takes. They are the ones who can break out of their comfy place and be more!

It's time for you to be crazy enough to be everything that you were put on this earth to be. Put on your ninja jammies or your snow pants and go get the job done!

TEN

You Are Not Alone!

ONE REASON THAT people resist making changes in their lives is because they feel like they are doing it all by themselves. It's scary to take that first step, or join that new club, or share who you really are when you feel like you are the only person in the entire world in your situation.

The details may be different, but I guarantee that you are not the only person on earth who struggles with depression, or emotional eating, or a fear of clowns, or a negative self-image, or self-doubt, or anxiety, or whatever it is that you are dealing with that led you to buy this book.

When you are ready to do something new and scary, ask yourself, "Is there someone who would be willing to take that first step with me?" Maybe it's a friend or a sibling. Maybe you know someone online. If not, there are so many clubs and groups you can join where you will be able to meet someone to share your journey with. Don't be afraid to Google local groups and organizations that are filled with people on the same path. You could also meet someone in an online group and share your struggles and your victories. It doesn't need to be an "in real life" person.

When I started my adventures in go-go land, Marissa was there for that first step in the door. Even though it took her a little time to join me and begin dancing as well, once she did, we worked together almost all our shifts for the first few years. We pushed each other when we didn't feel like going to work by begging each other, "Don't leave me there by myself!" We dared each other when we needed a little extra motivation to ask a customer for a lap dance or to try a new move onstage. We took the job of supporting each other to the next level by doing as many double dances and double champagne courts as we could. That always worked out better for us in the long run. If we told the customer that he would get a better show if he sat on his hands, we would have fun with each other and not have to be groped or fight off unwanted grabs from some random man.

Marissa and I eventually parted ways; I certainly had a part in that because I was not always a good friend, and for that I am sorry. Later in my career, I had other work buddies who encouraged me in the same ways at work (and who also enjoyed occasional shenanigans).

When I bartended at Warlocks and the other two clubs in the franchise, my favorite partner in crime was Madison. We would have the best time together no matter how many customers were in the bar. She was an amazing Shenanigator!

Shenanigator (*noun*): A person who instigates shenanigans.

Madison was a pro. One time when I was working a Saturday night shift with her, the customers kept barking at me when I walked up to them to ask if they needed anything. I was perplexed to say the least. It took me over an hour to discover the note she had placed on the back of my register where the patrons could see it, but I wasn't able to. It said, "Bark and I'll show you my tits."

We would pass the time when it was slow by coming up with games to keep us occupied. The bar was an oval with a rectangular stage inside. The opening to get behind the bar was on the side of the building where the back door was located, so the bar was at the corner of two major roads, with the front door around the block. Madison would slap my hand like a wrestler tagging in their partner to indicate that I was up. I would pound a shot, run from behind the bar to the back door and outside. From there, I would run around the corner of the block to the front door and come back in and make a lap around the bar before getting behind it again to tag Madison in by slapping her hand. It would then be her turn to do the same. We would usually only do this a few times because we couldn't get hammered while we were working. Also, we both smoked cigarettes, so we couldn't run for too long before we got winded and had to take a break.

My favorite story from when we worked together took place during a bachelor party. Warlocks was the biggest of the three bars where I worked. It had two separate private bachelor party rooms, and each room had its own stage and bar. One day, she was bartending in one bachelor party room while I bartended in the other. Her party ended before mine, so she came into my room and jumped up on my bar. She commanded the room by doing her best *Braveheart* impression and yelling, "They can take away our lives!

They can take away our freedom! But they can never take . . . our Black Haus!"

If you have never heard of Black Haus, here is an interesting factoid. For the last two decades, I have said that it is black cherry schnapps. However, I just Googled to make sure that I was spelling it correctly, and Google says it is blackberry schnapps. I'm so confused! How could I have been so wrong for so long? (Insert joke about my first marriage here.) Either way, the amount of Black Haus that I used to consume can explain why I no longer have the required amount of brain cells to retain the correct information. There is no way I would ever consider drinking it now, but I used to think that it was very yummy.

(If you are curious and want to give Black Haus a try, here are a couple suggestions: We used to mix Black Haus, vodka, and cranberry juice to make shots that taste like Swedish Fish candy. Another favorite with the customers was mixing Black Haus, Blue Curaçao, and lemon-lime soda to make shots that taste like blue raspberry snow cones. Either of these can also be made in a tall glass over ice as a drink.)

Unfortunately, my favorite way to drink Black Haus was cold and straight. I have no idea how many shots Madison and I did that night. I can only guess that it was "too many" by the stories I was told after the fact.

There was a one-seater bathroom in the hall outside of the bachelor party room. I was told that I kept closing the door and then opening it again while one of the bachelor party guests was trying to exit the bathroom. I had drunkenly decided I was playing the old board game *Dream Date* where you would open a door and get a new "date" each time. This poor guy had to deal with me opening and closing the door in his face multiple times while assigning him different personas.

After that, apparently, I crawled on my hands and knees from the bachelor party room to the manager's office. The thing is, in order for me to have done that, I would have had to crawl down the hallway, past two champagne court rooms, up three steps, across the side of the bar that went past the DJ booth, through the door that led into a restaurant-sized kitchen, and down a second hallway to the manager's office. All while the club was open and packed with a Saturday night crowd! I'm not excusing my behavior; I'm just saying it would have been nice if someone had helped me to get up and walk there instead.

I do remember hanging out in the little bathroom that was attached to the manager's office. I'm sure I must have gotten sick, but I don't specifically remember that. I do remember Madison coming in to check on me. At her prompting, the two of us sang one of my favorite songs I had learned at summer camp. Multiple times. It's called "The Weenie Man Song," and the lyrics go: "I know a weenie man; he owns a weenie stand. He sells me everything from hot dogs on down . . . boom boom boom. Someday I'll share his life, I'll be his weenie wife. Oh, how I love that weenie man. Hot dog! Hot dog, I love that weenie man . . ."

I remember Madison calling up her friend so I could sing the song to him, too. We were way too amused by the weenie man that night. Sometimes, you not only have good people to help you get through the tough times, you may inadvertently wind up having a theme song too.

The last thing I remember from that fateful night was my manager placing a pizza in front of me and encouraging me to eat some of it. Instead, I passed out cold face-first into the pizza. Cheese up my nose, sauce all over my face . . . out! My manager was kind enough to hang out in the bar until 8 a.m. when I woke up. Madison had given him my tip money from the night before, and he gave me that. He made sure I was sober and could drive home safely.

I have only had a couple of crazy incidents with alcohol in my go-go years, and I am grateful that I worked with good people who took care of me. If I had not had them to look out for me, there were all kinds of horrible things that could have resulted from my poor choices. Madison knew how to have fun, but she always looked out for the people she cared about as well. She's been a great friend inside the bar and in real life as well.

Our antics weren't only restricted to her and me. We used to bring the bouncers, DJs, and dancers into our world of happy chaos. To be fair, the customers weren't off limits, either.

One of my favorite customers was a little person named Aaron. He would typically order a soda when he came in, but sometimes he would want an alcoholic drink. We had to save his life one night when he got drunk and passed out face-first, feet off the floor, in the toilet. That was so scary! I'm glad that was a one-time occurrence and that we all cared enough to keep tabs on him. As a bartender, I had to be especially careful to keep tabs on what he was drinking because he physically couldn't process a lot of alcohol.

He loved coming in and hanging out, and we loved it when he was there because he was always willing to have fun and be silly with us. He worked the door for us on Saint Patrick's Day in a leprechaun costume. We would dare him to go smack a girl in the ass and hide under the bar. She would have no idea who got her! My favorite of his shenanigans was when he stood outside of the ladies' restroom and told every woman who came out, "Your hair smells lovely today." (For those of you who are scratching your heads: his nose was at the same level as their pubes.) Wherever Aaron is now, I hope he is healthy and happy!

Not all of the customers were kind, good people. Some were until they drank a little too much. I was always glad that most of the bouncers, DJs, and dancers had my back when I found myself in situations that could have ended badly. Some of the most memorable moments with customers involved no alcohol; they were just naturally a little left of center.

I worked shifts at all three bars in the company as a bartender. One was in the south part of the city, one in the center of the city, and one in the north. They were nowhere near each other, but I saw Timmy at all three. He didn't drive; he rode a bicycle. Timmy always drank beer. Slowly. Out of the corner of his mouth like a baby goat with a bottle. We had this conversation more than a few times:

"Hi, Timmy!"

"My name is Superman . . ."

"Hi, Superman!"

"My name is Superman. Superman is the man of steel. He's the man of steel; he can fly! My name is Superman . . ."

"The usual?"

"Yes."

He'd get his beer and hang out. He wasn't a big drinker.

He would call me over and say things like, "Two things really piss me off!"

"What are they, Timmy?"

"My name is Superman . . ."

"What are they, Superman?"

"They keep lions . . . in cages!! They are stronger than we, are they not??"

"Well, yeah . . . so they won't eat us . . ."

He never told me what the second thing was.

Another time he called me over and then pulled the neck hole of his shirt down to expose his shoulder blade and asked me, "Have you ever seen a back this hairy? I think not!"

Whenever he was in, I would ask the DJ to play "Kryptonite" by 3 Doors Down because of the line where the singer asks if the person he is singing to will still call him "Superman" if he goes crazy.

I sure will, Timmy!

Another character I came across was in a go-go bar I had never worked in. I used to meet up with a friend of mine named Vaughn to play pool in a bar that was halfway between us. At the time, he lived in Pennsylvania and I lived in Jersey. Vaughn was a big biker guy with a great heart. We had originally met at one of the places I worked and became good friends. We used to refer to the place where we met to play pool as "the club where old dancers go to die." It made me sad to see these women who had been dancing for decades and who would have probably had a nice retirement if they had saved their money, instead of just scraping by. I always tipped everyone well.

One time, we met there for a quick game and went up to the bar for drinks. Across the bar was a man who kept repeating the same thing over and over.

"Hi! My name is Lancelot. And I like to watch girls dance a lot. And when I watch girls dance a lot, my pants . . . dance . . . a lot!"

After our first game of pool was over, Vaughn went to use the bathroom, and ol' Lancelot worked his way over to me.

"Hi! My name is Lancelot . . ." he began his speech.

I just stared straight ahead and tried to ignore him. Vaughn came out of the bathroom and immediately ran over to me when he saw what was happening.

"Hi! My name's . . ."

"YOU!" (Dramatic pause.) "LEAVE!!" was all Vaughn had to growl, and Lancelot was out the door. He hopped on his bike and rode away. (I'm starting to see a pattern with go-go bars and bicycles . . .)

There were also the customers who stick out in my mind because of the lies that they told. Everyone embellishes the truth from time to time, but these guys were over achievers!

Several guys came in over the years wearing team jerseys with the names of players on the back and telling us they were actually the players. I have met several professional athletes in my time and none of them wear their jerseys when they go out socially.

One guy just hit the unlucky lottery. I was going around for tips, and we got to chatting. He told me that he was a poet and asked if I would like to read his latest poem. I shared with him that I also write poetry and would love to read it.

I carefully unfolded the piece of notebook paper he had placed in my hand and began to read, "It was an early morning bar room and the place just opened up. And a little man came in so fast and started at his cuffs . . ."

I raised my head and looked him right in the eyes when I said, "You didn't write this!"

He looked back at me in complete shock and said, "Yes, I did!"

I continued reading, "Now the broad who served the whiskey . . ."

I'm not sure how he picked me. I think it's a safe bet that not many of the other girls in the bar would so easily recognize the lyrics to "A Better Place to Be" by Harry Chapin. I am a huge fan of Harry Chapin and was frankly insulted that this man was trying to pass off Harry's lyrics as his own creation.

He tried over and over to convince me that had written it. When he saw that I was not going to back off, he walked away.

In retrospect, the dancers took liberties when telling the customers who we were so turnabout is fair play. Just don't plagiarize and never, ever steal from Harry Chapin!

In addition to all the characters who were customers, I have worked with countless bouncers over the years who liked to start trouble or joke around. It meant the world to me to know that in addition to having my back if I were ever in danger or needed back up, I could count on them to make my job more enjoyable. In all the time I worked in various gentlemen's clubs, no bouncer was as much of a shenanigator as Rob.

Rob was a big, bald, goofy man who did amateur wrestling and would fight anyone at the drop of a hat. In the rare times when a fight would break out, he would hop right on in, kicking ass and dropping insults the whole time. He wouldn't just physically kick your ass but would also make you feel bad about yourself at the same time. His signature move was to pull an "Al Bundy" with the guys he had to physically remove. Meaning he would have the guy by the neck as he headed for the door, but the guy would hit the wall next to the door before going through the doorway.

When Rob and I first worked together, I was a bartender, and he was supposedly my barback. I say "supposedly," because every time I needed Rob to get me more beer or ice or whatever, he was off bending over one of the dancers or finding some other way to fuck off.

The walk-in refrigerator and beer storage in this bar were located in the basement. The basement steps were so steep that they were almost a ladder. I'm not tiny, but I'm not beefy either, so hauling cases of beer up the vertical steps made me nervous. The other issue with me having to get my own beer was that the walk-in was Rob's number-one place to lay some pipe. I would literally scream, "Put it away, I'm getting beer!" before rounding the corner to the walk-in. Even after issuing a loud verbal warning, I still witnessed Rob "in flagrante delicto" multiple times. Rob loved to have a dancer do a line of coke off his dick. I saw that move way too many times. His second favorite place to have sex with a coworker was in the corner of the bar. It was a dark corner, sure, but it wasn't exactly hidden away. People were literally that oblivious that they didn't realize what was happening in plain sight. I wish I could remove the images that have been burned into my retinas.

Rob understood his uselessness as a barback and would refuse to let me tip him out, even on the nights when he was doing his job. He and I had a great time together because he would do just about anything to get a laugh, and he understood that he would never, ever be in the walk-in with me unless I was grabbing beer and heading back up the ladder steps.

When I became a manager, Rob was still working as a bouncer. One of my duties was making sure that we always had batteries for the DJ's wireless microphone. There was a grocery store nearby, but the neighborhood wasn't great. I would make Rob go with me because I did not feel comfortable going by myself.

One day as we walked through the produce section to get to the back of the store where the batteries were located, he decided to yell, "Hey honey! Are you going to do the cucumber trick again?" in an attempt to embarrass me. I give him credit because there were at least four senior citizens who whipped their heads around to look at us while their jaws dropped. I refused to let him get his kicks and immediately responded, "You want me to stick it in your ass in front of all of these people?" He got mad, an old lady clutched her pearls, and I laughed my ass off.

We scooped up all the nine-volt batteries that they had in stock and headed to the checkout lane. After dumping all the batteries onto the belt, Rob waited for the right moment to ask (loudly), "Wow baby, are all of these batteries for your new vibrator?" I gave him the biggest doe-eyed expression I could muster, flashed a wicked smile, and responded, "Oh no, baby, my new vibrator uses a car battery." He got mad and stomped off like a toddler, the cashier snorted, and I was once again the winner.

Rob did not understand that I had grown up with two brothers and had learned at a young age that it is no fun to pick on someone who does not give you the reaction you are looking to achieve. I understood that a lot of times, people show how much they love you and have your back by knowing they can have fun with you. In this instance, much like with my brothers, trying to embarrass me showed how much Rob cared.

Some of the fun Rob and I got into involved a woman we'll call "Molly," who shared managing and bartending duties with me. Molly was awesome, but she was also the type of person who didn't let a lot of people in. She could be misunderstood and labeled a "bitch" when she wasn't. It was just her personality to not be as outwardly goofy as the rest of us. This made her the prime target for Rob's shenanigans.

On days where I worked the day shift and Molly came in at night, Rob and I would conspire to get her. Typically, Rob would find an item behind the bar and stick it in his ass. I don't know how this started or why; he just thought it was funny. I specifically remember a hairbrush one time and a lighter another. We would wait for Molly to come in, and I would ask her to hand me whatever the item of the day was. Right before she'd give it to me, I'd say, "Oh wait, never mind, I don't want it anymore." She would ask, "Why not?" and I would smile and answer, "Because it was in Rob's ass."

She would scream and throw it, which would cause me and Rob to crack up. She tried to get me with the same trick one day, but I wouldn't take whatever object she was offering to me. I just knew from the look on her face that I had no interest in touching it. (I think it was a roll of Life Savers or something.)

When it came to messing with coworkers, Rob could definitely be ornery. But when all was said and done, he always had my back. All I had to do was point to a customer or do the universal head jerk with my eyes looking at someone to motion, "This guy!" and he would remove anyone who was giving me a problem. No questions asked. He was very protective of me and made sure no one ever messed with me.

I clearly remember a customer who was teetering on way too drunk. He ordered another beer, and I told him that I couldn't give him one yet, but he could have some water and hang out for a bit and then I could give him another. He started arguing with me and asking why he couldn't have a beer. I tried to explain that he was over the line but was welcome to hang until he sobered up a bit.

Most of the time when people started getting indignant because I had flagged them and demanded to know why, I would say, "Because I'm a bitch. I'm a cunt. I suck. It's not fair. I hate me. Was there anything else you were going to say?" and they would usually leave. When it came to this guy, I gave him a glass of water and told him to just take a little break, trying to be nice instead of flagging him completely. He looked me dead in the eye while he poured the entire glass of water out all over the bar. I just yelled, "Rob!!" and he took care of it.

Another time when I was bartending and cleaning up at the end of the night, a dancer got into a fight with her boyfriend. He had her money bag and wouldn't give it to her. Rob went up and started with diplomacy. He asked the guy nicely to give her the money. The guy refused, so Rob said, "Give her the money, or I'm going to have to pick you up and throw you into the wall." The guy looked right at Rob and said, "I guess you'll have to pick me up and throw me against the wall."

So . . . Rob did.

The guy bounced off the mirrored wall, off a table, and onto the floor. He quickly hopped up to his feet and exclaimed that he was going to come back "with guns blazing" while mimicking pulling two guns out of side holsters and circling his arms around like he was in an old Western getting ready to face off at high noon. He could have just left at that point; however, he decided to pick up a Corona bottle and throw it as hard as he could.

At me!

I wasn't involved in the fight at all, so I don't know what had caused him to pick me as a target. Thankfully, I ducked at the last second because it would have smashed me in the face.

Rob lost his mind. He picked the guy up and literally threw him out the back door and onto the sidewalk. We all stood around in the bar for a few minutes trying to compose ourselves and figure out what the hell had just happened. I cleaned up the broken glass from the beer bottle and finished cleaning the bar. When we were ready to leave, I turned to Rob and said, "You go first. If that dude is waiting by the door to hit someone over the head, it's not going to be me!"

After the manager set the alarm to lock up the bar, we filed out through the back door, and the finger-gun-toting customer was out there, waiting. He had a completely different demeanor this time. He was very repentant and apologized to Rob. (Not me or his girlfriend, but whatever.) He gave the dancer her tip bag and asked Rob for a ride home. Which Rob gave him. Boys are weird.

It was by all accounts a wacky night, but I can laugh about it because I knew Rob had my back and would keep me safe. I mean that in the literal sense, but I also mean he was there to cheer me on and be a friend, too, and pipe up whenever I needed to be told to let things go or if I was being irrational. Certain weeks of the month, I certainly could be!

It's important to have a success partner, or a group of people to help encourage you, push you, have your back. When you have "your people," you will go so much further than when you try and do everything yourself. When you find *your* people, you will soar. They say it takes a village to raise a child, but it also takes a village to raise you up to be the person you were put on this earth to be. And not just people who will constantly "yes" you but who will also provide constructive criticism. If it is destructive criticism, close your ears, put your head down, and get back to work. While cheerleaders are amazing and definitely needed, look for someone (or someones) who will not be afraid to speak up when you are not doing the activities that will bring you closer to your goal. Or worse if you are doing things that are moving you backward away from your goal. Make sure to also look for the people who will take the time to lift the other members of your tribe up, too. No one likes to be around people who only take from others.

Your tribe is out there, and the only way that you can attract them is by being unapologetically, authentically you. If you are putting up a front instead of being your-self, you are going to wind up attracting people who are attracted to the front, not you. Keeping up appearances to keep them near you is not only exhausting, but also disingenuous. It's scary to take off the masks that society can make us feel like we need to wear in order to be accepted. It's easy to hide behind the expectations that others put on us and try to be who we feel others want us to be. It is also exhausting.

When you know you will be accepted for your actual face, it makes taking the mask off easier. Just as removing layer by layer of clothing onstage left me—almost—fully exposed (we discussed the hoohah angle earlier) and feeling unrestricted and free, removing your false truths will leave you feeling free and unrestricted as well.

ELEVEN

Getting Good At Saying Goodbye

IN THE LAST chapter I shared some of my favorite stories of the people with whom I either connected and felt really understood me or just make me smile when I remember our interactions. However, there were many other people that either did not like me for one reason or another, or with whom I was close for a time but had to distance myself from later. I used to take those things to heart, but I don't quite as much anymore.

If you share your authentic self with someone and don't get the reaction that you were hoping to get, that simply means that person is not part of your tribe. If it is someone with whom you will continue to have contact (family, friends, etc.), just be wary of what you share with them. I have had goals in my life that certain family members have pooh-poohed, and I have just chosen not to share those parts of me with them anymore. We have plenty of other topics we can discuss.

At the same time, note that people don't need to be exactly like you (no one is) to be considered part of your tribe. They just need to love you for the real you. They will be there to support you and your dreams and love you enough to help you see when what you are doing is not healthy. Differing opinions are not the same thing as not having your best interests at heart when it comes to your dreams. Some of my family members whom I am super close to and love to pieces have vastly different opinions than me, especially on things like politics and religion. We don't agree, but we respect that we don't see eye to eye on those things, so there isn't a reason for me to cut them out.

There are certainly circumstances where relationships can turn toxic, however, and those are the times when it is in your best interest to cut someone from your life. I have found myself faced with having to make that decision on a few occasions, and one of the hardest times was with someone whom I had considered to be one of my best friends. We had known each other for decades, and I shared with her a lot of what was going on in my relationship at the time. She had encouraged me to leave my partner, paid for me to run a credit check on him to see if things he had been telling me were adding up, and given me advice on ways to take care of myself after moving on from this person . . . so I did.

Granted, her input was far from the only reason he got the boot. But the kicker (Get it? Boot? Kicker?) is that once I made the decision to cut this person out of my life and end our relationship, she sent him Christmas presents and called and messaged him frequently. Now, to my knowledge, there was never anything between them physically or romantically, but that is still shady as hell! How could I possibly trust her again? In the beginning of our breakup, he would "mysteriously" be aware of certain things I had told her. For all I know, they're still calling and messaging now. She got the boot, too.

Trust your gut. Realize when someone in your life is trying to keep you from success because they want to keep you down on their level (like the crab story earlier in this book) or when they are a toxic influence and need to be cut out of your life completely. Love yourself enough to follow through and remove them. In some cases, you will be able to phase the person out over time. The easiest way is to take longer and longer to respond to their texts and calls. Make sure you are always busy when they ask you to get together, etc., until they decide to stop calling, texting, and inviting.

Other people will try and hang on like a tick on a dog's ass, and you will need to have a conversation on the way out. If they are the type of person who will play twenty questions and try and explain into the ground why you would be better off keeping them in your life, prepare to be busy five to ten minutes into the phone call.

"I only have a few minutes before my doctor's appointment, but I really need to address this. I love you, but we've grown in different directions, and I need to move on for me from now on . . . oh shit, my doctor's office is calling me back. Gotta go!"

Do not listen to their excuses, and do not let them pack your bags and send you on a guilt trip. Example: "Are you crazy? Don't you remember when I was there for you when_____?" Instead, respond, "I truly appreciated you being there for me then, but I am me here for me now and need to work on myself."

I have what I refer to as "broken wing syndrome." I am always trying to fix people who are broken emotionally, and in the process, I wind up hurting myself. Over the past few years, I have been working on myself in that area and am working on getting better at setting boundaries. I used to think that setting boundaries meant that I was being mean or a control freak. I have since realized that boundaries are not set to keep people away from me but rather to keep them in my life. If I don't set my boundaries and make it clear what I can and can not handle, there is a good chance they will unknowingly push me to a place where I explode and push them out of my life.

I'm realizing that it is not my job or my place to try and fix anyone else's life. Even still, I give people more chances than I should. I excuse away bad behavior and don't always speak up when I am disrespected. I have made improvements but am still on that journey. Chances are if I have cut you out of my life, it's because you handed me the scissors!

And please don't think that you must wait for a major betrayal to cut someone out of your life. Sometimes we outgrow other people, and that is completely normal. As they say, some people come into our lives for a reason while others come in for a season. I believe everyone who enters our life is there to teach us something. But having taught us a lesson doesn't mean they are meant to share your life for the long haul. Not everyone needs to know all the nooks and crannies of your business either, so be intentional about how far you allow people to get in.

In the same way that a tree needs to be pruned when its branches start growing out of control, or a plant needs to have its dead leaves removed to thrive; we need to prune the people out of our lives who are no longer helping us live to our greatest potential.

I don't have any feelings of ill will toward the people with whom I have parted ways just because we took different paths. That's all good! In fact, I really hope that they are all living fantastic lives and are making their dreams come true. I can cheer them on and wish them well without having them be active participants in my life.

One person whom I had been friends with since high school fit into this category. We had lost touch though our twenties and reconnected in our thirties over social media. We hung out and had a great time for a while, but I was married and a mom of three, and she was still single and enjoyed more "single person" stuff and would get annoyed when she perceived that I was putting "bros before hoes." I, on the other hand, think that when the "bro" is your husband and you are raising your family (and you have made it clear that your family is your first priority), that means you can't be offended by your girlfriend not wanting to go out barhopping as often as you do.

I tried to work on one-on-one time with her, but it wasn't always possible. Our schedules were completely opposite: I had more free time during the day and would have been able to get together for lunch just about any weekday. Her job was during the daytime, so it wasn't possible. My ex and I had split the time we would have with the kids fifty-fifty, and my parenting days were Thursday to Saturday and every other Sunday. Naturally, if I had my kids for half of the week, I was going to want to spend my time with them first. I would guess that most parents would feel that way, but I can only speak for myself. However, she would be annoyed that I wanted to spend time with my kids.

Unfortunately, she needed more attention than what I was able to provide. So, I made the choice to break away. We're still connected on social media, and I am thrilled when I see her post that things are going well for her. But that doesn't mean that I am open to having the kind of relationship that we had before.

During my last couple of years in the industry, I worked with a girl named Victoria in several bars, and we always had a blast. We would give "double dances" where the customer would pay double to get a lap dance with both of us at the same time. It's funny—if you got a lap dance with two of the girls, it would cost you double. If you got another type of "double dance" where there were two customers (typically a couple, not a guy and his buddy) and one girl, it also cost double. Those types of dances were rare in my experience. When it was slow, we would entertain ourselves by picking music for each other to dance to during our time onstage. Typically, we picked the most awkward "nothing you would usually hear in a strip club" songs we could think of. When it was her turn to pick songs for me, she always picked "Beast of Burden" by the Rolling Stones, "The Thong Song" by Sisqo, and the one that immediately conjures up my memory of her standing by the stage pointing and laughing every time she made me dance to it: "Step by Step" by New Kids on the Block.

We always found ways to have fun together, and people knew we were two peas in a pod and that we had each other's backs. We would call the local late-night talk radio show on the way home from work and chime in. They called me "Sydnee the lap dancer," and the DJ would have us share our stories from that evening. But when I stopped working in that environment, I quickly learned that Victoria and I had little else in common except our musical tastes. It wasn't enough to keep an active friendship together. Like I've said about other people, I hope she is happy and healthy and doing well. We have just taken different paths.

Don't feel obligated to keep people in your life who no longer align with who you are. You need to change and evolve and grow to become the person that you are meant to be. That includes giving yourself permission to separate yourself from the people who do not add value to your life, or worse, who fill your life with negativity.

When it comes to relationships, having healthy boundaries and expectation-setting are a must! Not just in our friendships and with coworkers but in romantic relationships as well. Think of your top three must-haves and your top three no-ways. We all have deal-breakers. There are certainly some things that people do and believe that are completely against our own core values. Those are the things that we can't see past in order to have a close friendship or romance.

When it comes to romance, some people would put sharing religious beliefs in the category of deal-breakers. Or wanting (or not wanting) to have children. These are big deals and should be taken seriously when choosing a partner. Don't ever enter a relationship expecting to change the other person. That is not fair to them. When I talk about deal-breakers, I don't mean things like, "I have to have the sink empty when I go to bed, and he waits 'til morning, so that's it!" Things like that can be compromised. However, if you have always wanted kids and your potential partner has made it clear that they do not, don't think, *I'll make them see how awesome kids are, and they'll give in!* or even worse, *I'll get (them) pregnant—"by accident."* That is a horrible thing to do to someone and shows complete disrespect.

Are there people who have changed their minds on deal-breakers like kids and religion? Of course! People convert to different religions and may decide suddenly, "Hey, maybe I really would like to have kids," every day. But you need to ask yourself if that is a gamble you want to take or if the odds are leaning more toward you winding up frustrated and sad because your partner is on a different path than you that ultimately does not lead to the same destination.

Make sure, however, to keep the people in your life who do have your back. My best friend and I met when we were eight years old, and we've had our ups and downs. We stopped talking for a couple of years when we started high school because, well, we were teenage girls, and teenage girls can be nucking futs!

We began talking again between tenth and eleventh grade and quickly rekindled our close friendship. Through living in different states to living in different countries on opposite sides of the world, from being students to being moms, from having several different jobs and crazy schedules, we have always made the time to stay in touch. We wrote letters in the nineties, then talked over email. Our occasional short phone calls to avoid humongous long-distance bills have now turned into long calls several times a week thanks to Facebook Messenger. If we had believed that we could have only been friends if we hung out in-person weekly, we would never have maintained our friendship.

We have vastly different points of view on some subjects but have many interests that we share. The bottom line is that we respect each other. When it comes to the things we don't agree on, we don't berate or belittle each other. (We bust balls of course because we're from Jersey, and that's how we show affection!) The bottom line is, we just love each other and know there will always be some things that we see differently.

Sometimes it's not, "Goodbye" but "see you later." Only you can determine who you would like to share your time with, and which seasons of your life they will share with you.

TWELVE

Managing Your Time and Interacting With Others

WHEN SOMEONE IS your tribe, make sure you make time for them. It's easy to blow off plans or not feel like it because your life is so, so busy. Guess what? Busy doesn't make you special. We're all busy! In order to live the life you are dreaming of and share that life with the people you want to include in it, you are going to have to make the time.

Making time has not always come naturally to me. Partially because what does come naturally to me is procrastination, but mostly because I believed the lie that I did not *have* the time. I began using a planner to organize my time. Seeing everything I need to accomplish in my day has helped me to be able to visualize when I can make time for others, projects, and things I would normally blow off using the excuse that I am "too busy."

I recently realized that while the practice of blocking out time in your daily schedule may not be hereditary, my daily practice is more than likely learned behavior.

Since as far back as I can remember (and most likely since before I was born), my father has carried a Day-Timer in his front shirt pocket just about all the time. If you are unfamiliar with a Day-Timer, it is a pocket-sized planner. The pages are organized into hourly blocks of time that have kept my dad on track with his schedule since God was a boy. Okay, not that long, but certainly for decades! I'm sure that watching him schedule his time in his Day-Timer since I was a child made an impression on me and has helped me to use a planner as my tool of choice to organize my own time. Even if I don't keep mine in my pocket.

To make things easily recognizable immediately, I use a different-colored gel pen for each member of my immediate family. I use a purple pen for my activities, red for my husband, green for our oldest, blue for our middle, and pink for our youngest. I use the gel pens to write down what each person has going on in the appropriate block of time each day. It helps me to plan out my time, and the different colors help me to visualize where I need to be—and who I need to be taking with me—at what time.

My planner has become an invaluable tool in starting my day. There are certainly days when life throws me a curveball, and things don't work out exactly as I've blocked them out in my planner. But most days I am on track for the most part, and honestly, if I don't get to the laundry until a couple of hours after I had scheduled it in my planner, life will still go on. This practice has helped me immensely when it comes to making plans with family members and friends. In addition to my planner, I have a simple black-and-white calendar that is secured to my refrigerator with a magnet. My mother has given me this calendar for Christmas every year for decades. (Except for one year, which completely threw me off. No worries—I just printed out my own and used last year's magnet. Creativity can help solve even the smallest of problems.) I make sure that any activities, doctor's appointments, birthdays, etc., are on the fridge calendar so the family can see them at a glance.

While my calendar helps me to see at a glance where I need to be and when, my planner helps me to map out my day every morning. In addition to those two tools, I have become more and more reliant on reminders in my phone calendar to make sure I don't completely flake on an appointment or event as well. I update all three tools so that they are in sync and keep me and my family on track.

When I look at the calendar, there are times when it seems like I couldn't possibly add one more thing. Still, I try and make sure that I say yes to invites whenever I am able. I know it would be easy to use my full schedule as an excuse to always say no because the thought of going out can stress me out. As I've gotten older, I have unfortunately lost several friends. I seem to be leaving the time in my life where everyone seemed to be getting married and having babies and entering the time where funerals are more common. I'm not going to lie, it sucks! Especially when I kick myself for not actually going out to lunch or for a drink like that friend and I always discussed doing, but never did. Make sure that you make the time to get together with the people you care about before it's too late. Tomorrow is never promised.

It can be hard to follow through when the thought of going anywhere gives me anxiety. I keep pushing myself though because it is important. I can be characterized as an extroverted introvert, otherwise known as an ambivert.

I recently listened to a podcast by Chalene Johnson, one of my favorite fitness trainers but also a successful author, podcaster, social media influencer, and business builder (she is theBomb.com), where she talked about the differences between extroverts and introverts and the people who fit somewhere in between. I had always oversimplified the definitions of the two terms as extroverts loving to be out and about, to start the conversations, and to hop onstage to speak in front of a thousand people, while introverts are shy, hate being in social situations, and never leave the house. While some of those traits may fit, there is another dimension to the definitions that I had never heard before Chalene's podcast, and it makes so much sense. She discussed how the title has less to do with your outward actions and more to do with how you get your energy and recharge yourself. Extroverts become more energized around others, such as in crowds, while introverts need alone time to recharge. Some introverts are perfectly happy to get on a stage and speak to a crowd, but when asked to be in a small gathering of strangers, they will freak out. I guess that is because you are alone on a stage, while the gathering is more . . . "people-y." Small gatherings are even more so compared to larger crowds because it's harder to fade into the crowd and not be noticed. You are more likely going to be expected to interact with the other people in the room.

Some people don't believe me when I tell them that I am a naturally shy person. Especially when they find out that I used to take off my clothes onstage. But the truth is, in most social situations, I am uncomfortable starting a conversation. I used to walk away from the deli counter at the grocery store if they didn't ask me if I needed help; I just couldn't open my mouth to say what I needed to order. But if someone talks to me first, I can talk with them for hours. I just need them to give me the invitation.

Part of me wonders if my hesitation to speak up comes from a lifetime of being talked over when I open my mouth and start speaking. It may have started in my childhood (I am a middle child) but it has certainly continued into my adult years. I must make sure that when I am in a position where my voice needs to be heard, as opposed to just chit chat, I speak up and don't allow myself to be drowned out by the voices of others. It's still not easy for me to do but if I find myself in a situation where something needs to be said, I push past the fear and speak up.

The extroverted introvert title I have given myself makes sense because I get exhausted in large crowds of strangers (at a networking event or in the local mall during Christmastime, for example). I absorb too much energy from other people, and it wipes me out. However, I am all about having my friends coming over to my house to hang out. I love to plan parties and gatherings because I decide who is going to be there and what the energy will be like. I will host, do all the food, decorate, and be an awesome bartender because I know that if I am the one making the invites, it will be a party or an event filled with people who know how I am and won't be offended if I need to say, "Thanks for coming, but I need to decompress now. Be safe going home, eh?"

However, when it comes to the idea of me leaving my house? Well, I will have a full-fledged panic attack leading up to the time when I need to get in my car and go somewhere. I will dream of the different illnesses I can suddenly contract that would make it impossible for me to leave the comforts of my home. Then, I will put on my big-girl panties and go. Once I walk out of the house and get in my truck to leave, everything is okay. I have no idea where this agoraphobia began or why, but I refuse to let it hold me hostage. I can do breathing exercises, remind myself of how much fun I am going to have when I do go out (or that I need to go because it's important, like if it's a doctor's appointment or the supermarket), and then I just do it.

The older I get, the more I find that I am capable of just doing the hard things if I just do it. I wind up making mountains out of molehills and getting in my own way when I start overthinking and letting my fear take the wheel.

I love cheese. I know that seems random but follow me here…Many people are sugar addicts or have a mega sweet tooth. I have a cheese tooth. I love all kinds of cheese and enjoy eating it in everything from nachos, mac 'n' cheese, on burgers, with crackers and pepperoni, straight into my mouth …My husband owns a deli, but I swear that unlimited access to cheese is not the reason I married him!

I recently did a nutrition program that was designed to reset the bacteria in my gut. It involved eliminating certain foods from my diet for 28 days. I was not too concerned about not having gluten or processed foods for a month. However, not having cheese or alcohol made me a little nervous.

Instead of overthinking it, I made the decision to follow the plan and I just did it. I wound up feeling great and losing eleven pounds.

I still have my limitations. My best friend lives in New Zealand, and I am so grateful when she and her family come to the States to visit. Because I will never, ever be on a plane for the crazy number of hours it will take to get to New Zealand. I do love her dearly, and I also believe that I would really enjoy New Zealand, and I think that if you ever get the chance to visit, you should go. Then you can tell me all about it. I learned years ago when I lived in New Jersey and she lived in Los Angeles that somewhere after five to six hours in an airplane, I start to freak the freak out. Whenever I booked my flights to visit her, I stayed up the entire night before my flight to make sure I would fall asleep on the plane. Unfortunately, I typically snorted myself awake after I dozed off on the plane, and then I'd be screwed. I have taken medications designed to take the edge off, with no luck.

There will be some situations where you will have success on your own from digging into your own power. Other times, you may find that you can get farther when you allow yourself to be part of a team.

When it comes to attending events that take place closer to home, I've found more success with the help of my amazing group of friends. Whenever I try something new or we go out somewhere, they have not allowed me to be maimed or killed by anyone. We wind up having a lot of fun, and by the time I get back home, I am always happy that I went. It's important to me to keep pushing myself to overcome any ridiculous fear I have and to do things with my friends. To take it a step further, I have even challenged myself to attend events alone—either because the person I had been supposed to go with was no longer able to make it or because it was something I really wanted to experience but had no plus-one. In each of those cases, I wound up chatting with new people and have even made a few new friends.

There will be times in your life when you believe you are alone, but you truly are not. It's up to you to look around to find the types of people with whom you want to spend your time. A lot of times, there will be someone else in the crowd with whom you can make a connection and have a great time, even if it is only for the duration of the event and you never speak again. I have many friends on social media whom I had met randomly at events, concerts, on vacations, and in airports. I honestly believe that there are many more friendly, cool, and caring people in the world than people who are mean, obnoxious assholes. You just have to be open to meeting new people when you are out and about.

Don't be afraid to talk to new people, especially in places you don't usually frequent. What is the worst thing that can happen? You accidentally say something stupid? No one has ever died from embarrassment and odds are you'll never see them again anyway if you don't make a connection.

Start small to get used to the idea of being more social. I frequently just smile and say, "How are you doing today?" to elderly people in the supermarket. Nine times out of ten, their faces light up and they say, "Great! How are you?" or something similar. I answer and then we'll part ways to continue checking items off our shopping lists.

It's nice to be nice. I try to treat people the way that I would like to be treated. It seems like such a simple and obvious way to go through life, but unfortunately not everyone feels the same way that I do.

I used to rate the bars in which I worked by the "asshole ratio." I would decide if it was a good place to work at by comparing the average number of assholes to the number of friendly people there. If the asshole ratio was low (a zero-asshole environment is impossible!), it would be a more enjoyable working experience. If it was high, especially with the employees, I would seek out a new place to work rather quickly.

Now to be fair, those numbers could change day to day. Moods, circumstances, hormones, etc., can all play a part in affecting both the customers and the dancers, too. You know how they say that women who spend a lot of time around each other sync their menstrual cycles? There are certain weeks of each month that you may want to stay far, far away from go-go land!

When I was a manager and was asked what it was like to manage dozens of dancers, I would answer, "It's like being in charge of a bunch of middle schoolers who can legally drink." Now imagine a bunch of drunken middle schoolers who are all "riding the dragon" at the same time. When there are that many hormones pumping in one environment, it's easy to see why there were times when heels and weaves would be flying across one corner of the dressing room while another girl sobbed in the opposite corner because she felt fat and ugly. There were times when it was absolute chaos. I would be tempted to open the dressing room door, throw in handfuls of chocolate and tampons, and run for my life! Instead, I had to be the responsible one and keep it all together.

Speaking of tampons . . . there is nothing more embarrassing than bending over onstage and seeing a fuse sticking out of your G-string. Unless you didn't realize you needed one before it was too late! All I'm saying is, if you ever decide you want to be an exotic dancer, make sure you either keep a pair of scissors in your bag for string trimming or learn how to tuck it in a flap and keep it out of sight. No one wants to see that! It's also a good idea to track your cycle and only wear white thongs when you are comfortably in the "safe zone." When I was the manager, I made sure to spend most of my shift on the floor, so my girls were never alone. I was always there for them to (discreetly) make sure they knew if they had a tag sticking out of their thong . . . or more.

Have you ever been out somewhere and spent time talking to people, doing your thing, and then when you look in the mirror, you see a big piece of food in your teeth? Or a stain on your shirt? It's hard to not feel betrayed by the people with whom you were interacting. "I wish she would have told me?" you might think, or even worse, "She wants me to look like an asshole!"

Don't be afraid to speak up if you see someone who could use a heads-up. The situation may be a streamer of toilet paper stuck on a shoe as a stranger leaves a bathroom. Perhaps its spinach stuck in your best friend's teeth, or something even more embarrassing. In the end, the person you reach out to will be very thankful that they were made aware of the humiliating situation instead of being left to wander around clueless while people made fun of them or pointed it out behind their back.

Also, don't be afraid to just say, "Hello!" or compliment strangers as well. You never know what someone is dealing with, and a small act of kindness can make a big difference in their day.

When we all take the time to look out for each other, we are never alone.

THIRTEEN

Fantasy vs Exploitation:

You Have To Follow The Rules

SEVERAL PEOPLE AND organizations have spoken out against gentlemen's clubs over the years because they claim that these establishments exploit women. I feel it is important to add this little nugget of information to the fact pack of those who consider gentlemen's clubs exploitative: when I worked as a secretary, I was subjected to as much, if not more, sexual harassment than when I walked around a club in a thong and heels. I was typically the only female in the office, which made me the only target for inappropriate jokes, innuendo, touching, etc. I used to have to keep my guard up whenever I went to the Xerox machine because while I was busy making copies of documents, I would have to avoid the rubber bands being shot at my ass.

Over the years, I've tried to take the apparent well-meaning speeches to which I've been subjected in my stride. Whether it was friends of friends in a social setting, wives or girlfriends of my husband's friends, or women who were actively protesting the establishments in which I worked, I tried not to take it personally. I'd hate to think that the women who spewed their message of being concerned for me and my well-being were only doing so because they were in turn affected by negative influences in their own lives. Some women deal with a partner who is less than respectful, who has poor self-esteem, or who is jealous. Others are held back by beliefs that make them feel like they must treat their sisters as "less than." I hope that was not the case with these women. I would hope that they were confident enough with themselves and honestly believed what they were saying because they had come to that place of their own volition, not because they were forced to.

I do not judge anyone for having the beliefs that they do. According to Merriam-Webster, *belief* is defined as:[5]

(noun) something that is accepted, considered to be true, or held as an opinion: something believed

Whether those beliefs are religious (God is watching, so don't be bad! God loves you! God is a man. God is a woman. God is nature. There is no such thing as God), political (pro-life, pro-choice, pro-gun, anti-gun, conservative, liberal, independent) or something really important like Miracle Whip or mayo . . . most of your beliefs were planted in your head during the years you were a baby to when you were a small child.

For example, most of us have deep-seated beliefs about money: "Money makes the world go 'round," or one that I struggle with personally: "Good people don't have money." Growing up in a belief system that speaks very strongly about how we, as lowly humans, deserve nothing, I was brought up feeling guilty about wanting to have money. I developed the belief that wanting to be able to afford things without having to scrape by meant that I was greedy. The problem is that me not having money doesn't help anyone else who also does not have it. It completely closes the door to my being able to use my money to help others in need.

The flip side, which a lot of people have been conditioned to believe, is this one: "You have to have a lot of money to be successful." Again, this belief is flawed because there are many people who have material wealth but who are miserable and empty inside. There are a ton of people in this world who are successful in terms of happiness, not being in debt, and doing things that feed their soul, but who are not making excessive amounts of money. I choose to define success by happiness rather than the size of someone's bank account, how many vehicles they own, or how large their house is. Think about all the people who are working themselves into the ground, sacrificing time with their families, and putting their health at risk just to be able to afford to buy homes that have rooms that they will never use. We need to stop living our lives based on other people's beliefs ("If you don't live in _____ neighborhood or drive a _____, you're a piece of shit!"), and start spending time doing the things that feed our souls. Take a lower-paying job, live in a smaller home, and spend time with the people you love!

The reason why many of our beliefs were implanted in our brains when we were young is because at that age, we take everything we are told and shown at face value without question. But now that we are adults and can choose for ourselves, whether you are an atheist, Christian, Muslim, Hindu, vegan, cyclist, Crossfitter . . . that is *your* business. Whether you are still following the cues from your childhood or have decided that your truth means something else, that is entirely your call. Personally, I love learning new things and like to hear about other people's belief systems. I may not believe the same things, but if you aren't trying to force me into sharing your feelings on the subject, I can still be curious and respect that you feel the way that you do.

In the last few years, I have changed my eating habits, my daily routine, and my mindset by listening to others and taking to heart what they have had to say and share. However, some things that people have shared that work for them and make them happy are not a good fit for me and my life. Much like how size zero jeans can look amazing on someone else but would never be a good fit for me, even if I greased myself up with a tub of lard and used a shoehorn to try and get into them. That is why I have a huge problem if someone shares their beliefs with me and it doesn't come from a place of respect. If you share your beliefs, and I thank you for taking the time to do that but express that I do not feel the same, please do not try and bully me. If I say that I'm not interested but you try and guilt me into coming to a gathering (passive-aggressive comments to guilt-trip others are the worst, by the way) or raise your voice at me or use other tactics to corner me, then that is not cool.

Stop belief-assaulting me. No means no!

Social media platforms make sharing your beliefs to a wide audience easy but can also mean you will receive a lot of backlash and negativity for what you decide to share on the internet.

When it comes to online debates, I have found that when someone has reached the point where they know you are right but would never, ever be able to say it because they have decided that their argument is their mountain and they will die on it, they either:

1. Accuse you of "attacking" them.
2. Accuse you of being like "Hitler," bring up an example of how Hitler felt the same as you, or any other way of bringing Hitler into the conversation.
3. Say, "Well, I'm not going to change your mind, so I'm just going to stop talking," or some other "wah wah wah" or "I'm taking my football and going home" type of response.

Don't be a pussy. Just say, "I totally get where you're coming from, but I feel differently. Thanks for sharing your views with me," and move along.

When it comes to getting into social media arguments, especially about subjects like politics or religion, most of the time you will not wind up opening anyone else's eyes to see your side. It will just result in arguing, name-calling, and bad vibes, so why waste your time locking horns with someone who feels just as strongly about the opposite point of view?

There are still people on this earth who believe that other people are not on the same level as them because of gender, race, religion, or education. There are racists, homophobes, transphobes, chauvinists, and assholes who fully believe that they are entitled because they were born one way and someone else was born another. Knowing this, is it worth it for you to scream your views at these people if you do not feel the same way (and I really hope that you don't)? You could yell those same views at your water heater with the same result. Only the water heater won't yell back.

If you feel compelled to share how you feel about your religion, political views, lifestyle, or beliefs, create posts focusing on how your life has been positively affected by said religion, political views, lifestyle, and beliefs. The approach is to influence others from a place of love. Show them how your belief, organization, community, etc., could benefit them, rather than coming at them from a place of accusation and trying to point out how they are stupid for not agreeing with you. Showing someone how your beliefs can benefit them increases your chances of them opening up and being willing to hear your message. Remember the Rule of Seven from Chapter Four.

To put it in terms of exotic dancing: if you are concerned that a go-go bar has opened in your town and are trying to get rid of it, please . . . I beg you . . . don't say you are concerned "for the children." Every titty bar I have ever seen is windowless and does not allow underage people to enter. Dancers do not spend time outside of the bar in heels and thongs, so you would not see anyone clad in dancer wear unless you are in the establishment. Most women I have worked with showed up to work in pajama pants and a messy bun, as if they had come straight from shopping at Walmart.

You have a better chance of seeing someone walking around in heels and a G-string in Walmart than in the parking lot of the titty bar!

If you are concerned that an establishment is breaking the law: allowing minors to come and drink, selling illegal drugs, sacrificing virgins, etc., then, by all means, you have a valid argument to be upset with said establishment, and I suggest you take any proof you have of those violations to the proper authorities and allow them to investigate. However, if the problem is that you are simply terrified of nudity, or that you are concerned that your husband may go spend the rent money on an exotic dancer, or, god forbid, your man may have the audacity to look at another woman when you believe he should have blinders on to never get a glimpse of any other female on the planet, then the issue is something you need to take care of within yourself and your marriage.

I had only been working at Farts for a few months when a group of people in the surrounding community started making a fuss because they decided they didn't want us in their town. The people in this community group were so insecure that they decided to go after a bar that was located literally in the middle of nowhere. Because of the location of the bar, they were unable to use the argument that it was offensive to the neighborhood. It wasn't next to a church or a school or any other buildings at all. It was in the middle of pine trees.

Plus, it was just an establishment that featured girls dancing in thong bikinis and heels. (This was in New Jersey, so the tops stayed on. No nudity aside from butt cheeks). When they found out that the bar was doing nothing illegal so that they couldn't force us to close legally, they tried to convince management to force the girls who danced there to wear visible ID cards stating their real name, address, and age. When I say, "wear visible ID cards," I mean they wanted the girls to dance and then walk around for tips while an ID card that clearly stated all their personal information was hanging off the side of her thong. Picture a luggage tag hanging from your undies. This group of people was attempting to spoon-feed this information to anyone who came into the bar. I have no idea what the point of this practice would be if not to intentionally open the door to causing harm to the women who worked in the bar.

The members of the community group were so worried that the bar infringed on their rights, yet they were completely fine with the idea of completely stripping away a dancer's privacy and her right to not let customers know her real name or where she lived. In case you are blissfully unaware, not everyone in the world is a nice person. These people were so terrified of butts that they would never have to see unless they physically entered the building that they encouraged having a young woman get followed home and attacked. That way, they could say, "See?" and argue that the environment bred harmful consequences (even though it would have been the result of a situation they had created). That was more important to them than to just agree to disagree and let others to enjoy go-go bars alone while they continued to live their own lives and activities outside of go-go bars.

I'm happy to report that none of the girls were ever followed home and attacked because the owner told the community group to go scratch. But it all goes to show how some people are so entrenched in their belief systems that they are blinded to other possibilities and unable to accept other people. When those beliefs cause you to stop caring about the safety of other human beings, and in some cases deliberately cause them harm, that is both sad and dangerous. It is especially maddening when the groups responsible are screaming out of one side of their mouths about love and acceptance while condemning and attacking other people out of the other.

There is only one true judge, and that is God. "Love thy neighbor as thyself" does not continue to say:

"Unless . . .

they work in certain industries,

are sexually attracted to _____,

are a different color than you are,

spend their time doing things you wouldn't choose to do, and so forth."

I've said it before: just because you think something is "icky" does not give you the right to make it go away for everyone else on the planet. There are people in this world who think that chocolate is icky. Could you imagine if people were lobbying to make chocolate illegal just because it wasn't their jam? If you don't like chocolate, don't eat it. If you don't like exotic dancing, don't go into go-go bars. I think the likelihood of someone coming into your house uninvited and forcing you to watch them take off their clothes as they gyrate to some funky music is as likely as someone forcing their way into your home to make you eat chocolate. Live and let live, as long as you are not being forced to do something that is harmful to your own well-being.

Helpful hint: something that is perfectly legal that you don't agree with and that is located in the vicinity of where you happen to be located is not the same as you being forced to participate. If you would have no firsthand idea what was up without taking yourself into the environment on purpose, you are not being forced to participate in whatever goes on in there. You are going in because you are nosy.

When I was married to my first husband, one of his best friends got engaged. Let's give this friend the stage name of "Francisco." I had been there to witness Francisco's first two relationships, which also happened to be his only two relationships. Ever.

I can understand why, when he got engaged to his second girlfriend, he felt compelled to hold on for life. He was older than what would be considered the typical age in the dating pool when he got into the relationships with girlfriends one and two. He was genuinely nice and not a bad-looking guy. I think he was just very shy when it came to women.

Francisco and his fiancée held an engagement party. It was at a lovely venue. The banquet hall was very classy, and I was thankful that it was close to home. My husband at the time and I arrived, and we were having a fantastic time. The groom-to-be's friends began to rib him about having a bachelor party. Where would it be? What sort of debauchery would they all be privy to? They got louder and more vocal in their suggestions of the different types of establishments that they would expect to host a proper bachelor party.

Suddenly, the bride-to-be busted in and started yelling, "No strippers! No strippers!" then looked at me and said, "Sorry, [Sydnee.]" (She said my real name.)

Okay . . . just a couple of points here:

Point #1: much like no one could tell that Clark Kent was Superman when he wasn't dressed in his tights and outside undies, when I was not at work, no one would have looked at me and assumed I was an exotic dancer. I had dressed appropriately for the event I was attending. (Yes! It's true! Exotic dancers do not walk around outside of the bar in nothing but thongs and stilettos!) More times than not, if I was not in jeans and a T-shirt or sweats and found myself in a situation that called for dressier attire, I would dress conservatively. In any case, I had said nothing in response to the ribbing of her fiancé, so there was zero reason for her to out me in front of a room full of people who were unaware of what I did for a living, unless . . .

Point #2: she was one of the most insecure people I have ever met. When my first husband had his bachelor party, his best man took him and his friends out to Hooters and then to the local nude club (knowing that I would more than likely not know anyone who worked there—see former chapter about "gina juice"). That night, Francisco wound up calling his fiancée for a ride home because he was not "allowed" in Hooters and especially not in a nudie bar. My former husband and his friends left him at the pay phone waiting to be picked up by his fiancée. Francisco had made his choice.

Point #3: questionable behavior apparently ran in the family. When she had her bridal shower (Same venue. Woot! I like to stay close to home), a mutual friend who had originally RSVPed that she would be there was in a car accident the week before and could not attend because of her injuries. She called the mother of the bride as a courtesy to let her know. I don't know about you, but if I was holding an event and one of the guests called to inform me that she could no longer attend because she had been injured in a car accident, my gut response would be to ask, "Oh my god, are you okay?" The bride's mother's response was, "Shall we be expecting a gift from you?" Not anymore . . . bitch!

Point #4: when the time came for Francisco and his fiancée's bachelor and bachelorette parties, there were major discrepancies between the two. Francisco and his friends went into Philly and attended the local lacrosse game, followed by hanging out at the local corner bar. His fiancée went into New York City to barhop and attended a strip show. When Francisco's bride-to-be decided that he hadn't come home early enough from his bachelor party (which was the night before their wedding), in the argument that followed, she clawed his face. Hand to god, he got married wearing makeup to cover the scratch marks.

Yet the biggest threat to their marriage, in her mind, was that Francisco may look at someone else's butt in a gentlemen's club.

Okay, then.

Note: I feel the need to add in this space that anyone can be a victim of domestic abuse. It is not right to put your hands (or nails) on another person unless they are attacking you and you are fighting for your life. Period. No matter which person has the penis. Or if you both have a penis. Or if neither of you have a penis, except for the one in the drawer.

There also needs to be clarification in the realm of adult entertainment when words like *exploit* and *objectify* are being thrown around. According to Merriam-Webster.com, the definition of *exploit* (as a verb) is as follows:[6]

1. To make productive use of: utilize

Examples: *Exploiting* your talents; *exploiting* your opponent's weaknesses.

2. To make use of meanly or unfairly for one's own advantage.

Example: *Exploiting* migrant farm workers.

In my humble opinion, the exotic dancing industry is exploiting heterosexual men and their inability to resist turning to mush in the presence of naked breasts. Don't get me wrong: as a bisexual woman, I appreciate a nice set of tits. I think no matter whether you are gay, straight, bi, pan, or identify in any of the other options in the sexuality buffet, you can appreciate boobs. But hetero men get the trophy for becoming blathering idiots in the presence of a pair of chesticles.

To be honest, the industry does objectify women in terms of the dictionary definition of the word. The definition of *objectify* is as follows:[7]

To treat as an object or cause to have objective reality

Example: They believe that beauty pageants *objectify* women.

There is no argument that if men didn't put women in the "objects used for sexual gratification" category, there would be no gentlemen's clubs. It's a simple supply-and-demand situation. When I say, "supply and demand," I am referring to dancers who have decided on their own volition to get into the industry as a way to better their situation, not the very small percentage who have no say in how they got there.

Are there women in gentlemen's clubs who are being exploited in the sense that they are being taken advantage of? Especially those who are shipped in from other countries under the guise of getting citizenship and a better life only to be taken into clubs where the money they make has to be given to their handlers?

Absolutely!

There will always be exceptions to every rule. Just as there are plenty of women in the world who have never stepped foot into a gentlemen's club but who are still constantly being exploited.

I have worked in clubs that hired dancers from foreign agencies. These women knew little English (or shaving practices) yet raked in the dough.

Looking back, I'm sure it was out of fear that they worked their customers into submission so that they could reach their quotas. But at the time, that hadn't occurred to me; I was just sick of being passed over for dances so the guys could go back with one of the foreign girls instead. I started walking around the bar, grabbing my boobs and squishing them together, then pulling them apart over and over while saying (in my best accent to mimic theirs), "Hi! Couch dance? Hi! Couch dance?" Since I worked so many shifts and the customers knew me, my clever ruse did not work and was met with "Shut up, Syd!" and a dollar between the breastisis. Can't blame a girl for trying!

There are also many addicts, abuse survivors, and mentally ill women who wind up in go-go bars. In my opinion, if these women did not have the option of dancing and holding a legal occupation, they would be out on the street and most likely would have wound up as prostitutes. It's nice to say, "No, no! These women could get a job as a cashier! Or go back to school!" Sure, they could have, and if a frog had wings, it wouldn't bump its ass when it hopped.

Some of these women did eventually leave the bars and got "regular" jobs, but can all of them do so immediately? Probably not. There are many reasons for people to not be able to just move on to something else—for example, some of these women need the time to heal. This place of "in between" is an important one that gives a lot of women the chance to transition at their own pace.

You also need to understand the feeling of empowerment that comes with knowing that the crowd is looking at you as a sexual object. That they want, more than anything, to connect with you at the most primal level. In that moment, you are the one in charge of their minds . . . and the other bits.

So many people, women especially, give away that power, and it's sad. If you harness the power within you rather than feeling shame about it or giving it away to someone else to control, you can gain a whole new level of confidence.

Of course, we would all like to be loved and respected for our intelligence and personalities above anything else. There is nothing wrong with having that expectation. But I refuse to see the notion of "using your feminine wiles" as a negative. It would be like using a screwdriver to build a house instead of an electric drill. People may say, "Wow, that's impressive!" but at the end of the day, you're wasting a whole lot of time and ignoring a powerful tool that can help you to complete your goals faster.

I'm also not saying that women are only made of sexual power and nothing else, nor am I condoning the act of providing sexual services in exchange for getting something else. I am saying that the combination of body and brains can be a powerful alliance. And I don't mean a certain type of anatomy, age, hair color, weight, chest size, etc. When you exude the confidence that comes with being a woman who is secure with who she is on all levels, that grabs the attention of everyone who encounters you.

Here is the thing about me. Call it vanity, call it insecurity, whatever. The label doesn't matter. I want to be wanted. That doesn't mean that I want to have sex with multiple partners, but rather that I want multiple people to *want* to have sex with me. This sounds so horrible as I type those words, but I'm just being honest. The fact is I get off thinking that other people—male, female, trans, nonbinary, asexual, whatever—can look at me and think, *God, I wanna hit that!* And that's enough. And even though I may be a frequent participant in your "spank bank" but have chosen not to engage in anything sexual with you in real life, that does not mean I want you to remain unfulfilled. By all means, please be fulfilled!

Which brings me to another point: as of my typing these words in October 2022, there are currently 7.9 billion people on this planet. You may have read my previous confession about wanting to have people want to have sexual relations with me and thought, *What a conceited bitch!* or *How dare she?!* Yet on a planet with 7.9 *billion* people living on it, you honestly believe that your partner's mind has never drifted to a celebrity or a coworker or a former sexual partner or some stranger they saw in the grocery store while they are "doing the deed" with you?

Sure, I'm the conceited one.

Let me break it down in the simplest terms that I can: I love my husband with all of my everything. He is my number one, my world, my best friend, my heart! But if we are being intimate and I start thinking about something I saw in a porno flick we watched, I don't feel guilty. I would be willing to bet our house that he has also thought about other people in a sexual way in the eleven-plus years we have been together. He is a human being!

While I know it happens and I do not take it personally, to be honest, I *do not* want to know about it. I want him to give me the illusion that he thinks I am the hottest woman on the planet. There is a part of me that is so ridiculously insecure that I need to hear that if he could have his pick of any woman on the entire planet, he would still pick me. My Sydnee persona would say to him, "Of course you would pick me. What are you? Stupid?" The bottom line is, I know how happy we make each other, and that's all that matters.

A lot of couples have their "celebrity pass." This is an agreement between the two of them that in the extremely unlikely event that either person would find themselves able to have sex with a certain celebrity, it can happen with no retribution or consequences in the relationship. It's easy to make these kinds of deals because the odds of someone meeting a celebrity are slim. The odds of someone meeting a celebrity, and then experiencing a mutual attraction and opportunity to do something about it, are even slimmer.

My celebrity pass had been Chris Cornell, may he rest in peace. I had also considered Robert Downey Jr., but in the character of Tony Stark. I am a huge Avengers fan, and I love Black Widow, too. In my next life, I want to have an ass like Scarlett Johansson's in her Black Widow black leather outfit, or at least I would love to know what her ass feels like (with her permission, of course!). I also love Brendon Urie, lead singer of Panic! At the Disco. I had a dream about him once where I was at a Panic! show and had somehow made it backstage to meet Brendon. When Brendon invited me to come back to his hotel room with him, I wasn't going to pass up the opportunity. We get to his suite in the hotel, poured a couple drinks, and sat on the couch. The remainder of the dream consisted of me giving him financial advice and him being super impressed with my knowledge of the stock market and mutual funds.

I literally woke up laughing! First, because I have absolutely zero knowledge about investing and finances, and second, because even though my dream had seemed so real, I couldn't step outside of my marriage. Not even in the dream world.

I think that is the bottom line when it comes to fantasizing about other people when you are in a committed relationship. There is a part of all of us that drifts to what-if scenarios. I truly believe that no matter what the celebrity crush or person whom your mind drifts to when you are alone with your thoughts, if given the flesh-and-blood opportunity to make that fantasy a reality, most people would not take that step. Well, most people wouldn't take that step if they are genuinely committed to their partner, anyway.

If your spouse finds themselves in a position where they are tempted to get a little side action, and he or she decides to take that step, that is on them. They are either inherently a cheater, or there are deeper issues in your relationship that need to be addressed.

When I was dating my first husband, he confided in me that he was finding himself attracted to a woman at his new job. Looking back on that conversation now, I am shocked with the levelheaded response I gave him, as I am typically a very emotionally driven person. I told him to explore his feelings with her. Go on a date. If it wound up in bed, use a condom. I guess I subconsciously knew that if I hadn't said, "Go ahead," there would be a few ways this could have played out:

1. He could have seen her behind my back, which would have been much worse.
2. He may have gone down a "what if . . ." path, and I would have been the victim of the comparison game with a person he had created in his head.
3. He may have decided that he'd rather end our relationship to explore other opportunities.

He wound up meeting her for coffee and realizing that she was "annoying as fuck", so nothing happened. Could it have? Sure. All it would have done was make me realize that we weren't the match I had thought we were sooner. The two children we have together make me see why I married this man. They are why we were together because they are amazing!

Not everyone can tell their partner, "Give it a go, and let me know." The timing was important: this was when we were dating, not engaged, or married yet. I may not have been so willing to say "go ahead" when we were first married. Later, when we decided to open our marriage, I probably would have approached it as I had when we were dating. I must share, though: in my experience, most times when a couple decides to open their marriage, someone is bound to fall out of it. If you have a successful open relationship, then bless! The people I know who have been in them (myself included) have not fared the same.

Also, he had shared those feelings with me himself; I hadn't found out that he was planning anything or seeing anyone behind my back. No matter what the status of the relationship, if he had stepped out without telling me how he had been feeling, the outcome would have been completely different. Whether she was annoying or not!

I think that the comedian Sam Kinison (rest his soul) said it best when he did a bit on anal sex. He explained that, when it comes to sex, most women tell their man that he can have her boobs, her mouth, and her vagina, but there is no way he is getting her ass. In response, most men would think, "I didn't even want it until you told me I couldn't have it!" You know how when you're a kid, the thing you want the most is the thing you're not allowed to have? I could tell my kids, "You can have the brown, orange, yellow, and red M&Ms, but not the green ones!" and there would be hours of "That's not fair!" and them sneaking away with green M&Ms. But if I had asked instead, "Why do you feel like you need the green M&Ms?" it would open a discussion that would ultimately end in either my realizing why they wanted them or them realizing that they aren't missing out on anything. All the other colors are equally delicious!

My point is: opening a discussion can only help your relationship. A lot of times, people think they're "missing out" because they would like something from their partner that they assume their partner is unwilling to do. If you just talk it out, you may find that your partner is willing. Especially if you explain why this particular thing is so important to you.

Sometimes people go behind their partner's back because they like the dopamine rush that comes from being sneaky. Playing the game of seeing someone else on the side makes them feel more important or more desired. In those cases, that is disrespectful, and it's no longer a "My partner isn't willing to . . ." situation but rather an "I am lacking in self-esteem, I am a jerk, and I need to be a sneaky asshole to feel important" situation. I have watched enough fights on daytime television in my younger years (Jerry! Jerry!) to sincerely make this request: ladies! (I am asking you directly because most of these situations are on you.) Can we please start holding the right person accountable when your man steps outside of your relationship? We have so many reality TV shows and so many posts on social media that are based on drama created by the woman scorned going after the woman her man is seeing on the side.

No!! That is not the right thing to do.

Go after your man! Or let him go, and he can become her problem. My husband and I fall asleep every night to the Discovery ID channel or *Forensic Files*. One thing I see over and over is how, in many cases, the "other woman" has no idea that *she* is the "other woman" and not "*the* woman." Ultimately, one of the women winds up dead, and the other one winds up with a sentence of life behind bars with no parole while the guy goes out and finds some more suckers to have sex with. So not worth it! Best idea: the two of you catch him together and kick his ass out on the street. If you need inspiration, go to YouTube and check out the video for "The Boy Is Mine" by Brandy and Monica.

Now guys, I haven't forgotten about you! I know there are women out there who are cheaters as well. But I rarely hear the man saying he's going to kick the other man's ass. Is there a double standard when it comes to men and women cheating? I feel that men, in general, can separate sex as just a physical activity whereas most women are perceived to have an emotional attachment to it. Perhaps a man can see that a guy laying some pipe with his girl was just looking to get off and there isn't the same kind of deep reaction toward the "other guy." If the man has truly had enough of being disrespected by his woman, he will break it off and kick her cheating ass out. (Or he may decide to stay in the relationship because . . . boobs.)

This chapter is not only for those in an exclusive relationship. Rules should be followed whether you are a couple, throuple or single and ready to mingle!

If you are not tied down and want to "sample the buffet" sexually, there is nothing wrong with that, as far as a few simple rules are in place:

1. Be safe! No one needs the modern-day STD version of Typhoid Mary running around. Use condoms, get tested, and if you catch a treatable cootie, then by all means, treat it and make sure the only sex you are having is with yourself until it is cleared up completely. No one else wants your cooties. If you catch an untreatable cootie, make sure your partner is aware *before* you "do the do" so they can decide if they want to take a sexual gamble

with you or not. You are not to make those decisions for other people!

2. Make sure that your bed buddies know that they are just that: bed buddies. You need to make it crystal clear to your partner that your intentions are sexual and nothing more. If you are both adults, you should be able to have this conversation. If you are not mature enough to talk about sex with a potential partner, then you are not mature enough to be having sex. You don't want to wind up crushing someone's feelings (unless you're a total dick!) or come home to find a bunny boiling in a pot on your stove.

3. Gauge how you are when it comes to sex and relationships. Do you easily become emotionally connected to others? For example, do you kiss someone (or less!) and then immediately start fantasizing about your wedding? If so, you may not be capable of a no-strings-attached sexual relationship, and that's okay! Just don't put yourself in a position where you will wind up crushed. Or boiling a bunny. It's important to know yourself enough to realize if you are the type of person who can explore your sexuality with many partners or the type who is fulfilled with one partner for the duration of

> your life. There is no right or wrong choice. It
> is all up to the individual and their personal
> beliefs. Just keep your sexual exploits age and
> species appropriate!

All of this to say, make sure you know all the players in the situation before making assumptions. Please know that if a man likes to go to the titty bar, the "thing" in his pants that the dancers are all trying to get are his dollars, not his dick. Most customers who go to go-go bars are there to just take in a show and enjoy the view, like . . . dirty Disney. A fantasy land where you can go escape from the daily grind, the stress of your job, the commute, whatever, and enjoy a couple of hours in a magical space. Only instead of dressing up in a princess dress, you can watch a woman take one off. The odds of a customer leaving with a dancer from a strip club are slim, no matter what he was told in the couch dance room. While there are exceptions to every rule, of course, statistically, he is more likely to have a woman try and pick him up in a regular neighborhood bar than at a gentlemen's club.

I worked with a girl once who was selling her body on the side. She was in a dark place after an abusive childhood, which had led her into an abusive adulthood. All she had ever known was being used and tossed aside by people who were supposed to love her. It was sad to see her desperately trying to meet the quota that her pimp demanded by the end of her shift. I'm happy to say that she wound up clawing her way out of that situation and getting a job at a fast-food restaurant. She is the exception to the rule. Most women who have fallen that far do not have the self-worth or self-esteem to get out of the cycle of abuse or out of the circumstances that had put them in that place to begin with.

If dancing is a legal halfway point, then I see that as a good thing. It's a legal way for women to use their "assets" to create an income without having to take it to the next step of selling their bodies for sex. Not everyone can be a model, but the black lights can mask a lot of imperfections. Is there prostitution in gentlemen's clubs? Absolutely. Just like there is in regular bars, casinos, and online. But for every hooker, there is a larger majority of chicks like me who would just put on a stage show and walk around to get compensation for said show. And maybe a hug. No more. I had a reputation for being "conservative" with the customers, and that was fine with me. It was a title that made me feel proud.

Gentlemen's clubs are a unique place where the customers' fantasies and the reality of a dancer making a living to give them that illusion collide. If the dancer is able to call the shots of what she will allow, and the rules of the relationship are being respected by both parties, there is no reason why this type of environment should not be able to exist and thrive. It is not exploitation but rather a place where women can use their bodies as they see fit while customers are able to pay for the experience. A win-win!

As a customer, you may even get to experience an adult version of "Mr. Toad's Wild Ride." Just keep your hands down at your sides until the ride comes to a complete stop.

FOURTEEN

Standing Out from the Crowd

IN THE CURRENT age of constant content, from TV ads to social media posts to immediate input from every corner of the globe, it's so easy to get caught up in trends. You may want to wear the latest clothes, have the most popular hairstyle, the "right" shade of lipstick . . . and there's nothing wrong with that! But know that if you are actively trying to be like everyone else, you are going to blend in with everyone else. If you want to be noticed, make sure you put your own spin on all the trends you are enjoying to really make your unique attributes shine.

I have never been someone who follows fashion trends. Mostly because, to be honest, I suck at it! I've never learned how to put pieces of clothing together to make a trendy outfit. Basically, I need someone to come out with an adult line of Garanimals or hire someone to dress me. I used to wear all black in the eighties and nineties because I was able to throw together an outfit without worrying about them clashing. (And because I was all about vampires. More about that in a bit.) I have a few basic guidelines that help me pick out clothing. I know that red, black, and purple suit me, as do the burgundy and maroon shades that fall into the same color family. I know that I look better in actual halter tops than halter-neck tops. Since I've had my kids, high-rise waistbands are more complimentary than low-rise pants or skirts.

And that's all I know about dressing myself. Now, I usually wear jeans, a T-shirt and Chucks because that is my level of fashion.

I have worked in gentlemen's clubs that allow "costume ladies" to come in and sell outfits to the dancers. It's impressive how many of them show up with a rack of dresses and outfits for sale that they've sewn themselves. Many people aren't aware of this, but there are trends in go-go wear just as there are in mainstream fashion. I have seen girls get into physical fights over outfits when they both wanted to buy the same one. I've also seen physical fights break out when two girls had the same outfit and wanted to wear it at the same time. It's crazy how emotional someone can get over a piece of clothing that is going to wind up in a heap on the floor of the stage.

Stage wear can be expensive. There were certainly girls who could not afford to buy multiple outfits. Most clubs expect you to change after wearing an outfit for two songs, max. Some places expect you to change for every set. Whether you can afford fancy costumes or not, you should be able to wash said outfits regularly. Some girls wore the same thong for so long it was glued into place. Not for nothing, you can get cheapo thong undies at Walmart so you can swap them out while the others are in the wash. No need to be disgusting.

Whenever the costume ladies came in, I would ask if I could try on an outfit. We had the same rules as bathing suits in a store: you could try on a bottom over the thong you were wearing, and then walk out to the bar wearing it to see if you could get a customer to pay for it. Most of the time, I was able to find someone to finance my outfits if I promised him a first private dance in it (which would be the first private dance *out* of it since those were topless). It was pretty genius, actually. "Buy me this so you can pay me for that."

The advantage to trying on clothes in a room full of other people is that you can get an opinion from the group. Assuming that they like you and will give you an honest opinion, that is. I could always count on Marissa for that. She would be the first one to be like, "Absolutely not!" if an outfit wasn't a good fit. I would do the same for her. I may not be able to dress myself, but I have a pretty good eye for what looks good on other people.

When I first started dancing, I wore all kinds of crazy things because I was clueless and relied on outfits that either came from my underwear drawer or that I could get for cheap. These were the pre-online-shopping days, and I would go to local adult stores and occasionally find something in Victoria's Secret that would work. I never wanted to look like everyone else and always created my own style. I remember one of my outfits—a white thong bikini with fringe and turquoise embellishments. Whenever I wore that, I danced to "Wild, Wild West" by The Escape Club and "Wanted Dead or Alive" or "Blaze of Glory" by Bon Jovi. I had a long-sleeved yellow top with a matching yellow thong that I would wear with a denim vest and Daisy Dukes that were cut to a thong. My favorite outfit was a black thong one-piece. It laced up in the front, and if I bent over too far, I could have cut myself in half. I thought it looked hot with the denim vest and my thigh-high leather boots.

I mentioned that I had no clue what I was doing, right?

After playing around with different looks using the outfits I had bought off other people, I knew I had to be true to myself. I was definitely me in the other outfits, but they didn't portray my personality as well as when I finally got down to my inner Sydnee and made the choice to build on what made me . . . me!

As I mentioned earlier, I had been a vampire fan for a long time, ever since I first watched *The Lost Boys* in the eighties. I was thrilled when I found out that a girl I worked with was dating a guy who had a side business molding custom-made fangs. He could create top and bottom fangs, but I only wanted the two top ones. They were caps made from the same material that they used to create dentures, so I could eat, drink and smoke with them in my mouth. They were easy to care for as well because I would soak them in denture cleaner and brush them with a toothbrush and toothpaste. She brought me over to his apartment after work one night to get the molds taken. The next week, he came into the bar with my fangs. I happily gave him the (tax deductible!) eighty dollars and took a seat next to the mirror. He showed me how to slide them over my teeth and secure them, and how to remove them. He gave me instructions on how to clean and store them.

I wath tho happy! (There was an adjustment period before I could talk without a lisp.)

After a few weeks, I could drink and smoke with the fangs in. I never did like eating with the fang caps on, but I didn't eat at work most of the time if I was working night shifts, so it wasn't an issue.

Fun facts about dancing with fangs:

1. Be prepared to answer, "Are those your real teeth?" a gazillion times a night. I had long since mastered keeping a straight face while spewing all kinds of levels of bullshit out of my face hole, so I was able to answer this without laughing or rolling my eyes as well. When asked about the validity of my fangs, I would look the customer right in the eyes and go on a long diatribe about my Romanian heritage (lie) and how my great-grandparents had come over in the 1800s (true—just not from Romania) because vampire hysteria had taken over their village and they feared for their lives (lie) and that my parents were concerned when I was a baby and my teeth came in pointed (lie) because only 0.01 percent of the population was born with natural fangs (I guess that's a lie. I never looked it up).

2. If you flash a big, toothy grin at customers from the stage, it will most likely spark curiosity, so they will keep watching your show unless . . .

3. Some customers are wussies and scared of vampires. I was walking around for tips one

night, and when I walked up to one customer, I smiled, and he shrieked! Full-out screamed in my face and ran away. I did feel bad about that one because I'm certain he had some sort of PTSD when it came to the undead. He was the exception, though, because there were several other customers who feigned fear just to get out of tipping.

4. You will hear "Bite me!" a gazillion times a night as well. After a mental eye roll, I would say, "Sure! If you have your results from recent blood work. I can't just be biting people not knowing if they're clean! I have one blood partner and we get tested monthly. I mean, it's not like they make fang condoms, and you just can't be too safe; I'm sure you wouldn't want someone with dirty fangs biting you? I'm not some sort of blood slut after all, and oh my god! Is that what you think? Are you calling me a blood slut? That is so insulting . . ." That exchange usually ended with them tipping me to go away.

5. If you keep your fangs in a 35mm film case and get pulled over on your way home from work, be prepared to take them out of the case, pop them in, and smile. That is if the officer pulling you over is like the one who stopped me. He couldn't believe it when I

showed him. He thought they were "So
cool!" and asked me a bunch of questions
about them before letting me go with a
warning. Thank you, sir!

Here is another trick that I learned early on: when you dance, people are comfortable asking you to do things that they would never ask someone outside of a bar in a million years. (Unless they are hiding behind a computer monitor. That tends to make people ask and say all kinds of stupid shit that they would never have the balls to say if they weren't speaking online anonymously.) I guess being the one not in their undies gives you confidence. I have been asked several times to go back to someone's hotel with them at the end of the night. No matter how clearly you convey, "I am a dancer, I am *not* a prostitute," or, "I'm married," or, "No!" those answers are always met with more questions or stupid statements, like, "Aww, don't you like me?" or "What he don't know won't hurt," or, "Eating ain't cheating."

One time, I happened to be at the right (wrong) place at the right (wrong) time just as a customer came in through the door. He made a beeline across the bar at me and immediately asked me for a couch dance. I said, "Sure," and we proceeded to walk to the couch room. He was a rotund man with glasses and a pocket protector in his dress shirt. That's all fine, but I could tell rather quickly that showering wasn't one of his daily pastimes. I had a knack for attracting large guys and learned early on how to maneuver giving a couch dance when there is . . . let's just say a lot of ground to cover.

I settled in and started moving to the music. He began to tell me all about how much he loved to jerk off to Shannon Tweed movies. For two full songs, he went on and on in more detail than I cared to hear. In my head, I kept a steady stream of "La la la la la la la" playing while I smiled and nodded.

The second song ended, and I got up and gathered my things. He looked me dead in the eye and asked, "If I come back at two o'clock . . . could we . . . do it?"

"No," I answered point-blank.

"Why not?"

At this point, I could have gone through the laundry list of reasons why not, from my being in a committed relationship to my not being a hooker. Instead, I channeled George Carlin and said:

"Because I wouldn't fuck you with a stolen pussy!"

I spent years being point-blank honest about why I wouldn't leave with a customer, and let me tell you, they don't care! They will push and push until you flip out. Then you just get angry and closer to having an ulcer, and they'll tell everyone you're a nutcase. I finally decided to change my approach since it was obvious that while I genuinely believed I was speaking English, the customers were hearing Charlie Brown's teacher.

Let's start again from the top:

Customer: "Hey baby, why don't you come back to my hotel room after work tonight, and we can have a little fun?"

Me: "Fun?! Fun sounds awesome! I love fun! Sure! But my best friend, Marissa, has to come too because I give her a ride home, and we like to go everywhere together. Oh, and we'll need pizza because we'll be hungry after work. But we have to order it from Domenic's because their pizza is the best! Have you ever had it? It's so much better than Franzino's. One time I got Franzino's and the crust was soggy, and the cheese smelled like old gym socks. It was so nasty! Have you ever gotten a pizza like that? Well anyway, I like pepperoni and extra cheese, but Marissa likes veggie, so I guess we can order two pizzas, or if you just want to buy us one then we can get the pizza half and half. And broccoli bites! Have you ever had them? They are so cheesy and good! And we'll have to swing by the convenience store for Mountain Dew because Domenic's only has Coke products. So annoying, right? But I'll need the caffeine, and Doritos would be awesome, too. I like the red, but Marissa likes the blue, so we can just get one of each, and some onion dip, and I need a pack of Marlboro Lights. You know what? This lighter is almost dead, so I'm going to need a new lighter too, unless you have one. Or do you have matches? I'm sure we can figure it out . . ."

I would say anything that popped into my head at the moment until they would be throwing money at me to get me to shut the fuck up and go away. They were going to wind up calling me a nutcase either way, right?

There is more than one way to reach the result you desire. You need to be steadfast in reaching your goals and flexible with the path to get there. We are never able to plan for all the obstacles that will appear in our path, and the journey from where we are now to our goals is almost never a straight line. (Remember what I said in Chapter Six about getting creative.) Don't get hung up on things having to play out "your way." If it were up to me, I would have danced to my set and then passed around a tip bucket to collect money. That way, no customers would have ever touched me. (Except the ones I knew and whom I would sit with to have a drink. Those were my buds and would always get a big hug.) But that is not the way it works.

I may not have been able to control the way that tipping worked, but I could decide on how I wanted to present myself. After trying several looks that were not "me," the vampire look was born. I naturally have dark eyes and brunette hair. I do tan, but when it's not summer, I fade to Casper quickly. I accentuated the vampire theme by using black eye shadow not only on my eyelids but also to hollow out my cheeks as well. I started with the raw materials I had to create a look that helped me to stand out from the pack.

Then I took it a step further.

Where most people would do an all-black-themed goth look, I wore bright-red stilettos. I know that's breaking goth protocol, but that's the point. There were several customers who gave me the nickname "Red" because of my shoes. Those heels made a statement without saying a word and made me memorable. This was especially true when it came to one of the managers. I found out quickly after I started working at a bar in the city that one of the managers, we'll call him "Mitch," had a foot fetish. Being that I have sexy feet, this was an advantage for me. He *loved* my red shoes. I would see him staring as I walked by, gazing at the red heels like a cheetah salivating at the sight of a gazelle.

Little did he know that *I* was the cheetah . . . looking at his chubby gazelle self like, "I know which manager to talk to when I need an extra shift or when I need time off." I would ask if I could speak to him in the office, then sit in the seat across the desk from him. I would cross my legs and let my shoe dangle off my big toe, spinning it slowly as it hypnotized him. Sure, I could have that day off. Of course, he could find room for one more on the Saturday night shift.

Game. Set. Match.

I love that my feet have always gotten attention. I know that sounds weird, but it's one body part that I have received positive feedback on for years. I'm not sure if it's because I'm a Pisces (the astrological sign that rules the feet) or just luck of the draw, but I have had men, women, gay, straight . . . all share with me how they find my feet attractive. I appreciate the compliments.

If you ever decide to dance, I hope you become a favorite of the foot fetish customers. I have had men pay me for couch dances and champagne courts who ended up spending every minute of the time they had paid for massaging my feet. Score! Is having cute feet a strange thing to use to my advantage? Maybe. But why not? I have been trying for the past couple of years to get someone to help me set up a website where I can make money with pictures of my feet. All my friends who are in the website building and hosting business think I'm joking, but I'm not. I have no reservations about taking foot photos by request. Want me to stick my foot in some chocolate cake? You got it! Glitter? Ocean waves? Want me to wrap some spaghetti around my toes? Sure thing! My rule when it comes to starting this website is that the only part of my body that will be visible in the photos is my feet. Other than that, if it does not cause me bodily harm, I'm game.

What attributes do you have that set you apart? These aren't limited to the physical, though if you have a unique look or body part that gets you attention, own it and use it. Nonphysical attributes that can set you apart could be:

A talent: Can you sing? Dance? Are you talented artistically or do your talents lie in writing?

It could be a skill you have acquired: Are you a fantastic carpenter? Mechanic? Sword swallower?

Don't be afraid to use what you've got to draw attention to yourself and be appreciated for your worth. You can use these parts of yourself for a personal boost, but also to move a business you have started forward. And don't be discouraged if you know someone else with a similar talent. Everything in this world that you can do has already been done by someone before you. You can't give up just because you are not the only person in town who bakes cakes, or styles hair, or does handyman jobs. (I said handYMAN jobs. Sheesh!) Sure, there are other people who do these things, but they don't do them the way that you do! Add your own twist, your own style, your own way of doing it just a smidge different so that it stands out among the crowd.

Also, don't be intimidated by people who say that "anyone" can do what you do. People who say that fall into the "I need to try and make others look 'less than' to make myself feel 'more than' " category. It's a bitch move. Once, I was at a craft show and perusing the items for sale on one of the tables. A couple came over to the same table and started picking up the items to inspect them further. The woman held up one of the crafts and rolled her eyes. She told her husband, "I could make this!" and the guy behind the table said, "Maybe you *could* make it, but I *did* make it."

If you are not sure how to stand out, think about the qualities you look for in someone who has the same skill as you. What draws you to that person that other people in the same field may not be doing? Find your niche, and then craft your social media posts and advertisements to speak to the target audience that falls into that niche.

If you use your time and money trying to attract everyone, you will wind up with very few people interested, if any. You don't want to take a "throw all of the spaghetti at the wall and see what sticks" approach to growing your business. You need to take the time to figure out what you're about and how you can attract like-minded people who will be interested in your products. For example, if you specialize in monster-themed cupcakes and have a talent for creating edible monstrosities that are spooky, gross, and frightening, concentrate your efforts on groups of people who love monster movies or Halloween. They are the ones who will more likely be having parties or get-togethers where spooky, gross cupcakes would be appreciated.

When you have gotten a following, politely ask those people to post about your products and share them with their friends. These days, businesses live and die by the internet and reviews. Give a quality product, and then request a positive review. You cannot offer an incentive in exchange for a good review, but you can do your best to make sure that your customer has no reason to give you any less than five stars. If the person you ask does not believe you deserve five stars, make sure to ask why. Don't get angry; get curious. There will always be people who will never be happy no matter what you do. But most people are not that way and can offer you solid advice to improve on what you are doing. If what they say is not possible, it can open a dialogue so you can explain to them why. Communication is key. In my experience, people are very forgiving when they know that you are honest. If you make a mistake, own it! If they are asking for something that isn't possible, politely thank them for their interest and be clear on why it isn't an option.

Figure out your passion and how you can use it to help the people you care about. Then find ways to make your passion grow! Whether you are focusing on goals in your personal life or trying to grow a business, the more you are true to yourself and your end goals the easier it will be to attract the people into your life that feel the same.

FIFTEEN

That Bitch Named Jessica

MOST OF US have what we refer to as an "inner voice." We might believe that this voice is intuition, God, a gut feeling, Spidey senses, or the souls of our ancestors . . . everyone is entitled to their own opinion. Regardless of what we call it, these inner voices echo in our minds.

I used to joke that I had a voice in my head that drove me insane because it stuttered.

"K-k-kill your p-p-p-"

"What are you saying?!"

(I wish that were my joke, but I picked it up from a cartoon years ago.)

I say this with empathy. When I was a kid, my uncle lived with us and legitimately heard voices in his head. He took medication, but it didn't always get rid of them completely. He used to scream at them, "Shut up, you goddamn billy goat!" I am not sure whether he truly believed that billy goats were speaking to him or if he thought that what he was saying was a legitimate insult, but I feel bad that he had to deal with a situation that was out of his control and completely infuriating.

When it comes to myself, I believe that I have two separate voices that ring between my ears on a regular basis. One of the voices is negative. She likes to pipe up when I am scared, feeling depressed, feeling unworthy, etc., and loves to pour gasoline on that fire of negative thoughts. Some of her greatest hits are: "Oh my god, look at how fat you are!" "No one could love you!" "You are a worthless piece of shit," and, "You may as well just eat all of the nachos and cheese because all of the working out and eating right you've been doing is pointless. You'll never have the abs you want."

Thankfully, there is a second voice as well. This one is positive, encouraging, brave, and confident. She is the voice that says, "Go for it!" "Check you out, sexy mama!" "You *will* be a successful author!" "You are loved!" "You are beautiful!"

The problem is that the negative voice seems to speak more often and at a higher volume than the positive one. I have found that the ratio of positive to negative self-talk can change depending on which week of the month it happens to be. I struggle a lot more during my PMS week every month (or in my case, every three weeks). I'm sure this isn't rare and that most women who deal with PMS would say the same.

Our bodies are made up of so many parts. From the top of our heads to the tips of our toes. Yet, for me, none of those other parts matter when I get completely hung up on my waist. On days when my stomach is more bloated, sticks over the top of my jeans, or is a muffin top and then some, I feel the worst about myself. I could have a zit on the tip of my nose the size of Rudolph's shiny red schnoz, and I would be less concerned about that than I am when I feel like my belly is on par with the Pillsbury Doughboy. "Tee hee" my ass.

It's so easy to let that voice take over and send me into a spiral of self-doubt, depression, and self-pity. But I know that this can only happen if I let it. I have been dealing with my inner voice since I was a tween. For me, there is a connection between when my hormones first came in and when my self-image turned to shit.

When I was going through the boxes full of stuff I have had in storage forever, I found old diaries and projects from summer camp where we had been asked to describe ourselves. I used words like *gorgeous* and *beautiful*. No self-esteem issues in my eight-year-old self, that's for sure! The inner voice that popped up to convince me how ugly, stupid, and worthless I was showed up around the time I was twelve years old. I'm not saying that I had never been affected by negative input hurled my way from others before that. I certainly got called names in school and by my brothers, had my physique picked apart, etc. I guess I had a tougher skin before the hormones came in. It could have also been because I wasn't as concerned about the opinions of others before I got to middle school.

When I entered the tween years, I started wanting other people (especially specific people) to find me attractive. There were times when I tried so hard! I would change my looks and interests in the hopes that I would be viewed as more attractive. Since I had already been trying so hard to be considered beautiful, funny, and interesting, it stung even more when insults were thrown my way. Especially when the specific people I had been trying so hard to attract joined in. Cue Garth Brooks's song "Unanswered Prayers."

I can't even imagine what my life would be like if I had wound up with some of the people I had been hopelessly in love with as a teenager. The people whom I wanted to be with so badly that I made promises to God that I would go to church every single Sunday, never cuss again, give all of my stuff to the poor, and a plethora of other barters if only this person could love me as much as I loved him or her . . . . As my best friend once told me, "God can see around corners." I'm so glad He saw the life I have now around my corners and didn't put me on one of the paths I had begged to be on instead!

Have you ever tried to make one of those bargains with God? Or the Universe? Offering up anything you possibly can in a moment of desperation because in that moment, you feel like you deeply *need* the thing or person? You feel like you've hit a brick wall when it comes to ideas or resources to achieve the thing you need on your own? These conversations with our higher power typically happen when we have reached rock bottom.

When you find yourself about to make promises to the sky . . . don't. You and I both know that you are going to drink again, cuss again, skip a Sunday, etc. Instead of making empty promises, make a "plan of action." Brainstorm ideas to reach your goals. If your deepest desire involves wanting to be in a relationship with someone else, work on yourself. If you build up your self-esteem and confidence to the point where you are radiating attraction, either the person you are trying to attract will have no choice but to want to be with you, or they are a complete moron. And you don't want to waste your time with a complete moron, right?

I have spent a lot of time working on myself and am a lot more confident than I was in middle and high school. Do I still care about other people's opinions? I can't lie, I do. However, I am no longer seeking approval and basing my worth on the opinions of other people the way I did as a teenager. I do still feel ouchy if someone insults me, but I can deflect it most of the time.

The thing that sucks the worst about outside negativity is that my inner voice loves to add those things to her script. The double whammy is that the negative inner voice latches on to whatever negative outside input I get and amplifies it. "So-and-so was right, you are stupid!" This voice also loves to bring up things that should be long buried: "Remember that time in fourth grade when you made fun of that girl and made her feel bad? I bet you feel like a real asshole, and you should!" "That person who left the comment saying that you are wrong was so right. You are always wrong! I don't know why you even bother sharing your opinion."

In a world where we as a society have become more focused on anti-bullying, zero tolerance, and teaching our kids the importance of being kind, it's hard to admit that our biggest bully may be ourselves. I was tired of saying shitty things to myself and feeling, well, shitty about it, so I knew I had to come up with a way to fight back against my worst enemy: myself.

I will never understand why I always give others grace so easily, yet when it comes to myself, I don't think I deserve it. I feel like if I don't do something perfectly, I'm terrible, stupid, and worthless. Who the hell do I think

I am if I believe that I am expected to be perfect? I am a human being, which means I am fallible. So are you. Let's all start giving ourselves grace and not expect perfection. Perfection is a myth!

I gave that negative voice a name of her own. She now has a separate identity so that it no longer feels like me being mean to me but some random stupid bitch instead.

I named her Jessica.

The name was inspired by the Sweet Valley High series of books I read as a tween. Jessica was the evil twin, so it seemed appropriate. Now whenever that negative voice starts yapping in my head, I can say, "Suck it, Jessica!" because I don't need to waste my time around random stupid bitches. It's a lot easier to do that than to say, "Suck it . . . me." So, if you find yourself being dragged down by your own negative voice in your head, give it a name. Then tell it to "suck it!"

When someone bullies you, you can either:

1. Take it and continuously get beaten up and lose your lunch money and self-respect.

Or:

2. Stand up to the bully. Show that you are not afraid and tell them to leave you the hell alone.

Like everything else, it takes practice. Over time, you will find that the more you tell the negative voice to "piss off" or "suck it" or even "fuck off," the less time you spend in a negative loop. There will always be times when Jessica pops back into my head. I don't think that I will ever get rid of her completely. Her visits just aren't as long now, so she can't do as much damage. I have found that when Jessica starts spouting her nonsense, I benefit from journaling, blasting music that makes me happy, dancing, petting my dog, and talking with friends. These are all ways to either drown her out or make her retreat to the darkest recesses of my brain. At least temporarily.

For the record, I thought it was only fair to name the positive voice as well. I tried to think of the perfect name to describe me when I am in the zone and feeling saucy and super confident, a voice that took me years to find. Finding it a name only took me a second because there was only one name that made me feel like my superhero self:

Sydnee!

I have learned to quiet Jessica's big mouth and to instead listen to the whispers that Sydnee is sharing with me. Most of the time, Sydnee isn't as loud as Jessica, but occasionally she raises her voice. When I am feeling really lost and in need of guidance, Sydnee speaks the loudest. She begins screaming at me that I need to love me for me. Her cries echo in my ears when I am in a situation where I must deal with a person who does not have my best interest at heart.

I have dealt with many people in my life who are bullies. Grown humans who genuinely believe that loud equals right. These people feel that they can get whatever they want by puffing up their chests and bellowing in my face. There was a time when they were right, and I would crumble. That is no longer the case. Sydnee is there to help me stay strong and shut them down. She reminds me that they can only take my power if I give it to them.

She is a powerful ally.

It does sound a little cuckoo, but just give it a try. You have nothing to lose except some negativity. If you want to share with me the name that you chose, just tag me in a post on social media with #suckitjessica and #suckit_____, filling in the name you have chosen for your own negative voice. Feel free to add the hashtag #notimeforstupidbitches, too, because you don't have time for that!

If you've never kept one before, start a journal. Writing can help to purge out negative feelings. If you feel like you could never share your innermost thoughts and feelings with another person, a diary is a great way to get those feelings out of your head without worrying about judgment. If you are afraid of someone stumbling upon the book and reading it, you can always (safely!) burn it. (By safely, I mean in a fireplace, firepit, etc. Don't light your paper on fire and throw it in the sink or tub. We all need to learn from Lisa "Left Eye" Lopes, rest her soul. You may think you're making a good decision, and then in a blink, you burn the whole house down!)

Another option would be to write down the negative things you are dealing with on a piece of toilet paper and flush it. That will ensure that you won't burn the house down. If you have a whole roll of negativity, make sure you flush a few squares at a time. You don't want to flood your house, either.

Recently, I noticed a pattern in the morning. I have tried several different approaches to stop hitting "snooze" when my alarm goes off and instead get up the first time my alarm starts blaring. I have put my phone across the room. (I'll hit "snooze" and climb back into bed.) I have labeled my alarms to say things like, "Get up! Now!" or "Winners don't hit snooze." But when it's first thing in the morning, I don't care, I guess, because I still hit the snooze button.

The kicker is, I never go back to sleep. Instead, I lie there wide awake and worried that I won't hear the alarm again. The entire process of hitting "snooze" in the hopes of going back to sleep is futile! The amount of time I would lie in bed with the covers up to my nose while I was trying to snuggle back into sleep was ridiculous. Instead of catching a few more Zs, I would be bombarded by thoughts of negative people and situations in my life. That would get my heart racing and my adrenaline pumping to the point where not only was there no way I would settle back to sleep in the nine minutes I had before my alarm went off again, but I would start my day in a stressed-out, shitty mood.

I started intentionally changing my thoughts. If a negative thought popped into my head, I would imagine the scenario as if the mental picture or thought were tangible. I would then clearly see myself in my mind's eye grabbing the thought, crumpling it up like a piece of paper, and throwing it away. I did this every morning, sometimes having to do that with the same thought multiple times. Over time, they have all but stopped. Now if one creeps back in, I just imagine myself crumpling it up and tossing it away. Then I clearly think about something for which I am grateful. I focus on something positive and make sure I start my day in a positive headspace before my feet even touch the floor.

When you change the dialogue in your brain, you change your life. Earlier, I mentioned that you need to surround yourself with people who will have your back during your journey. You are going to have an extremely difficult time moving forward and achieving your dreams if you don't have your own back. If you find yourself battling with a negative voice, it's time to give it a name of its own. Now that you've named that voice, tell it to "suck it!"

SIXTEEN

Oversharing

WE ARE IN an age where people are putting things on public display that they never would have in years past. And it can become very problematic if we start comparing ourselves to the social media version that others share. While we all know the people who constantly post "Woe is me!" content and thrive on negativity, most people post the best of what is happening to them daily. Some people post total bullshit versions of what is going on in their lives and embellish the truth to make themselves appear cooler, more successful, happier, or more "perfect" than they really are.

In either case, remember that what they are posting is their highlight reel and not their highlight *real*.

I am a self-admitted oversharer. I spend a lot of time on social media, primarily Facebook. I share what is going on in my day and what I've dealt with in the past, both my victories and my struggles.

There are several reasons for this. Some are attention seeking, but most are because I want others to see that they are not alone. I share the lessons I have learned and the skills those lessons have taught me in the hopes that others can use them to bring themselves to a better place. (I do not publicly share things about my kids because they are all teenagers, and I don't want them to be embarrassed by a post I've made.) I have frequently had things go from my brain to my page without stopping to censor it. Those posts sometimes result in me embarrassing myself, like stories about me peeing myself during cardio workouts to waking up with a hangover and being unable to find the dress I knew damn well I had been wearing when I got home the night before. (After spending several days searching everything from laundry baskets to trash cans to the freezer, it finally turned up inside the sleeve of a hoodie inside the laundry basket that I had checked multiple times. I am quite certain that drunk Syd had had an exceptionally good reason for hiding the dress in a hoodie sleeve. Sober Syd has no clue why it was in there.) However, I always know that what I shared came from a place of authenticity.

Have I lost Facebook friends and followers because of some of my posts? Sure. But the question is, have I lost anyone who really is a good fit for my life? When we let our true selves be seen, we attract people to us who understand our journey. They may relate because of their own personal experiences, or they may just be drawn to us because they find our stories intriguing or inspiring.

Oversharing on social media is one thing, but I will never forget a time when I personally overshared years before social media was invented.

Marissa and I had been dancing for a couple of years when my "real-life oversharing incident" took place. When Marissa and I worked the same shifts, we used to moon each other. A lot! I know that sounds stupid because we were wearing thongs, so really . . . what does mooning do when your whole ass is out anyway? But it was kind of a "kiss this!" gesture that we would frequently give each other while goofing around. It got to the point where we would pull the top of our thongs down and moon each other several times each shift. We did it so often that it became my natural reaction to her making a smartass comment. I would do it without even thinking.

When you spend that much time together inside the club, it's easy to have a momentary lapse of reason when you are outside of the club because you are so used to being in that work environment. One day we were at the mall, and she made some smartass comment to me. I have no idea what her comment was now, but I turned around and dropped my jeans and mooned her right there in the middle of the mall. It took a half second for me to realize that this was not the time or place, but (*butt?*) by then, I had already "overshared" in the middle of a mall full of shoppers.

Thankfully, no one called security on me for "making an ass out of myself," but I could have very easily gotten into a lot of trouble. Nowadays, they throw people on the sex offender list for that stuff. I'm grateful that anyone who saw my little . . . indiscretion didn't make a stink about it.

Speaking of oversharing and not respecting the time and place, there were multiple times when a male customer at the bar would whip his penis out, thinking that no one could see he was waxing the carrot on his barstool.

We had a regular customer at Sunsingers who was a chronic masturbator. Every single time he was in the venue, he would be beating the bishop at the bar. I can't imagine the heart-stopping, blood-pumping embarrassment he must have felt the first time he was confronted about his willy going out to explore. Even though I would have thought that being caught would have made him feel ashamed and "teach him a lesson," it wasn't enough to keep him from doing it again.

And again.

And then some more!

I would avoid going up to him for tips because I didn't want to feel his "tip" on my thigh. Instead, I would walk right by him. If I saw even a millimeter of his one-eyed trouser snake peeking out of its sweatpants-covered home, I would point and yell "Freebird!!" at the top of my lungs. I'm not sure why he was permitted to continue coming into the bar, or why he would even want to once he had been exposed (pun intended). In time, I had pointed and screamed at him so many times that all the dancers and staff started calling him "Freebird."

Most of the guys would have never risked a penis puppet show while they were sitting at the bar knowing they were surrounded by other customers, dancers, and bar employees. However, several must have had no idea that there were cameras all over the couch dance rooms and thought they were in a completely private space. Little did they know that was not the case. In their minds, the couch room seemed like it would be a great place to make a surprise introduction.

I learned early on that the guys who tried to show you their "John Thomas" when you hadn't given them any indication that you wanted to see it were just looking for a reaction. I'm sure the reaction they were trying to get was

"Oh baby, I want me some of that!" And if their attempt at making a couch dance *Love Connection* failed, a shocked "Oh my god! Put it away!" or shriek would be next on their list of desired reactions because negative attention is still attention.

Most of the men who felt the need to overshare their genitalia didn't know me from a can of paint, so they weren't expecting any of my personal go-to reactions. If I were giving a guy a couch dance and he whipped it out, I would either:

1. Point at his dick and laugh my loudest, most maniacal cackle that made everyone in close vicinity immediately whip their heads around to see what was going on. That usually resulted in him putting it away with the quickness because now the other customers had gotten a peek, too.

2. Point at his dick and yell, "OH MY GOD!! THAT IS SOOOO CUTE!! WHERE'S THE REST OF IT??" That also usually resulted in the customer quickly returning Mr. Happy to his pants.

Or:

3. Point at his dick and yell as loudly as I could, "HOLY SHIT! I'VE NEVER SEEN A COCK THAT'S AN 'INNIE' BEFORE!"

Any of my responses would typically end with the customer returning his junk to his pants or running out of the private dance room, or both.

Take a little advice: do not just go whipping your dick out. Especially when you have not been invited to do so. First of all, ew. Second of all, ew. And third of all . . . ew!

And any dancer who willingly hops on, gargles, or plays handball with your lil' man in the couch dance room is not a newbie at it, and you deserve whatever blisters or crotch rot you get.

Let me say it one more time . . . ew!

There are degrees of oversharing, and when your over-sharing crosses boundaries (especially legal or other people's personal ones), you have shared too much. When my husband and I were first dating, we went to a fundraiser at a local bar. There, I met a woman whom I would see again several times later. Our first interaction involved an overshare. I said, "Hi! It's nice to meet you." She immediately told me all about the hysterectomy she had been through years before, how they had taken her ovaries, too, how much pain she was in, and various other parts of her gynecological history.

I stood there thinking, *I'm sorry, what was your name again?*

Knowing when and where it is appropriate to share the intimate parts of yourself, whether they are emotional or physical, is important. While I share so much about myself on social media to attract the people who are my tribe to me, I know the line where I need to stop sharing. I understand that some people just lack social awareness. Some people have medical conditions that cause them to not be able to pick up on social cues, while others have gone through their entire lives without ever learning them. If you do not have a health condition that makes you unable to interpret the behavior of others, you need to learn how to pick up the cues that others are giving you. If you are sharing how big your morning poop was to other people in the checkout line, and they look at you completely disgusted, make a note to yourself: that is not the time or place to share that information.

Most of us have at least one friend who knows all the nooks and crannies of our day-to-day, as well as all our darkest secrets. Well, at least the darker ones. That doesn't mean everyone in your life wants or needs to know all those same details. If you are unsure if the person you are talking with fits into the "nooks and crannies" category, maybe you should find a topic to discuss that isn't so personal. Then if the conversation works its way into a space where you are getting cues that the person is open to hearing more personal details, you can start to tell the more intimate stories.

Most importantly, if your stories involve other people and not just yourself, do not divulge the details of who they are (yay, stage names!) unless they have told you that it's okay. If you are going around sharing other people's business when it is something that they have told you in confidence, that just makes you a gossiping asshole.

I used to have a friend who loved to gossip. Every time we hung out or talked on the phone, she would spill the tea on people we had gone to school with, coworkers, etc. It didn't take me long to realize that if she was talking about others to me, then she was talking about me to others. I stopped sharing any personal details of my life with her that weren't already available on social media. Then I stopped hanging out with her. Seeing her smiling in pictures on her social media captioned "Besties" with the people she so viciously shit-talked about to me made me realize my time was better served elsewhere.

I used to stress about the things I had shared with her before I broke off our friendship. Then I realized that if she was talking to anyone who really knew me or cared about my well-being, they would talk to me directly. If not, why should I waste any of my time worrying about their opinions of me? I just blessed and released. And unfollowed.

While I am extremely active on Facebook, my husband is the most anti-social media person I know. He has no social media. He wants no social media. He would live out the rest of his life being totally content with not having any sort of involvement in social media at all. (Including never hearing me say, "This post is so funny, listen . . ." or "Check out this meme!") But because we are married, and I am so pro-social media, there are times when he is involved in my posts and photos. I always check with him first before I post something that includes him. I would never want to make him uncomfortable or embarrassed. I love him and respect him, so his feelings mean more to me than any post.

It is up to each individual person to decide how much they want to share of themselves and with whom. But if you are about to tell stories about someone else, stop and think about how it would make you feel if they said similar things about you to other people. If you would be hurt, embarrassed, or angry, that is a good indicator to keep your trap shut. If you feel compelled to share someone else's story, ask yourself: Is it to lift them up? Or do you just like to share gossip? If you are running your mouth just to spill the tea, ask yourself, "Why?" Do you need to tear someone else down to make yourself feel better?

Guess what? Blowing out someone else's candle will not make your own candle shine brighter.

The number-one reason for dressing room fights in go-go bars, in my experience, is when one dancer finds out that another dancer has been telling her business to customers. The gossiper may have thought that she would get the attention of a customer by trying to make him feel like the other girl wasn't who he believed her to be. Spoiler alert: customers love to play the gossip game, too.

"Oh my god! I can't believe you never told me that [fill in the blank: you're married, have kids, have an STD, etc.]."

"What? That's not true! Where did you hear that?"

"[Insert name of dancer]."

Storms into the dressing room and smacks a bitch.

I have made a conscious effort to stop the middle-school-level shit-talking. It serves no purpose. On top of not initiating those kinds of conversations myself, I will also not engage in those conversations when they are started by other people. It's a waste of time and only breeds negativity. I encourage you to do the same.

As I mentioned, I am incredibly open on social media, whether it is about my personal struggles with depression, when I fall short of my goals, and when I screw up something new that I am trying out. I will be the first to admit when I am having a rough time because it helps others to see that they aren't the only ones who drop the ball sometimes or deal with shitty situations. However, I never take my issues with someone else in my life to social media.

Okay, full disclosure, I *have* shared if a random stranger does something that makes a good story. Like the day I was in the local Walmart and this old lady in an electric scooter cart kept showing up in the aisle I was in. She would move the scooter halfway up the aisle and center it so I couldn't go around her with my cart. At first, I thought it was a coincidence, but she would park her cart in the middle of the aisle and stare right at me. I went a few aisles down just to test my theory, and she showed up there, too, and stopped dead center in the aisle!

Just when I had convinced myself that it was all just an odd set of accidental circumstances, another older woman showed up. She looked at the woman in the scooter and said, "That's it! You're not getting nothing!" The woman in the scooter asked, "Why not?" The other woman replied, "Because I've been watching you, and you're being a total b-i . . . you know!"

I was flabbergasted. It was probably just "unlucky lottery" that she had picked me. From their conversation that I overheard; it was not the first time she had been a "total b-i . . . you know" to someone in public. I'll never know why that happened, but it was so out there that I had to share it on my Facebook page.

Sharing stories about run-ins with crazy strangers is one thing. But when it comes to those in my life I know by name, I do not vent about them online. When I feel the need to vent, it is typically to my husband or my closest friends (the ones in the "nooks and crannies" category) because they understand that I'm just blowing off steam privately and not on social media. Most of my vents are because I can't stand when people don't play by the rules of common decency; are bullies, hypocrites, or passive aggressive; or just lie through their teeth and get away with it. Especially when, for a variety of reasons, the people I am venting about are people I am not able to remove from my life currently.

It is a healthy practice to let out steam to one person whom you trust. Bottling up your feelings when you are frustrated, upset, and angry only builds pressure up in your body, which causes stomach issues and will eventually end with you letting all those feelings out at once. Usually at an inappropriate time and to an inappropriate person.

Have you ever heard the saying that many divorces happen because someone left the toothpaste cap off? Obviously, dried-out toothpaste is not a reason to end a marriage. It just illustrates how, if you don't deal with your feelings and keep them bottled up, they will eventually explode over something silly. For example, perhaps one of the people in the marriage has been sitting on a time bomb of emotions for years. They've been feeling that their partner does not respect them, is neglectful, doesn't listen, etc. However, they've never expressed those emotions to the other person. Then, maybe on a day when their inner emotions happen to be particularly active, they walk into the bathroom and see the capless tube. Just sitting there on the edge of the sink. Maybe there is a little blob of toothpaste coming out and sitting on the countertop. Maybe their partner has squeezed from the middle of the tube instead of rolling it up from the bottom . . .

This is the moment when their brain can go to "See?! They can't even put the toothpaste cap back on! How many times have I asked them to do that, but do they ever listen? Do they ever listen to anything I say?" and the snowball starts rolling and growing until just about every instance in the relationship when they have felt disrespected is mentally listed as evidence to what a shithead their partner is.

Maybe the relationship was destined to end at some point anyway. Or maybe discussing the feelings you have been experiencing along the way would have helped to heal the cracks before they got too big. At any rate, sharing what you're going through can provide clarity and give the other person the chance to support you along the way. Or it could have given you a chance to see that they really were a tool-pants before you invested any more time, and stomach lining, into a relationship that wasn't meant to be.

You will find that the more you remove negative vibes and people from your life, the more room you make for positive people and experiences. It may seem impossible at first to envision yourself being surrounded by positivity and people who are not constantly being negative. It will take some work on your part, but you are the captain of your life and time. You decide who you let into your space and for how long.

As I mentioned earlier, we are sometimes not able to fully remove certain people from our lives without a barrage of consequences that we are not prepared (or don't want) to deal with. In fact, the only way to guarantee that we never have to deal with anyone else's negativity would involve removing everyone from our lives and going to live in the middle of a desert or out in the woods where we don't have to deal with human contact at all. That's just not practical for most people. But even if we can't remove people completely from our lives, we can still limit the amount of interaction we have with them.

Make yourself unavailable; don't answer or return calls and turn down every invite. Eventually, they will stop asking and if they talk shit about you, oh well.

At any given moment, someone may also be saying something negative about you to someone else. You can drive yourself crazy trying to change other people's behavior. (Friendly reminder: you can't control anyone else's actions, so don't even bother.) The alternative is to just let them go and embrace your newfound peace instead. You decide who you will allow to affect your mood and mind. Letting go does not mean that you no longer talk to them (you can still peek at their social media to see what they're up to). It means removing their input from your daily activities completely.

As an empath, I especially need to limit the amount of negative energy I am exposed to for my own health, or the negativity and complaining will drain me and break me down. I often find myself on the phone for an hour or more listening to negative stories of how the person on the other end is being mistreated by others. (Never mind that in previous phone calls I had already pointed out several reasons why the "others" that my friend was bitching about were toxic to my friend's well-being, not a good friend, using them, etc., and should be removed from said friend's life.) But my friend would continue the relationship because . . . boobs!

"Why don't they listen?"

"That's what I said!"

"If they had only _____."

"I told you so!"

If you care about the person, "I told you so" is never going to be the thing to say. It is neither loving nor compassionate. I've learned that it's important to stop trying to be right and be compassionate instead. Even if it makes me want to slam my head into the wall repeatedly when I have given advice to others that was ignored, then someone calls to bitch to me because they ignored said advice and I was right.

As you share your life and experiences with others, don't be like Freebird. Know your audience and don't overshare to the point that it repels the people you are trying to attract. Stay authentic and share just enough to show others who you really are. This will not only attract the people who will be a positive influence in your life and create curiosity, but it will also weed out the people who are not a good fit for you. Not everyone is someone you will want in your day-to-day, and that's okay!

When all is said and done, you are ultimately responsible for every decision you make. At any moment, every other person in your life may not be there anymore. Decide who is adding positives to your life and let them in with open arms. Anyone who consistently adds negativity to your life needs to be cut out. Blood, water or . . . vodka. Doesn't matter. No one can suck the life out of you without your permission so stop granting it!

SEVENTEEN

Kindness is Key

FROM THE TIME kids start going to preschool (and even before then in a lot of homes), they are encouraged to "be nice." "Treat others the way you want to be treated." "Help out when you can."

I've mentioned before that I have always been a helper. I will happily volunteer my time, knowledge, and money if I am able to help others get into a better space. I am registered to be an organ donor when I pass away and am and will continue to be a regular blood and platelet donor while I'm still on this plane. I encourage everyone to give blood if they are able and become a registered organ donor as well. Seriously, what are you going to do with your spleen in the afterlife?

There are so many organizations and causes that need support. I am a believer that what you put into the Universe will always come back to you. I try as often as possible to help with causes that are close to my heart and spread positive energy because I believe it causes a ripple effect and creates more positivity. Whether it is donating to a local animal shelter (I would love to adopt all of the homeless pets, but we do not have the room to provide them with suitable care . . . yet!), donating board games to the local retirement home, donating food to the local food bank, etc., there are all kinds of things you can do to help out in your community.

So far, my favorite contribution was when I participated in uplifting a community that I am not only a part of but support completely. In 2019, I gave out free "mom hugs" at the Philly Pride Parade. It was my first Pride Parade as I had only recently shared that I was bisexual with people outside of my close circle. Even though, in the grand scheme of the LGBTQ+ rainbow, a bi woman is not typically ostracized as much as the people represented by the other letters, I have experienced being treated poorly because of my sexuality. I was happy to be in a situation where I could be openly myself, and not only be accepted but also celebrated.

Well, celebrated by other members of the LGBTQ+ community and allies anyway. As we walked up the street a group of protestors was screaming at us that we were all going to go to Hell. "God hates fags." And my favorite was when they targeted me personally and called me a "labia licking lesbian." Like that's a bad thing? It was only half true anyway. Instead of hurling insults back at them I decided to blow kisses at them and yell how much I loved them. They quickly decided to ignore our group and started hurling their insults at others who were there to celebrate Pride.

I connected with a couple of awesome people (who honestly were more interested in getting a free "dad hug" from my husband) and gave two of them my contact information so they could use me as a support system. They had been kicked out by their parents for being trans. I told them I would happily step in as a "bonus mom" and said, "Let me know what's going on in your life so I can be there to support you when it's hard and cheer on your victories. I will remind you to eat your vegetables and change your undies but will also listen when you need an ear with no judgement."

This is just the tip of the iceberg when it comes to suggestions on how to give back to your community. I hope we would all be willing to do whatever we can to support those who do not have a support system of their own.

I am only human and have had less-than-stellar moments as well. I don't always treat everyone with kindness, even though I try to. Several times, there have been situations where I started off treating someone with kindness only to have them continually return that kindness with doucheness. As a human, I finally reached my limit and acted out.

Victoria and I worked at a club called the Firehouse with a girl we called "Sméagol." As in Gollum from the *Lord of the Rings* series. She looked exactly like the character in the movie but with long dirty-blond hair. When we saw her across the bar, Victoria and I used to laugh and say, "She is tricksy, she is false!" in our best Gollum voice. Especially after she pulled her shenanigans. She would "claim" customers like Gollum claimed the Ring.

"That's my customer, you can't talk to him."

The hell I can't!

She may have thought that he was her "precious," but ultimately, it was up to the customer if he wanted to tip me or not. Most of the time, the guy would give me a dollar or two, and she would lose her shit.

I know that customers have their preferences when it comes to dancers, but you can't stick a flag in someone and claim them as your own. It's the customer's choice if he or she wants to share their wealth with other dancers, as well as how much of said wealth they would like to share. Side note: if you are a customer who is in the club to see one dancer and no one else, then don't be staring holes through my ass while I'm dancing and then tell me you won't give me a dollar because you're only there to see so-and-so. Keep your eyes to yourself or pay for the show. It's a dollar, not a kidney.

The other reason that Sméagol drove me nuts was because she would go into my bag when I wasn't in the dressing room and steal my makeup, use my hairbrush, etc. I told her several times not to use my stuff. That's just gross. She took my concealer once and tried to deny it. The concealer she was holding had no cap, and she didn't know where the cap had gone. I knew I had had my concealer on the counter with the cap off, and the cap was still in my cosmetics bag. Perry Mason wasn't needed to solve that case.

I could have once again told my water heater to leave my shit alone with the same result. I had asked her, nicely, multiple times, and she just didn't care. I then told her several times more firmly, and she still didn't care. Ultimately, I had to take an "unkind" approach to dealing with this situation.

At the time I worked with her, my younger daughter was in preschool. Unfortunately, she came home from school one day with head lice. It was a terrible case and took several weeks to eradicate, but I stayed on it. I used several rounds of over-the-counter delouse shampoo and combed her waist-length hair for hours with the teeny-tiny-toothed comb. After becoming frustrated with the number of hours it took every day to go through her long hair with said teeny-tiny-toothed comb, I lost my patience and chopped her hair up to her ears. It took a couple more weeks, but I finally got rid of the lice.

But . . . not before I took the brush I used at work and brushed my daughter's still lice-ridden hair with it for ten minutes. I put the brush in a zippie bag and sealed it. That night at work, I took out the brush and left it on my spot on the counter. I went out to check in with the DJ and hung out at the bar until it was my turn to go onstage. After my set, I went into the dressing room to find Sméagol brushing her long hair with my lice-filled brush. I looked her straight in the eyes and said, "I thought I asked you not to use my brush?" She started to stammer some bullshit response, but I cut her off and said, "You know what? Just keep it."

I know it's probably not "proper" to suggest that you be kind to others because if you are not, they may come back at you with a lice brush. But maybe that image (and the head-scratching that can result from the thought of said lice infesting your head and crawling around on your scalp and laying eggs in your hair that are going to hatch into more bugs crawling on your head . . .) will be enough of a catalyst to encourage you to respect other people's property.

When Marissa and I worked at Sunsingers, there was a dancer there with the same lack of understanding that Sméagol had. I'll call her "Micki." I have mentioned before that it was common for us to order food while we were at work. A little inside info: dancing burns a lot of calories, so dancers tend to eat . . . a lot! I've seen girls chomp down an entire cheesesteak with a side of fries in between their sets onstage and manage to stay thin.

By the time I was bartending and managing, I was aware of the way things were. Whenever I would order food at work, I would make sure to also order an extra side of fries. I would leave that out for the vultures, I mean dancers, to pick at so they would keep their grubby little fingers out of my food. It was like working with a flock of seagulls. There were days when I wanted to run so far away . . .

In the strip mall where Sunsingers was located, there was a pizza place and a Chinese restaurant. Both places hired delivery guys who were more than happy to bring in food for us. I'm sure that it took them a lot longer to walk food into the bar two doors down than it did to get into their cars and deliver to someone's house miles away. I can see how a wiggling tushy could be a distraction when you are a twenty-one-year-old (or younger) delivery boy.

Marissa and I were working with Micki one day when Marissa decided to order Chinese food. When Marissa brought her spring rolls and pork fried rice into the dressing room, Micki made some comments about how good it smelled, how hungry she was, etc. Marissa and I both told her that it was indeed yummy, so she should order her own. She just gave a little laugh, but we never saw her heading to the pay phone to place an order for herself.

Marissa and I went out to the bar and came back to the dressing room to find less pork fried rice in the carton. We were convinced Micki had been digging in while we were out of the room, but we couldn't prove it. And while I am not a medical professional, the crust and bumps on Micki's lips and mouth were enough to convince us that Micki was not someone with whom either Marissa or I would want to share a spoon.

We couldn't just throw the food away and pretend like nothing had happened because we felt the need to make a point. We came up with a plan that was certainly not kind. I kept an eye out while Marissa went into the bathroom and peed into the carton of pork fried rice. After stirring it all around, she put it back on the counter and we went back out to the bar to do our sets onstage and walk around for tips. When we were done, we walked back into the dressing room to change our costumes. When I opened the door, there was Micki chowing down on the pork fried rice that now had "special seasoning."

It was not my proudest moment, but I would be lying if a small part of me didn't believe she had it coming. Treating others with kindness is not the same as letting people run all over you or disrespect you. If Micki had said, "I'm really hungry and don't have the money today for food, mind if I share?" I'm sure Marissa would have gotten a cup from the bar and divvied out some of the food for her to eat with her very own spoon. However, when you aren't invited to share, especially when you (allegedly—again not a doctor, so not confirmed) have herpes sores all over your lips, don't just help yourself to someone else's food. A good rule of thumb is to not touch anyone else's anything if you have not been invited to do so. Not their food, not their makeup, not their boobs, not their husband . . . not their anything! That is not being a kind human.

I had to share the Chinese food story because of the sheer ridiculousness of it. Thankfully, situations like the ones with Sméagol and Micki were few and far between. There will always be people who have zero boundaries or think they are entitled to grab anything they want just because they want it. Most of the time, we were all happy to share food, hair spray, etc., if we were asked. We just didn't want to share the things that could ultimately end in us contracting a communicable disease.

There will always be times in our lives where we have spent time with someone, look back and think "I had no idea they were dealing with (fill in the blank) and I wish I had been kinder." Being kind is your best bet most of the time as we can never know what other people are dealing with in their own lives. People do take advantage so be mindful of when kindness crosses the line into enabling or hurting yourself for someone else.

The bottom line is, you never know what someone else may be dealing with and how your actions can influence them. What you say and do influences others in a positive or negative way. I have heard stories of people on the edge who had gotten to a place where they felt like they were done with everything and everyone. They were planning on taking their own life or, in other cases, taking other people out with them. They had lost all hope in people, but then someone showed them kindness and changed their view and their plans. As the old camp song says, "It only takes a spark to get a fire going."

Whenever possible, err on the side of kindness. I donate money when I am able. I donate clothes and shoes every few months because I hope they can help someone in need. I compliment strangers; I hold doors; I say, "Thank you!" I'm not pointing out any of this to give myself credit. I'm only pointing out that it feels good to help other people, and it can help spread positivity. The more you practice it, the easier it will become. It doesn't have to cost you a dime.

Also, as you are on your journey of differentiating between kindness and being a doormat, please be aware that the people who have become accustomed to taking advantage of you will not appreciate your epiphany one bit. Brace yourself and be prepared to deflect all the insults and attempts at them packing your bags and sending you on a guilt trip that are inevitably headed your way. When users are no longer able to use you, they start talking shit. They will accuse you of being mean, or crazy, or call you a bitch. Manipulators can't stand boundaries and will throw the biggest fits when they feel trapped. You need to recognize this behavior for what it is. They are terrified of losing you as a means to get what they want, so they will come at you with both barrels to try and convince you that in order to be a "good person," you cannot tell them no.

Don't fall into that trap. Sometimes the kindest thing you can do is to get another person on the path of caring for themselves and being a productive member of society rather than allowing them to suck the life out of everyone who cares for them. Tough love is love.

When you are an enabler, you are not looking out for someone's best interest. You are just looking for a way to keep them quiet and, in a place, where you feel like they are happy, even if that means you are not. In some cases, this could make you feel like you are an even better person because of your martyrdom. That is tricksy, that is false! Recognize that if you genuinely love someone, the kindest thing you can do is help them to stay on the path to success. No matter how hard that may be.

What spark of kindness can you share to start a fire of positivity in the world?

EIGHTEEN

Party! Party! Party!

I MENTIONED IN the prologue that the bachelor party experiences that I've had would need their own chapter. There is just nothing quite like a bachelor party, no matter where it is held.

At Sunsingers, we had a private back room that was off from the main bar. The entrance was very wide, with a couple of steps leading up to it. Curtains hung all over, creating little mini rooms with cushioned chairs and low tables. It was rarely used for anything more than a space for the girls to hide out and do lines. Occasionally, the club hired a psychic who set up his table at the top of the steps and charged for readings. I always wondered how that had come about. I'm sure he had known someone who had known someone. It was so loud in the club you could barely hear what he was saying, but he was a nice guy, so I hired him to do readings for me a few times.

The first bachelor party I ever worked was in that gross back room. I was required to walk around and "work the room." I stayed in the middle of the room as much as I could, afraid of what might hop out from behind a curtain and grab me. I tried to sneak out of the room and back into the main club, but the manager spotted me and threw me back into the lion's den.

While it is possible to make good money working the bachelor parties, most of the time, the customers figure that since they've already paid for the room, they don't need to spend any more money. They will grab you, pull you into them, grind on you, and not give you a penny. Most bachelor parties are open bar, so in addition to the lack of money and extra grabs . . . these guys are usually trashed. They could be a nightmare to work. In clubs that host bachelor parties, it is also expected that all the dancers working the shift need to work the bachelor party in addition to the main room.

I have worked in clubs like Warlocks where there are rooms for bachelor parties that are in completely different areas of the club from the main bar. In the bar with the spiral staircase, there was a bachelor party room upstairs, so the guys who came to the club for bachelor parties weren't even on the same floor as the rest of the patrons. I remember the room in that club being rather small. There was no stage, but there was a pole that went directly from the ceiling into the carpeted floor and that was roughly the diameter of a garden hose. There wasn't a whole lot spinning going on because between the lack of a proper stage and the skinny poles being hard to get a hold of it was too dangerous. You could easily kick someone else in the room or get a heel caught in the carpet and hyperextend your knee.

One night, three or four of us were in the room goofing off while we waited for the party to come into the room. I was trying to spin on the pole when the door opened and twenty or so men came in for their party. One of them was holding a leash. On the other end was a completely naked woman crawling on her hands and knees and wearing a dog collar.

I have friends who are dominatrices (Thank you, Merriam-Webster! I didn't know the plural of *dominatrix* until just now!), so bondage situations are not something I find shocking. In fact, I find them quite pleasurable. However, seeing a grown woman butt naked and crawling around on all fours in the club did catch me off guard. How did she get to a point where she was renting herself out to parties as a "slave"? How was she permitted to be in the club with completely exposed genitals? How did I wind up in a room full of men who would rent a slave and parade her around while we held on to our garden-hose-sized pole trying to make a few bucks?

Life is strange.

She was the only "slave for hire" I have come across at a bachelor party. However, she was not the only "slave" I have ever met. One of my coworkers, Candy, was a domi-natrix and had a slave. She was a petite lesbian, and he was a big guy who was completely in love with her even though he knew it was never going to happen. Through Candy, I learned a lot about the slave-mistress relationship and found it fascinating. A lot of people think that dungeons and dominatrices are about sex, but in Candy's case, she never had any sort of sex with her clients. In the simplest terms, he was there for her as a bodyguard and did her housework and anything else she told him to do. He enjoyed doing what she said and got a lot of pleasure from the dynamic. It wasn't so much a sexual thing but rather about their roles. It was all about control and power. Her clients paid for the interaction, but the relationship between her and her slave was mutually beneficial. He was a great guy, and because she and I were friends, he had my back, too.

Once, Candy asked me and Marissa if we could help her out with one of her clients. He was a long-time client and was looking for a "multiple mistress experience." I said, "Sure!" because the curiosity was killing me, and I found the idea exciting. On top of that, she gave us each fifty bucks.

We put our little black dresses, stockings, and heels in a backpack and drove to the high-rise apartment building where Candy lived. She had two apartments that were across the hall from each other. It allowed her to conduct business in one space and live in the other. What she didn't tell us was that she lived in a building that was occupied by her and senior citizens. It was an "assisted living community" even before that phrase would become commonly used. Thankfully, Marissa and I didn't try to waltz into the lobby in our mistress outfits! We were wearing sweats and T-shirts, which allowed us to make our way to the elevator with no questions asked. We didn't want to walk into the apartment in our sweats, however, so we got changed in the elevator. I'm glad no one else needed to use it at the time. I would have felt horrible if Marissa and I had caused an elderly man to have a heart attack!

We walked from the elevator to Candy's apartment, and when she opened the door, I wasn't sure what I was expecting to see. A middle-aged man who was blindfolded and kneeling on the living room floor completely naked with one end of a thigh-high stocking tied around his penis and the other in his mouth wasn't even in my top ten guesses. From the purple color that crept up from his neck to cover his entire face, I gathered this was one of those situations for him that had seemed like a good idea in his head but had become embarrassing once it played out in real life. Candy guided us through the session. He was supposed to make ten dollars by giving us pony rides around the room, rubbing our feet, etc. He earned his money a penny at a time. Poor guy had no chance, but it was an experience, and after we left Candy's place, we laughed ourselves stupid.

The smaller clubs typically didn't have a designated area for separate entertainment, so the bachelor parties would be in the bar along with everyone else. Because of this, there weren't many "extras" for the guys like private rooms and bartenders; they just hung out at the bar and watched the show like everyone else.

I was onstage once when I heard my real name being screamed at top volume. I looked out to see who the hell was in the crowd who knew me and was completely horrified to see several of my former male teachers from high school staring at me. One of them was getting married, and they had chosen to visit the club where I worked. I was awfully glad that this was a Jersey club, so my top stayed on. The whole situation was weird enough without any of them seeing my nipples.

I encountered other awkward situations, though awkward in a different sense. When I was at Warlocks, a bachelor party came in and sat in front of one of the satellite stages. I went up to do my set and immediately recognized the bachelor. He had been a junior camp counselor when I was a camper in middle school, and I had been head over heels about him at camp. As I danced to the song that was playing, I tried to make eye contact. I just wanted to see his reaction and gauge if he recognized me.

He had no idea who I was.

When I went around for tips, I walked up to him and confidently said, "Hi [his name]." His face was priceless! He stammered out, "D-d-do I know you?" I smiled a big smile and said, "You broke my heart when I was thirteen years old!" and walked away.

In the next few sets as I walked around for tips, I let him in on how I knew him. He absolutely remembered me, and we reminisced about camp and talked about his wedding the next day. To me, the funniest part about his wedding was that my father was officiating! It was all very strange, but I was happy to see him again.

Weird is one thing, but disgusting is another. One of the most disgusting experiences I have ever had in a club took place during—surprise, surprise!—a bachelor party. The bar where I worked had a raised area that had tables and chairs. If no one reserved the space, it was open to the public. I don't remember if partygoers were able to get open bar, what was included, or how the perks worked, but no matter what had come with the bachelor party reservation, this particular party needed no more alcohol.

I remember not wanting anything to do with this party. As an empath, I feel energy, and I could tell by the vibe this group was giving off that it was not going to end well. At the very least, I would leave that area pissed off and most likely with no more money than I had had when I walked into it. But like I said, you can't get out of working the parties, so I was stuck. (I mean, I'm sure it was possible for a dancer to get out of working the parties, but I was not willing to perform whatever sexual favors the manager would have wanted in exchange for skipping them.)

I trudged up the steps and put on my happy face. The majority of what comes with being a dancer involves being an actress. My plan was to make this group of drunken douchebags laugh and hopefully get paid for being entertaining while not having to smack unwanted hands off my no-no square. I walked up to the first guy who was sitting in a chair at a table. I said, "Hey, baby! You having a good time tonight?" He looked up at me, then with no warning at all threw up all over my leg! This man projectile vomited all over me, and I was frozen into place with barf running down my leg and into my shoe.

Should I run? Scream for a towel? It took me a good few seconds to figure out how to handle this situation. I decided on the latter because the last thing I wanted was to try and make a run for it and slide in the puke puddle and fall. I took off my shoes and got as much of the vomit off me as I could with bar towels. Then I made a run for the bathroom and did the best I could with soap and water to scrub down my legs and feet. All the while, I was trying not to puke myself.

I packed up and went home. At that point, I didn't care if I got fired; I just tipped out the DJ and left. I had to walk past the group of partygoers on my way out. Not only did no one in the bachelor party apologize for their friend covering my lower body in vomit, not one of them gave me so much as a dollar! This group most definitely gets filed under the category of "drunken douchebags." Plus, they get the distinction of receiving the award for being the worst bachelor party I've ever worked.

I did enjoy bartending for bachelor parties more than dancing for them. There is something to be said for having a three-foot barrier between myself and grabby hands, along with a selection of bottles that I could use for self-defense if need be. The other advantage to bartending the parties over bartending in the main bar was that the drinks would have all been paid for with the room rental. I didn't have to worry about ringing anything up. I was given a couple hundred dollars in ones to give to the guys who wanted to trade in bigger bills for tipping. When I set up the bar, I would divide my money into stacks of ten one-dollar bills to make change quickly and easily.

There was one party that completely perplexed me. They paid for a two-hour party, which includes the private room, private DJ, open bar, etc. They barely drank anything and sat around basically ignoring the dancers. Maybe the guy really didn't want to get married? Maybe something bad had happened that day and they weren't in the mood? Either way, it was two hours of all our lives that we'll never get back.

The funny part about bartending bachelor parties is sitting back and scanning the room. I loved watching out for "Paw Paw" who probably hadn't touched a naked ass aside from his own in decades and who would be smiling like a kid on Christmas morning. Then there would be the one guy who didn't want to be there but who had come anyway to support his friend, cousin, etc., so he would set up shop at the end of the bar and talk to me the whole time. I also loved coming up with the kind of shots that everyone wanted to do, all while balancing the partygoers having a great time and not puking. I'm puke-scarred for real!

One way that bachelor parties enjoy humiliating the groom-to-be, especially when they are in the main club and not in a private party room, is to get him on stage in front of everyone. This is commonly referred to as a "hot seat." Hot seats are not reserved only for bachelors but can also be done during birthdays, job promotions, or any number of other celebrations. The victim, I mean the customer, is brought onstage and sat in a chair with his back to the pole. Then he places his hands behind his back so his wrists can be tied up. Depending on the club, the customer is secured to the pole by handcuffs, cable ties, or sometimes his own belt. He is helpless and must endure whatever the dancers have in mind.

In the clubs where I worked, they would normally pick three girls to do a hot seat. I would typically give a lap dance while getting the crowd to cheer at a volume that would determine how hard I would grind, how fast I would move, and so on.

But first at Warlocks and then at the Ballet, there was this one girl . . .

Gigi had been in the go-go game for a long time. You would never guess her age in a million years because she looked amazing! She was petite and very athletic. She incorporated gymnastics and lots of pole work into her stage show. She gave zero shits that the Board of Health required shoes while you danced. She would dance barefoot most of the time. She was serious about making money, but she was also hilarious and had us cracking up often in the dressing room.

Gigi had a streak in her that can only be described as "mean" when it came to giving hot seats. She would get in front of the guy and gyrate for him. This poor man would think that things were heading in a direction that would get him all kinds of excited. Then she would take off his belt (if he was wearing one), open the fly of his pants or pull the waistband out (if he was wearing sweatpants), and pour a cup of ice into his pants all over his crotch. Usually, she would rub the ice into his groin for good measure. As if that wasn't enough, she would climb up on top of his thighs, stand over him, shake her boobs and egg him on right before she jumped in the air and landed spread eagle on his ice-packed package. I can't imagine how "very ungood" that must have felt to both of them!

Depending on her mood, she would rip elastic bands off underwear, do all kinds of moves I had only ever seen professional wrestlers pull off, and make sure that, if nothing else, the guy's night would be memorable. One guy had a complete shit fit because she had ripped the waistband off of his "good" undies. They were apparently a gift from his fiancé, and she was going to "kill him." I wonder why he would have worn his good undies to his bachelor party if he had thought no one was going to see them. Hmmm.

My favorite hot seat of all time was one that was given to a club manager who was particularly mean to me. I'm not sure why he treated me the way he did; he was just a dick. He had exactly two outfits that he wore for days at a time before switching. One was jeans and a crusty sweater. The other was a crusty sweat suit. He was overweight, smelly, and liked to pick on me.

When I worked the day shift, the club provided a lunch buffet. The dancers could eat from it after the customers had had a chance to get their food first. The buffet consisted of things like lunch meat, cheese, rolls, chicken nuggets, chips, etc. One day, I was walking away from the buffet with three chicken nuggets on a plate. He looked at me and said, "You better stop eating that shit, you're getting fat." At the time I was five-foot-six and weighed 125 pounds. Not for nothing, but at five-foot-nothing and 350-plus pounds, he had zero reason to talk about what anyone else weighed.

I happened to work the night of his birthday and was informed that all the girls had to go onstage and give him a group hot seat. I would have rather used an Epilady to remove my pubes than touch this man, so I hung out in the back of the crowd of dancers, hoping to be forgotten. (It worked! I didn't have to go up and dance for him.) The other manager got him onstage for his hot seat. He was in a chair, handcuffed, the whole shebang. The DJ announced that he would be getting a special hot seat from all the girls in the club. They had a couple of his favorite girls tease him a little and then blindfold him. I watched as a humongous, sickening grin crept across his face. He really believed he was in for the ride of his life. I guess in some ways he was right! A couple of girls climbed onto the Asshole Express and gave him a ride before they snuck the special surprise of the evening onstage.

Unbeknownst to all of us, the owner and the other manager had hired a gorgeous, young, obese stripper to give this guy a hot seat he would never forget. She jumped up and down on his lap so hard I thought he was going to break! I'm still completely in shock that the chair stayed in one piece. He tried to act like he thought it was funny, but I could tell he was pissed. That made my heart grow three sizes. I have always been a believer in karma, but you don't always get to watch karma in action with your own eyes. When you are given that gift, it is truly magical!

Most of the parties that happened in the clubs were for the customers, but the Christmas parties at Warlocks were *legendary*! I'm saying this even though I never hung around until the wee hours of the morning when all the real debauchery happened. I have seen some pictures that I am surprised were able to be printed. These parties took place in the nineties and early 2000s, so there were no smartphones, and camera phones were in their infancy. Someone had to take pictures with a camera and then take the film to be developed. With a straight face.

As they handed the film to the photography department employee.

I am truly shocked that no one has ever gotten pregnant by just sitting on a couch in the private dance area. If someone ever went into the couch dance room with Luminol and a black light, no one would ever buy a lap dance again for fear of sticking to the cushions. But I digress . . .

In my years there, the owner and management gave presents to the dancers that ranged from chocolates to jewelry to nothing. Warlocks Christmas presents were on par with Forrest Gump's famous line about life being like a box of chocolates: you never knew what you were going to get, if anything. Meanwhile, bartenders and managers got bonuses. I appreciated those for sure! During a couple of the years when I danced, the owner thought it would be a fun present to hire male dancers to put on a show for us at our Christmas party. However, the owner was a bit tight with his wallet, and my guess was that the dancers he had hired for us were the totally green newbies he could get for cheap. They were all in the physical shape you would expect to see. One guy got my attention. He had long black hair and great abs, and he came onstage in tight jeans and a leather jacket. First, he wiggled out of the leather, then he tore off the jeans—and I lost interest. I've just never found the sequined banana hammock look appealing. (Get it? Banana? Appealing?)

No matter how much these guys were lacking in the dance skills department, they were a much more welcome sight to my eyes than when one of our regulars did his annual dance onstage.

Mort had been coming into the bar since forever. He would frequent all three of the establishments that were in our company. He had been sober for years and only drank club soda. He had quit smoking years earlier but would always bum a cigarette to hold in his fingers while he sat at the bar. He never lit it; that was just his way to keep the cravings at bay when he was in an environment where he had used to smoke.

Mort was an older man; I would guess in his seventies. He was five-foot-three, tops, and was just as wide in the front. He looked like he was eleven months pregnant. Every year at the Christmas party, he would get onstage in nothing but a G-string and a Santa hat and dance for us. It was like a train wreck—you didn't want to look but you just couldn't tear your eyes away. One year, he took it even further and whipped off the G-String. That image has been burned into my retinas, and I would love to be able to remove the specific brain cells that hold that memory. Mort was a sweetheart and was always genuinely nice to me. But I never, ever needed to see him naked.

Ever!

The last shift I ever worked as a dancer was a Christmas party at the Firehouse. I had started working there with Victoria while we were also working at the Ballet. I had decided at the beginning of the shift that I was just done. I had uncharacteristically been calling out at least one shift a week for weeks leading up to the party because I was having bad stomachaches. Looking back, I know they must have been caused by anxiety. I was in a place in my life where the thought of letting strange men touch me while playing the games I needed to play as part of the job were things I was no longer willing to do. It was time to "hang up the heels" and end my thirteen years as a woman who worked in go-go bars.

I told the owner but asked him not to say anything during my shift. If the other dancers know someone is leaving, they are more likely to try and steal her stuff because they know she won't be back. This was at the club where I had worked with Sméagol who had stolen my shit, so I wasn't taking any chances! The owner was disappointed because, other than those few shifts in the weeks leading up to my leaving, I was the most reliable dancer with the least amount of drama he had ever hired. He told my husband, "If I could have twenty girls like Sydnee, I'd be set." I always showed up early, tipped out at the beginning of my shift, didn't do drugs, minded my own business . . . . Not to toot my own horn, but I was a stellar employee.

At the end of the night, the DJ made an announcement that I would be leaving after that night, and I danced to an extra set. The club was packed because of the party, so it was a good night to pick for my last. I got some extra tips. Victoria had the DJ play a silly song for me, then my now husband asked the DJ to play "Bawitaba" by Kid Rock for my finale. It was a fitting way for me to spend my final four and a half minutes onstage as Sydnee. When Kid Rock opens the song screaming, "My name is Kid!" I would scream "My name is Syd!" because, for many years, to a lot of people, it was. It was bittersweet for sure.

I pushed myself to do a great performance and go out with a bang, singing along to the music, making sure to do every pole trick I knew, and ending the song as a sweaty, panting, pile of exhaustion on the stage floor.

My final trip around the bar was filled with a lot of laughter, hugs, and I'm not ashamed to admit, a tear or two. The people in those barstools had all impacted my life in one way or another, no matter how great or small. I was going to miss some of them a lot. Others . . . I was ready to bless and release.

While part of me was scared to make the transition, most of me was ready to move on to new adventures. I had learned to trust my inner voice and on December 22, 2008, my voice was telling me that it was time to close that chapter. A few months after leaving the Firehouse, it was shut down. While I'm curious to think of where I would have gone next, I'm glad to have gotten out when I did. The industry had changed, and my patience had run its course. I was done.

But I do not regret working in gentlemen's clubs. Whether it was dancing, bartending, managing, or house-momming, the lessons I learned in those dark rooms will always stay with me. I hope that you have found them helpful as well.

As you go down your own path, please be true to yourself, be brave, and be confident! The personal growth I have experienced while working in an industry I never knew I would be a part of has benefited me in all the areas of my life.

Confidence and inner strength are universally impor-tant. Whether you find yourself daydreaming about going back to school, starting a company, exploring your artsy side or opening your heart to a new romantic partner; do it! Jump in with confidence and follow your intuition. No matter what the outcome, remember: at least you're not onstage with your boob hanging out.

Chase your dreams, take the time to cultivate your talents, and do the hard work you need to do in order to live the life you deserve.

I dare you!

EPILOGUE

I KNOW THERE are tons of people who will not be as amused with my story as I am. That's okay!

My motivation to write this book was to immortalize my experiences for my tribe. Meaning, the people who can either relate because they have felt the same way I have, or those who relate because they want to make the same changes in their own lives. It doesn't matter if they have ever stepped foot in a gentlemen's club or not.

I struggled for a long time before I started typing because I was afraid of being judged. I don't know why I am so worried about the opinions of people I don't even know. I have been working ridiculously hard to get past this, and I realize that the people I am meant to share my life with will love me no matter what. As far as the people whom I am not meant to share my life with . . . why should I care? As the popular saying puts it: "Those who mind don't matter, and those who matter don't mind."[8]

I also hope that by sharing my truths, I can show that there is so much more to people than stereotypes. People are all multilayered, and you can never tell by appearances alone what has brought someone to the place that they are in right now. Whether someone is in a great place or a dark place, we have all been through hundreds of experiences that have led us to where we are right now. Remember the times when you have struggled on your own journey and use that as a reason to treat others with compassion and empathy.

We are all where we are as a result of the choices that we've made. There are going to be times when we don't make the right or the best choices. The good news is, every time we wake up in the morning, we get a chance to choose again!

Over the course of writing this book, I have realized how much I miss dancing. Not the job part. I no longer have the patience to smile at people I'd rather kick. I'm generalizing of course. There were tons of awesome guys whom I am so grateful to have met and a select few who are still a part of my life over a decade later. I just no longer feel like doing the sorting process. In this day of camera phones, I am also in no hurry to find out that there are pictures that I did not authorize of myself on the internet.

Sure, clubs may have a "no phones at the bar" rule. But they also have "no pulling your dick out at the bar" and "don't grab the girls by the pussy" rules, too, and those aren't always followed. It's not worth it to me to risk having topless pictures of myself posted on the web. I have enough trouble knowing that an ex has pics that he's apparently keeping in his "spank bank" and has threatened me with in the past. I don't know about you, but if I were his current wife, I wouldn't be cool with my hubby keeping pics of his former wife that are that personal.

Different strokes I guess (ba dum dum).

At any rate, I miss the "spinning around the pole and moving onstage" part of my former occupation.

Reminiscing while I was writing this book made me feel an even stronger pull in my soul to dance again. Last year I took a chance and called up my old boss from my Warlocks days to see if he would be okay with me coming into the bar before it opened and using the stage to dance once a week. I figured it would not only satisfy my nostalgia but also be a great swap for one of my weekly cardio workouts. Traditional cardio is not my favorite, and I would much rather raise my heart rate while pole dancing than doing burpees. I was happily surprised that he was still managing.

I loved his reaction when he picked up the phone and I told him, "It's Syd, from the nineties!" He sounded genuinely happy to hear from me. It made me smile, because he has worked with hundreds, if not thousands, of dancers over the past few decades, and he remembered me. And not just remembered me but remembered me fondly.

At forty-three years old, I started dancing again. This time though, it was once a week as a workout. He told me that I could come in whenever I wanted, but part of the appeal for me is that I go so infrequently. If I started going in multiple days a week, it wouldn't be as fun, and it would interfere with my other workouts.

I bought some new stilettos from Amazon because I cannot dance flat-footed. I could dance in my bare feet (since I come in during off-hours, the odds of the Board of Health having anything to say about it are slim), but it would be dangerous. You never know if someone has dropped a glass or bottle and left shards of glass on the floor the previous night. Even if there is no glass, there is a good chance that I would wind up with some weave wrapped around my toe and a sequin or two stuck to the bottom of my foot.

The shoes I use to dance in now may be like the kind I used to wear, but instead of sexy thongs and mini dresses, I now wear shorts and a sports bra with a tank top. (Don't forget the super-sexy pee pad!) I bring my laptop and plug it into the bar's sound system to play my special "Titty Bar" playlist. I use a mix of my old dance songs as well as some new favorites. Since the bar isn't open, I can dance to whatever I want, and I do! From show tunes to Iron Maiden and all kinds of things in between. My old boss goes up to the office on the second floor and leaves me to it.

Even being alone on a stage in an empty bar, and so much older than before, with the cellulights blaring . . . I feel amazingly confident. Being on the stage once a week recharges my battery and gives me a major endorphin rush. I also feel pretty badass because when I got back onstage that first time, I was able to immediately do all the spins I used to do years ago. It was like riding a bike. Even if over the next few days, my muscles felt like I had fallen off a bike, gone headfirst over the handlebars, and landed in a sticker-bush-filled ravine.

I instantly fell back into the routine I described in Chapter Nine. Although I did the back flip once, I decided to remove that from the routine for safety's sake. Crawling across the hardwood stage can be dicey, too, as my knees are a lot older and not as forgiving. I have also been stuck a couple of times when I've tried to get back up. I have tendinitis in my right hip flexor, which acts up sometimes. I laughed when my doctor told me that it is called "dancer's hip."

Muscle memory runs deep. Whether it is in the physical sense or in the lessons you have learned. You never know how big of an impact your habits have on you until they come back years later. Make sure that they are the habits that you not only would like to revisit but would also like to serve you on your journey to succeed in your dreams.

I post my weekly dancing days on social media because they are that day's work out, and I am not embarrassed. I'm completely covered and find no reason to not share. As a result, I have been asked more than once if I could teach pole dancing. Part of me would love to. But I'm certain that would bring more liability to the club than just letting a former employee (who they know could fall off the stage and not sue) do whatever she does. I completely understand the owner not wanting to take on that risk. Plus, I find my weekly dance workouts so fun because it is no longer a job. Even if I were teaching and not walking around for tips, it would still be a job again. If I ever change my mind, I will let those friends know.

To the people who have talked about me behind my back for my choice of working out, y'all can suck it! There is no reason in the world that you can't just keep scrolling past my posts or choose to look the other way.

I've worked hard to become who I am now. Finding my voice, standing up to bullies, not giving in to the demands of narcissists . . . these are all skills that took me a long time to learn. Not everyone is born brave, and some of us have been raised to always put others first, even at our own detriment. In these cases, you need to dig deep to find your courage. Don't be upset if you are not able to achieve things the first time you try them. Lots of things in life take multiple times to get right. Careers, athletic achievements, marriages . . . . We can't beat ourselves up when things don't work the first time. Instead, we give them a go because most of the time life isn't a "one and done" situation. Our trials are what make us stronger, better, and ultimately successful.

There are so many resources available to us now, from books (thank you for reading mine!) to podcasts, YouTube videos, live events, etc. Make the investment in yourself to make your life the best it can be. As far as we know right now, we only go around once, so don't let fear hold you back from reaching your dreams!

As you go on through your life, I hope that you channel your inner dancer. The part of you that is confident, energetic, and willing to put it all out there to move yourself forward. Enjoy the music, move your body, have fun! Do not ever let anyone hold you back from becoming the you that you were born to be.

And remember no one ever died from embarrassment. The absolute biggest mistakes that leave us red-faced and mortified make for the best stories later in your life. So, jump in, take the dare, and if you wind up with a boob popping out of your top, it just may put you on the path to a new adventure!

LEAVE A REVIEW

If you enjoyed this book, it would help a lot if you left a review on the site you bought it from or on Goodreads. This can be a few words or just a star rating.

Thanks very much!

Sydnee.

ACKNOWLEDGMENTS

I had been writing this book in my head for years but lacked the confidence to turn my thoughts into a reality. Thank you to my amazing husband, Dave, for encouraging me to make my thoughts tangible. And for the extra push that I needed to achieve my goal of finishing the first draft by my forty-fifth birthday. I love you tons! I am so grateful and blessed to be your wife and appreciate you more than you will ever know!

To my three kids, I don't want to embarrass you by naming you in this book. So, to DA, ST, and LT, I love you all to the moon and back! I am so honored to be your mom! Thank you for everything that the three of you teach me daily, from social media hacks to sharing your thoughts and opinions on what's going on in the world. I know that you found out about this part of my life sooner than I would have liked, but you took it all in your stride, and I appreciate that.

I am sorry for all the anonymous online bullying that you have had to endure because I chose to have a legal job years before you were born that makes some people feel the need to act out. They act that way because they don't like themselves. I would have gladly taken that all on myself so you would have never had to. If you are going to deal with it anyway, I would rather use this platform to share some of the positive parts of this profession, some of the laughs, and maybe erase the stigma that comes along with it.

To my parents, in-laws, siblings, "sis-in-loves," and my awesome cousin—Karl, Evelyn, Joe, Debbie, Linda, Bob (RIP), Carolyn, Kim, Kevin, Karlyn, Danielle, Jennifer, Lisa, Angela—and also my nieces and nephews. I know I have not always been the easiest to get along with and that my choice of profession was not your first choice. Thank you for loving me anyway! I love you all!

To all my friends who have had my back over the years: Christina, Meliss (RIP), Deanna, Eric, Jen, Dan, Shanny, Gina, Steve S., Vin, Steve F., Becca, Scott, "Madison," Ann B., Glenn, Leah, Colleen, Sue, Mickey, Adam, "Camp Mom," and so many more! Thank you! I love you guys!

To my more recent friends and the ones with whom I've reconnected: Rod (RIP), Kelly, Lisa, Kevin, Mike, Dom, Anthony, Marty, Lana, Ann M., Charles, the "Witch's Brew Crew", "The pack that loves you back", and all the friends I've made whom I only know through my computer screen. To my awesome editor, Kim, and to my fantastic cover artist, typesetter, and amazing guide to help me through all of the mazes and pitfalls of publishing, Gareth. Thank you all so much for being a part of my life and sharing this journey with me! I love you!

Thank you to Al, Lisa R, Pete, Heidi, Scott, Jen, Doc, Jul, Chris, April, Mark, Annie, and Skip for seeing past my job and into my heart fifteen years ago. Love you all!

Even though we haven't spoken in years, thank you, Marissa, for daring me all of those years ago to step out of my comfort zone. I hope you are living the life of your dreams!

Thank you to Farnoosh Brock (ProlificLiving.com) for so kindly giving me permission to use some of her positive affirmations.

To all the haters who bet against me: thank you! To the shit-talkers, the cheaters, the abusers and the bullies: thank you! To the people who claimed to love me while they only loved themselves and used me, to the game-players and the assholes: thank you! Without all of you, I would not be where I am right now. Thank you for lighting the fire in my soul to prove all of you wrong. It has inspired me to become what I have always had the potential to be and what you had tried to keep me from becoming.

I am so thankful for my life and appreciate everyone whom I can share it with now. I appreciate all the authors, motivational speakers, and role models who have helped me to strive to be the best me that I can be. (Special shout-out to Kim Harrison for being especially awesome!) If it weren't for the hard lessons I had to learn along the way, I would not be able to be so grateful for the blessings I have been given. I am so thankful to have the life I do now with Dave, our kids, and our friends and family.

Gratitude is everything!

NOTES

1 See https://en.wikipedia.org/wiki/Crab_mentality

2 Rape, Abuse & Incest National Network (RAINN): https://www.rainn.org/, National Organisation for Victim Assistance (NOVA): https://www.trynova.org/, The Trevor Project: https://www.thetrevorproject.org/, Office for Victims of Crime: https://ovc.ojp.gov/help-for-victims/overview.

3 https://www.prolificliving.com/

4 https://www.dictionary.com/browse/visualize

5 https://www.merriam-webster.com/dictionary/belief

6 https://www.merriam-webster.com/dictionary/exploit

7 https://www.merriam-webster.com/dictionary/objectify

8 Percy Morris (1938); *The Journal of the Institution of Municipal & County Engineers*, *64* (16); Discussion, p.1277. See https://quoteinvestigator.com/2012/12/04/those-who-mind/